Professional Remodeler's Manual

Save Time, Avoid Mistakes, Increase Profits

R. Dodge Woodson

McGraw-Hill, Inc.

New York San Francisco Washington, D.C. Auckland Bogotá
Caracas Lisbon London Madrid Mexico City Milan
Montreal New Delhi San Juan Singapore
Sydney Tokyo Toronto

hc   1 2 3 4 5 6 7 8 9 DOC/DOC 9 9 8 7 6 5

Library of Congress Cataloging-in-Publication Data
Woodson, R. Dodge (Roger Dodge), 1955–
    Professional remodeler's manual : save time, avoid mistakes,
increase profits / by R. Dodge Woodson.
        p. cm.
    Includes index.
    ISBN 0-07-071797-4
    1. Construction industry—Management. 2. Dwellings—Remodeling.
I. Title.
HD9715.A2W6484 1995
690'.837'0286—dc20   95-9260
                                                                     CIP

Acquisitions editor: April D. Nolan
Editorial team: Robert E. Ostander, Executive Editor
               Sally Anne Glover, Book Editor
               Jodi L. Tyler, Indexer
Production team: Katherine G. Brown, Director
                 Rhonda E. Baker, Coding
                 Rose McFarland, Desktop Operator
                 Nancy K. Mickley, Proofreading
Design team: Jaclyn J. Boone, Designer   GEN1
             Katherine Lukaszewicz, Associate Designer   0717974

This book is dedicated to Afton, Adam, and Kimberley,
the best family I could ever hope for.

Acknowledgments

I'd like to acknowledge my parents, Maralou and Woody, who took me shopping to buy my first toolbox and tools. Thanks, Mom and Dad.

Contents

Introduction

Remodeling can be a very rewarding business. People are always looking for quality contractors to upgrade and expand their homes. If you
build a good name for yourself and stay financially healthy, your business can boom and see you through a comfortable career. But if you
step into the traps that befall many contractors, your business might
crumble all around you and take you down with it. Whether you are
new to the business or have years of experience, there are more than
enough surprises waiting for you that can all be potentially fatal in financial terms. This book is written to help you avoid the discomfort
and disaster that so many contractors suffer.

I have worked in the trades for more than 20 years. During many
of those years, I ran my own business. Most of my experience has
been gained on residential jobs. The work I've done has ranged from
simple handyman jobs to major building and remodeling projects.
Through these years of experience, I've learned a lot. Many of the
lessons were quite costly. In this book I'm going to share with you
my experiences, my knowledge, and my mistakes. You can learn
from these and save yourself the high cost of trial-and-error educa-
tion. I didn't have a seasoned professional to guide me through the
treacherous waters of remodeling, but you do, and together we will
make you a better remodeling contractor.

There are dozens of books written on the subject of remodeling.
Most of them are aimed at homeowners and do-it-yourselfers. A few
are written with the professional contractor in mind, but none offer
you what this book does. I'm not going to waste your time showing
you how to use a tape measure or how to hammer a nail. No, I'm going to devote our time together to teaching you how to avoid the
many pitfalls that are so common in the remodeling business. If you
want to know how to use a framing square, this is not the book
you're looking for. But if you want to discover how you can make
more money, have fewer on-the-job hassles, and enjoy your work
more, this is the book for you.

   This book covers all of the phases of residential remodeling. I'm going to take you, step-by-step, through these phases and show you what to watch out for. You'll learn about situations that you might not know exist and risks that you might take everyday without realizing it. Each and every chapter of this book will propel you higher in your chosen profession as a residential remodeling contractor. Thumb through a few of the chapters and read a few paragraphs. You won't read long without learning something new. If you're looking for a more rewarding career in remodeling, you owe it to yourself to read this book.

1

Site considerations

Site considerations are not a part of every remodeling job, but they can, and often do, come into play with major remodeling projects. For example, if you were hired to build an addition on a home, site conditions would be very much a part of your responsibilities as a contractor. If you are simply remodeling a bathroom or a kitchen, you probably won't have to concern yourself with potential site problems, but you might. Have you ever installed a bay window in an eat-in kitchen during a remodeling project? This type of work could put you in jeopardy of violating zoning regulations, deed restrictions, and covenants. Any time you are working with the exterior of a property, you might have to deal with site conditions.

Many large remodeling jobs involve the addition of living space to an existing structure. To gain this habitable space, new foundations are dug. Ah, here's a situation where site conditions come into play. Something as simple as installing a garden window could violate local setback laws. Many remodelers never stop to think that they might be setting themselves up for a lawsuit when they agree to perform certain types of work, but they can be. As a remodeling contractor, you are responsible, to some degree, for doing work within the confines of local laws, restrictions, and ordinances. To be competent at doing this part of your job, you must have some basic knowledge of what to look out for.

Building a small deck or enlarging a bathroom might not seem like much of a risk to you, but either of these jobs can stir up some serious trouble. Building a garage is another way to get yourself caught up in hassles. For that matter, just painting the exterior of a home can cause problems. Foundation work and grading are both areas where an inexperienced contractor can fall into despair. With so many potential pitfalls awaiting you, it pays to be well-versed in your field of endeavor. With this in mind, let's begin looking at some of the risks and responsibilities you might be faced with on your next remodeling job.

Zoning

Let's talk first about local zoning laws. These regulations can bring an abrupt halt to any job. Zoning regulations can govern everything from setbacks to the types of uses a building is approved for. For example, it might be in violation of zoning laws to convert a single-family home into a duplex.

If you are working in a progressive location, where code enforcement is done on a professional level, you will normally encounter any zoning problems prior to having a building permit issued. In some rural locations, however, things sometimes slip through the cracks until work has already started. This can be an expensive mess to straighten out. Your responsibility runs further than just finding out what zoning requirements entail. You must conform to the local laws, rules, and regulations as you proceed with your work. This part can get a bit tricky. To expand on this, I'd like to share a personal experience to illustrate how one remodeler thought he was in the clear but wound up in a conflict that nearly cost him his business.

Adding a family room

A general contractor I once worked for found himself tangled in a nasty legal mess. A couple had hired my boss to build a family-room addition on their home. On the surface, the job was pretty clear-cut. The homeowners wanted the addition to extend off an existing part of their home. It would be accessed from both an existing living room and the existing kitchen. This was not the best layout in the world, but it was what the people wanted.

My boss went through the usual steps involved with securing a building permit. Plans were drawn. Specifications were made, and a site drawing was rendered. A complete permit package went to the local code-enforcement office for approval. After a week or so, the plans were approved and a building permit was issued. We all got busy building the addition.

The first major step in the project was the footing and foundation phase. This went off without a hitch, and the framing crews were fast at work. Because this was an extensive, and expensive project, the homeowners had arranged construction financing for the job. Their agreement with my boss included a small deposit to start the job and a large payment when the addition was under roof and dried in. Our company was supplying all labor and material for the job. Well, when the time came to get the first large-installment payment, trouble popped up, and it did so in a big way.

My boss had submitted an invoice for payment of services rendered and materials provided. This bill included all work up to the present stage of construction, and it was a sizable sum. As the salesperson and estimator for the company, it was my job to go around and collect payments when they were due. I went to the job to pick up a check for the company, but I didn't get one. In fact, I felt as though I had walked into a hornet's nest. The homeowners, who up until now had been very nice, were raging mad. It seems they had just been informed, only minutes before my arrival, that the bank could not advance them any money on their construction financing until the zoning violations were corrected.

I made the mistake of asking them what zoning violations were at issue. The couple unloaded on me. As a company representative, I had to stand there and take what they dished out, but I had no responsibility or authority in terms of the problem. All I could do was let them vent their anger and wait until my boss could be contacted. I was confused from what the people were telling me, but I was young and inexperienced at the time. Looking back, it is easy to see what went wrong, how it happened, and why the customers were steaming mad.

What was at the root of this problem? Well, it seems that our company had built a portion of the new addition in a setback zone. This particular location had zoning ordinances that required at least 20 feet of open space from any structure to a property line. As it turned out, the foundation for the new addition encroached on this setback by about 2 feet. Technically, the local code office could issue an order requiring the part of the structure in violation to be removed. Needless to say, the customers were not about to pay a single penny for the work that had been done until the problem was resolved.

How could this have happened? Didn't the code enforcement office issue a permit? Yes, they had issued a permit, based on representations made by my employer. You see, he had drawn the site plan that showed property boundaries and structures. He also made a mistake in his calculations while doing this, and that is what caused the problem. If a surveyor had been brought in to draft a site plan, the odds of all this trouble happening would have been much lower. But, in an effort to save money, the site plan was done by the contractor, not a surveyor. This opened the contractor up to certain liabilities.

How was the mistake discovered? The bank required that a site survey be done before any money would be advanced. When the bank's survey team did their work, it disclosed a zoning violation. Therefore, no money would be loaned on the project until such violations were corrected. Well, this whole story goes on and on, and it involves lawsuits, nasty letters, angry phone calls, and a lot of other stuff that you wouldn't want to deal with. And it could have all been avoided simply by hiring a surveyor in the first place.

What was the final outcome of this tragic story? The local zoning board issued a variance that allowed the addition to remain in its existing location. Our company completed the job and was paid for the work as contracted for, with the exception of legal fees incurred by the homeowners. To make a long story short, the job was finished, everyone involved was sick of the whole process, and the remodeling company lost money on the project. All of this happened because the contractor was too cheap to pay for a site survey before beginning construction.

Setback ordinances

Setback ordinances are one of the most common zoning regulations that remodelers are faced with. Whether you are building a garage, a sun room, a deck, or a room addition, setback requirements might alter your plans. You might not feel that setbacks are your responsibility, but I wouldn't hang my hat on it in a court of law. As a professional contractor, you have certain obligations to your customers. It is not fair for me to say that you alone are to be held accountable for setback violations, but if you don't want to spend the next few years in and out of court, you will do well to avoid conflicts of this type.

The issue of setback requirements is not a complicated one. They are very simple, really. Most jurisdictions require a certain distance from every property line to any permanent structure, such as a house or garage. Portable structures, like sheds on skids, might or might not be affected by setbacks. Since every town, county, and state can create its own rules, you should check with your local authorities before commencing any work.

Setbacks vary in their rules. One town might say that front and back setbacks are 25 feet and that side setbacks are 15 feet. Another jurisdiction might set the front and back limits at 15 feet and the side setbacks at 10 feet. In the rural (or maybe you'd call it remote) setting where I live, there are no setback requirements. The point is this: setback requirements do vary, and you should be informed of what each and every one of them dictates in areas where you will be working.

If you are working in heavily populated areas, you are more likely to encounter trouble with setbacks than if you are working out in the country. I have found this to be true of my career. Setbacks in Northern Virginia, where I worked for several years, were much more of an issue than they are here in Maine. Anywhere where the price of land is at a premium, developers attempt to cram the land full. This means that homes and businesses are built on small lots and often are built right to the fringes of setback requirements. Something as simple as installing a bay window could trigger a setback problem. If the structure is in compliance, with 1 foot of space to spare, and you add a bay window, you might throw the property into violation. This might seem unlikely to you, but I can tell you from experience that there are buildings that have been built to such strict guidelines. Don't take anything for granted.

I remember an office building being constructed in Virginia some years ago. It was three or four stories tall and made of brick. Somewhere during the construction, it was discovered that the building was in violation of the side setback regulations. Unfortunately for the building owner, the adjoining land owner was a competitor who would not agree to a variance. A portion of the building had to be torn down. This is a pretty extreme case, but it gives you an idea of what can happen.

Above-ground structures

Above-ground structures, such as decks attached to second floors, are not immune from setback regulations. If you have a customer who wants a nice deck installed off the master bedroom on the second floor, you'd better check into zoning requirements. Even though no foundation work will be required, the deck will be an appurtenance to the building, and it might violate setback laws. This type of work is almost always ignored by contractors in terms of zoning. Many contractors assume that since the foundation footprint of the building is remaining the same, there is nothing to worry about. Don't count on it!

Would you ever stop to think of setback requirements when a customer asked you to install a large, garden window over a kitchen sink? I doubt it. If I hadn't been in the business for so long, I probably wouldn't think of it either. However, I have endured decades in the construction and remodeling business, and it has taught me a lot. Since a garden window will protrude farther than a standard window, it might trigger a setback violation. The odds of a house being this close to a property line is minimal, but it never hurts to check. It only hurts when you don't.

Freestanding structures

Freestanding structures might offer some of the highest risks to a contractor. If you are called to build a freestanding garage, gazebo, or other outdoor structure, you must check the zoning laws carefully. Whenever an outside structure is added to a property, it raises some risks for the contractor. Even if you are being hired only to build a barbecue pit, you should check the local zoning regulations. In short, if you are doing anything to alter the exterior of a property, zoning laws should be considered. But it is not only outside work that could put you in a mess. Some inside work can cause just as much, if not more, trouble.

Inside work

Inside work is not normally thought of as being a high risk in terms of zoning regulations, but it can be. Every now and then, a person buys a house or building with the intent to change its use. This is an extremely lucrative business when done properly, but a lot of rookie investors make mistakes. And you might wind up right in the thick of things with them if you don't know how to protect yourself. Keep in mind that different locations, laws, regulations, and rules can affect the level of responsibility that a remodeling contractor has to any of the subjects we are discussing. Your part of the country might not require as much of you as some other parts. But even if you are not held responsible for violations personally, the fact that violations are created can cut off your cash flow and force you out of business. This certainly brings the matter close to home and to the forefront of your attention.

A duplex that didn't work

I'd like to tell you a story about a duplex conversion that didn't work. There are actually two stories to be told here. I will start with the one where a young military couple purchased a large, rambling, old building with the intent to convert it into a duplex. The couple called me to give them an estimate on what would be entailed to section off the building and create two separate living quarters.

After talking to both the husband and wife by phone, I arranged a meeting to evaluate the property. As I walked through the large home, it was obvious that the size of the building could easily accommodate two families. The layout of the structure was conducive to a cost-effective remodeling effort, and it seemed that the pair had picked a good property for their plans. After walking through the building and discussing the goal of creating a duplex, I took a rough drawing, supplied by the couple, and returned to my office to work up some numbers.

As I mulled over various cost factors, something dawned on me. I couldn't think of any other multifamily properties on the street where this big house was located. On a hunch, I called the zoning office. The phone call didn't take long, and it saved me a lot of time. As it turned out, the property was situated in an area zoned only for single-family use. It would have been a violation of local zoning ordinances to create a duplex. Well, I didn't like seeing a big job go down the tubes, but I was glad that I had discovered the problem before I was too involved with it.

After my phone conversation with the zoning department, I called the couple and arranged a meeting to discuss what I had learned. The young couple was, to say the least, very unhappy with my findings—not with me, but with the information I had brought to light. They had paid extra for the property in view of turning it into an income property. After they confirmed what I had told them, they were distraught. As the bearer of bad news, I was not real popular, but the couple did realize that my professional approach had saved them time and, perhaps, money and future frustration.

A second story, of similar nature, involved an investor who purchased a property that was being used as a duplex. My first contact with this individual came when he asked me for an estimate to convert the duplex back into a single-family home. Since conversion projects are usually done to accommodate more families, instead of fewer, I had to ask why this unusual request was being made.

The investor had purchased the building thinking that it was a legal duplex. After his purchase, the local tax assessor came out to put a current value on the property. During his inspection, the assessor noticed that the property was being used by two families. This discovery triggered more research by the tax assessor and resulted in an ultimatum from the local code enforcement office to return the building to single-family use, as it was not zoned for multifamily use.

The investor sought legal action against the real-estate brokerage that had sold him the building. Did he ever recover any money for his damages? I don't know. After learning the history of this deal, I declined any interest in bidding on the work. This, however, is yet another example of how things are not always what they appear to be.

So what is the point to all of this? It's simple. As a remodeling contractor, you might be vulnerable. There was a time when courts were reserved for serious crimes. In today's arena of business, however, it seems that more and more people are looking for a good legal battle. You have to protect yourself. One bad deal can cost you your home, your business, and your credit. This, obviously, is a deadly blow to anyone's economic future.

Local code requirements

Local code requirements are another issue that can put you at risk. How many contractors do you know who cheat the system? Certainly you know plumbers who install water heaters without permits. And, I would guess, you can name a few contractors who do interior work without permits. It is difficult for a contractor to embark on a major addition that requires site work without posting a permit, but it's sometimes done. This is a very bad practice, and it's one that can put you out of business quickly.

Most jurisdictions require permits for any substantial amount of work done on a property. If these permits are not obtained in the proper manner, the contractor is usually at risk. Anyone who has been in the business for very long has had customers who wanted to forgo the permit process. Homeowners know that taking out permits is paramount to be reassessed for higher property taxes. This is the homeowner's problem, not yours. However, if you go along with this approach and do the work without a permit, you become a party to the infraction.

It might be hard to believe that contractors would actually try to build a garage without a building permit, but some do. This is work that is out in the open and easily spotted by code officials. Yet some contractors are so hungry for work that they will infringe on the laws and rules of the code-enforcement office to get work. This is a shame, but it is also a big mistake. Contractors, in general, don't enjoy a great reputation. There are many stories about rip-offs and fraudulent activity centered around contractors, especially home-improvement and remodeling contractors. Don't get caught up in this situation. If a permit is required for the work you are bidding, don't do it without a permit.

Deed restrictions and covenants

Deed restrictions and covenants are items that many contractors never think twice about. They aren't really a contractor's responsibility, but they can have a tremendous impact on your profits and stability. This is especially true in densely populated areas. Before you agree to do any exterior work on a building, you should seek some protection. Ask your customers to either provide you with a copy of their deeds or a release of liability for any violation of deed restrictions and covenants. A written release is your best course of action.

Land developers have the right to insert covenants and restrictions into the deeds of properties that they convey out to purchasers. There are no real limitations on what these restrictions might apply to. For example, a developer can prohibit the parking of commercial vehicles, such as your work truck, on the grounds of a property. Can you imagine living in a place where you couldn't park your truck in your own driveway? Well, my parents live in such a place. Their deed restricts not only the types of vehicles that may be kept on the property, but also the type of mailbox they may have, the colors their house may be painted, and other types of situations that might arise. Being an old country boy, I can't accept this type of control, but I do understand it.

Developers put restrictions in their transfer deeds to protect their investments. A high-class subdivision could be demeaned if someone decided to paint their home pink, blue, and yellow. I suppose work trucks can also lend a less appealing atmosphere to a neighborhood than some fancy sports cars. From my personal perspective, this seems to be snobbish and wrong. But, from a developer's point of view, I understand the need for such regulations.

If people are going to pay top dollar for a prestigious address, they want to make sure their investment is protected. This, in many ways, is good for the developer and the property owners. While I understand it, and perhaps agree with some aspects of it, I feel it goes against the grain of what America stands for. In any event, there are places where homeowners are limited in what they can do with the exterior appearance of their homes. This can affect you as a remodeling contractor. How does it bother you? Well, let's see.

Assume that you are awarded a job to install vinyl siding on a home. The customer has decided that routine painting is expensive and undesirable. For this reason, you have gotten the job to side the home with vinyl. It's a big house, and your profit margin is good. The only glitch in the deal is that the customer refuses to pay an up-front deposit. The reason you are given for this is the many tales the homeowner has read about dishonest contractors.

The house is in a great neighborhood, and the homeowner seems fine. Since you have 30-day accounts for your materials and the job will take less than a week, you decide to accept the job offer. After all, the homeowner has agreed to pay you in full upon completion. The next week, you set up shop and begin the new siding installation. Your crew finishes the job on schedule, and you submit an invoice for payment. But the payment doesn't come promptly. You call the customer and don't like what you hear.

When you contact the customer, you discover that the neighborhood homeowner's group has complained about having a house covered with vinyl siding. You never stopped to think that the house you were working on was the only house in the area with vinyl siding. The customer goes on to explain how the homeowner's board is bringing a legal suit to force the removal of the new siding. In your position, you could care less about the lawsuit. You only want your money. But the homeowner refuses to pay you until the dispute is settled. What are your options?

You can lien the house, but that won't automatically put money in your pocket. The supplier's bill for the materials will be coming soon, and you've already paid your crew. You are out money now, and you will have to pay your supplier by the 10th of the month. Still, you're getting nothing from the customer. Was it your responsibility to verify if your work was in compliance with subdivision restrictions? Probably not, but the result is the same. You're not getting paid. You could have avoided this situation if you had reviewed the customer's deed restrictions and covenants. Getting a release signed by the customer would give you more ammunition to go to court with, but you don't have any of this. All you've got are incoming bills and no cash. See how easy it is to wind up in a mess?

A new roof

If you were called to install a new roof, would you consider consequences for deed restrictions and covenants? You should. Roofing frequently falls into a category of control in subdivisions. There is often language in these restrictions that limits the types of roofing materials that may be used and the colors of roofing that are acceptable. Again, this is not an area where you should have to be on top of every deed restriction, but if you're not, it can hurt you.

Landscaping

As a remodeling contractor, you might or might not take on landscaping jobs. They can be a part of your overall project, or perhaps you do them for some extra income. In any case, landscaping can be affected by covenants and restrictions. If you are doing any work that affects the exterior of a property, you must be sure that the activity will not create problems that you can't deal with effectively.

Grading

Grading work can get expensive very quickly. Most remodeling jobs don't require much earth work, but some do. If your work will alter existing conditions or create new circumstances where existing grading will not be sufficient, you have to be aware of this. People can get pretty nasty at times, and the only way to avoid confrontations and lawsuits is to address the issues and objections before they become volatile. Let me give you an example of such a situation.

I worked for a contractor once who was hired to build a sun room on the back of a house. The house was on a sloping lot, and the addition's foundation was going to extend farther above the finished grade than the rest of the home's foundation. This issue was not discussed prior to the construction process. My supervisor was aware of the increased foundation exposure, but he failed to discuss it with the homeowners. I don't know all of the particulars, but I can fill you in on the key points of the problem.

A new sun room was built on an existing home. When the foundation was installed, which was made of cinder block, it extended well above grade. The customers were under the impression, for whatever reasons, that the foundation would be backfilled to match up with their existing foundation. The contractor didn't share their opinion. One thing led to another, and a major battle ensued. The property owners wanted the contractor to haul in dirt to conceal the ugly block foundation. My boss had no intentions of doing this, and they all wound up in court. I don't know what the outcome of the dispute was because I changed jobs shortly after the trouble roared into full force. This was a problem in communication, but it was a serious problem, nonetheless.

Environmental concerns

Environmental concerns have become an issue for remodelers to be mindful of. Excavating for a new foundation or filling in some low spot on a lot can get you in trouble from an environmental angle. There are state and federal laws pertaining to what can and cannot be done in certain areas. For example, here in Maine, wetlands are a big issue.

Maine has a lot of land that is considered to be wetland. This wetland is heavily protected from development. Building too close to a designated wetland or filling in such a piece of property is a major offense. This type of situation can affect a remodeling contractor.

Let's say that you are called out to build a terraced deck for a customer. The deck will start at the rear of the home and extend downward, towards some lake frontage. Your customer wants this deck for enjoying sunsets over the water. After looking over the proposed location for the deck, you agree to build it. The farthest end of the deck stops well short of the lake, but it terminates in some reeds where the land begins to get soft. If you build this deck, you are most likely violating environmental laws.

In the scenario we've just examined, you might be saved from big trouble by having your building permit request denied. However, maybe the permit would slip through. This gives you the right to build the deck, but if you construct it in a protected area, you might still be held accountable. At the least, you will have to defend your actions, and this will eat up whatever profits you might have made. There are all sorts of tricky situations like this one that can complicate your life.

If you will be doing site work in an area where erosion or runoff might occur, you might very well be required to install a barrier to prevent such occurrences. The barrier might be made of bales of straw or plastic. If you are unaware of this requirement when you bid a job, the cost of this work will come out of what you had hoped would be profit. You're in business to make money, not lose it, so do your homework before you commit to a quoted price.

Even if you believe that responsibility for site considerations does not rest on your shoulders, you should protect yourself at all times. Being issued a building permit should take you off the hook, but fighting in court to prove that you are innocent gets very expensive. Believing that your customers are responsible for what they hire you to do is not good enough. Ignorance of the law is not a suitable defense. As a professional contractor, it is up to you to know all of the laws pertaining to your actions and to avoid infractions of them.

Underground utilities

Underground utilities are common in many locations. If you start digging footings with a backhoe, without proper planning, you might wind up either in big trouble or dead. Digging up a buried gas pipe or electrical cable can bring your career to a quick end. There are usually agencies that you can call to help avoid underground mishaps. If there is no single agency in your area that handles all underground utilities, you should call each utility company that might have cables, pipes, or equipment in the area where you will be working. The agencies and companies will come to the site and mark the locations of their underground materials. There is still a chance you might find something buried where it is not supposed to be, so caution should still be observed. But if you have had all of the utility locations marked by proper authorities, you have at least removed yourself from any blame for negligence.

I've talked to a lot of general contractors in the past who don't worry about underground utilities. Their position is that they hire subcontractors to do their digging, so the problem rests with the subs, not with the generals. In theory, this might be true, but it doesn't take a lot of time or effort to make a few phone calls, and I always prefer to know that the calls have been made. For this reason, I insist on calling the utility agencies myself. If the diggers call too, that's fine, but I want to know that my office went on record as requesting underground utility markings.

Trees

It is not uncommon for trees to be in the way of large remodeling projects. This could be the case if you are raising a roof or adding an addition. Who is going to be responsible for removing the trees? If you're bidding the job with an open, vague proposal, the customer will probably assume that you are taking care of the tree removal. If you aren't, you had better spell it out in your proposal.

Cutting trees can be dangerous under any conditions, and the risk goes up when the trees are near homes and buildings. Professional tree cutters don't work cheaply, but they are a good investment under most remodeling circumstances. You could send a laborer to the job with a chainsaw to hack down the tree, but what will you do if the tree falls on a house or car? Worse yet, what happens if the tree falls on a person? In my opinion, the risk of cutting trees in populated areas is high enough to warrant the expense of a professional tree cutter who is properly insured.

Damaged lawns

I have heard various remodeling contractors complain about how their jobs turned into nightmares because of damaged lawns. In general, it seems that their customers were not prepared for the type of destruction that some remodeling jobs can cause to a lawn. When a backhoe rolls across a lush lawn to dig a footing, leaving deep tread marks in its path, unprepared customers have a right to get upset. The customers are not experienced remodelers. They don't think about the fact that equipment has to get to the job site in some way, which often means right across their lawn. Neither do they stop to think about how loose nails will wind up in the lawn when a new roof is installed.

As a business owner, you owe it to your customers to advise them of situations that might arise around your work. If you're going to have to dig up their yard to make a new sewer connection for an addition, tell them what to expect. If you will be setting up pump jacks or staging that might kill some of their grass, discuss it with the customers. Communication goes a long way in avoiding confrontations.

Be thorough

Be thorough in your site inspections. Look for circumstances that might lead to unexpected expenses. Check to see if there is likely to be anything happening that the customer hasn't thought of. If you don't do your own site work, take your site contractor with you on the inspection. After you have looked the job over carefully, check with local authorities to determine if there are any hidden problems with the work that the customer is requesting. Talk to the utility companies. If there is a gas main running underground where your customer wants footings dug for a new garage, something in the plan is going to have to be changed. Cover all of your bases before you commit to a firm price. This is the only way to be fair to yourself and your customers.

2

Foundation factors

How many times have you looked at a remodeling job and failed to take foundation factors into account? It happens, but it can be a costly mistake. If you are called to look at inside remodeling work, you might never think to investigate the foundation under the area where your work will be performed. It is understandable that you are concentrating on what the customer is showing you, but you can't afford to overlook foundation fundamentals. If you do, you might see all of your profits go up in smoke.

I have done a lot of remodeling in the past 20 years. Much of it has had to do with bathrooms and kitchens, but I've done additions, attic conversions, basement completions, garages, decks, sun rooms, and just about everything else there is to do. Some of the jobs have required the installation of a new foundation. It was easy to evaluate and compensate for the cost of this foundation work. But many of the jobs showed no obvious signs of foundation work, even though they wound up requiring it. And, yes, I have been caught on some of the jobs without being prepared for the time and expense involved with foundation work. If I hadn't made some mistakes, I wouldn't be able to tell you how to avoid them.

As I'm sure you probably know, foundation work is expensive. It can be very expensive, and if it is not covered in your budget for a job, the cost comes out of your profit. This is never a pleasant pill to swallow. You can, however, avoid most foundation frustrations by doing some extra investigation when looking over potential jobs. We're going to talk hard numbers and technical foundation terms in this chapter, but let's start with some examples of how you might get caught off guard with a faulty foundation.

Termites

If you live in an area where termites run rampant, you could be faced with some foundation problems. I inspected a job once where the owners wanted to have their kitchen gutted and redone. When I went to the house and looked all around the kitchen, I took notes of all the cost considerations. Or at least I thought I had.

After submitting my bid and being awarded the job, I sent my crew in for the demolition work. Then my telephone rang. It was my crew leader calling to inform me that the floor joists and pier foundations under the kitchen were going to have to be replaced. They had been damaged beyond repair by termites. Well, my quote didn't exclude floor joists or piers, but I had never planned on re-placing either of these items. Needless to say, I lost a good bit of money on that job.

No foundation

One of my first bathroom remodeling jobs taught me a lesson I've never forgotten. Don't assume that every house is sitting on a foun-dation. This job was in an old farmhouse. The customer wanted to re-model the upstairs to include a new bathroom. There was a bathroom on the first floor, almost directly below the proposed location of the new bathroom. I assumed we would run the pipes down through a chase in a closet and connect them into the pipes under the first-floor bathroom. Well, that's what we did, but the job didn't go exactly the way I had planned it. You see, there was no foundation under the first-floor bathroom.

The section of the house that we had to work under was sitting on large, old timbers. The only access was through a tiny hole used for ventilation. My helper and I had to dig our way under the house. I mean this most literally. We used small folding shovels to dig a trench so that we would have enough height to scoot up under the floor of the bathroom. Part of this house set on a cellar foundation, but the part where we were forced to work didn't. The job took much longer than I had planned, and again, I lost money.

Ledge

In Maine, there is a lot of rock. When it is bedrock, it is called ledge. This ledge can be deep in the ground or it can protrude up above ground level. It is frequently only a few feet below the grade level.

This situation can ruin plans for a full basement. The only way to deal with ledge is to blast it out, and this gets extremely expensive. I almost got burned big time on a job because of ledge, but a single clause in my contract saved me.

Basements are very popular in Maine. I had a customer who wanted some major work done on his property, and the job involved digging a new foundation. There were some warning signs on the lot that pointed to ledge being present, but there was not enough evidence to be sure. However, I had my doubts about being able to dig deep enough to create a full basement. With this reservation in mind, I included a clause in my contract, which is not one of my standard clauses. It basically stated that my price was based on so much per vertical foot of foundation. The clause went on to say that if ledge was encountered during digging, I would not be responsible for blasting, and that I would be allowed to work from the point where ledge was contacted. If this condition were to arise, the customer would be credited, based on the per-foot price, for however many vertical feet of foundation was not installed.

As it turned out, we hit ledge after digging down about 3 feet. The customer had been made aware of this risk before any agreement to do the work was made, so he was prepared for the possibility. He wasn't willing to go to the extra expense of blasting, so he got shorter foundation walls. His overall cost of the job was less, since the walls were not full height. Because the potential for the problem was addressed in our contract, I didn't lose any money or wind up in a court battle. It all worked out okay, but it could have been a horrible situation if I had contracted to provide a full basement without my disclaimer clause.

Buckled and crumbling

Buckled and crumbling foundations can pose serious threats to major remodeling jobs that involve adding additional living space on upper levels. Foundations where the mortar has turned to sand or where pressure has buckled them might not be structurally sound enough to support the additional weight of a second-story living area. If you run across a situation like this, you had better have an engineer look the job over before you make any commitments. Can you imagine the repercussions of doing a full-blown attic conversion only to have a portion of the foundation give way because of your work? I've never had this happen, but I sure don't want the first-hand experience of it.

Types of foundations

There are many types of foundations. Each type has its place in construction, and some are better than others, depending upon their uses. Remodelers are often hired to add living space onto homes. This involves the installation of new foundations. Choosing the best, and most cost-effective, type of foundation for your jobs will make your bids more competitive and your customers happier. To do this, you must take soil conditions into consideration (see Fig. 2-1).

Safe Loads by Soil Type

Tons/sq. ft. of footing	Type of soil
1	Soft clay—Sandy loam—Firm clay/sand—Loose fine sand
2	Hard clay—Compact fine sand
3	Sand/gravel—Loose coarse sand
4	Compact coarse sand—Loose gravel
6	Gravel—Compact sand/gravel
8	Soft rock
10	Very compact—Gravel & sand
15	Hard pan—Hard shale—Sandstone
25	Medium hard rock
40	Sound hard rock
100	Bedrock—Granite—Gneiss

2-1 *Sample load ratings for various types of soil.*

Slab foundations

Slab foundations are about the least expensive type to use for living space. This doesn't necessarily mean they are the best, but they usually cost the least. Since a slab foundation gives you footings and a subfloor all in one package, the cost of constructing a room addition on a slab is quite affordable, when compared to other foundation options.

There are some disadvantages to slab foundations. For one thing, underground installations such as plumbing, electrical wiring, and heating and air-conditioning work are not accessible once the floor is poured. Some people don't mind this, but others can't stand the idea of not being able to get to their mechanical installations.

Slab floors tend to be cold. Customers might not think of this when planning a job, but they will think of it when they walk around on the finished floor without shoes on. Carpeting helps to combat the cold, but there is a noticeable difference between a concrete floor and a wood floor. There is also the issue of concrete floors being harder than wood floors.

Moisture sometimes seeps into slab floors. This isn't a routine problem, but it can occur. If moisture invades a slab, it can cause floor covering to come unglued. It can also make carpeting damp and musty, and in the long term it can destroy the floor covering.

Storage under a slab floor is nonexistent. There is no room for mechanical equipment, such as a heat pump or water heater. This might not be much of a factor in remodeling work, but it is something to consider.

Pier foundations

Pier foundations can be very cost-effective for certain types of re-modeling projects. They are an obvious choice for decks, but they can be used for several types of additions. Screen porches do very well when built on pier foundations. Sun rooms can also be built on piers. Other types of rooms can be placed on piers, but they generally look more out of place and present some difficulties with mechanical installations.

If the room being built on piers is not equipped with mechanical installations, there is little need to block off the underside of the addition. I'm not saying that the floor joists shouldn't be insulated, but there will be no need to protect pipes from freezing or air ducts from exposure. Installing lattice around the perimeter of the piers will enclose the foundation to enhance its eye appeal.

When plumbing, heating, or air ducts are installed under the addition, additional precautions might need to be taken. Since exposure to outside elements often affects the performance of these systems, you might have to build an enclosed chaseway under the addition to protect the systems. This is still much less expensive than constructing a full foundation.

Crawl spaces

Houses built on crawl spaces are common. There should be at least 18 inches of height between the ground and any floor joists, but other than that, a crawl space can have as much or as little height as needed. Adequate ventilation is also needed (see Fig. 2-2). Crawl-space foundations cost much less to build than full basements. Additions built over crawl spaces make it relatively easy to install mechanical systems, and the enclosed foundation protects the systems from outside elements.

Crawl Space Gross Vent Area Requirements

	Multiply free vent area by:	
Vent cover material	*With soil cover*	*No soil cover*
¼" mesh hardware cloth	1.0	10
⅛" mesh screen	1.25	12.5
16-mesh insect screen	2.0	20
Louvers + ¼" hardware cloth	2.0	20
Louvers + ⅛" mesh screen	2.25	22.5
Louvers + 16-mesh screen	3.0	30

2-2 *Foundation ventilation recommendations.*

Having a crawl-space foundation allows access to mechanical systems and framing systems. This gives a lot of customers peace of mind. They know if anything ever goes wrong under their floor, it can be accessed. If new mechanical equipment, such as a heating system, is required to handle a new addition, it can often be tucked into the crawl space.

From an appearance point of view, crawl-space foundations normally beat out slabs and piers. The exterior can be veneered with brick, or it can be swirled with a stucco pattern and painted. Unlike a slab, where exterior siding must be installed low to the ground, additions built on crawl spaces can have their siding start well above ground level, avoiding some moisture problems. Most room additions work very well on crawl-space foundations.

Basements

Basements are nice from several standpoints. They make installing mechanical equipment easy. Access to building components is excellent in a basement, and an unfinished basement provides significant room for storage. Most people never seem to have enough storage, so this is a major selling point for a basement.

The drawbacks to basements include possible moisture problems and considerable expense during construction. Some basements fill with water on a regular basis. Subsoil drains, sumps, drain tile, and sump pumps can be installed to correct most water problems, but the effort and expense has to be accounted for. Excavation for a basement gets expensive, and so does the additional height of the foundation walls. If money is no object, then a basement is rarely a bad choice.

Foundation work

If your jobs involve foundation work, you must be sure to avoid missing details that could result in liability and expense. Most seasoned remodelers have the skills to do this, but if you're new to the business, don't be afraid to ask your foundation contractor to accompany you on site visits. Homeowners will be impressed that you are professional enough to bring a specialist out with you. A lot of young remodelers are concerned that customers will think of them as being inept if they show up with an entourage of experts for an estimate request. I've have found the opposite to be true. I often take specialists such as electricians, site contractors, and foundation contractors with me when working up estimates. Sometimes I make the initial visit alone, and then if the job looks promising, I arrange a second inspection to get my experts on the job. This makes the bidding process more accurate, and it reduces the likelihood of mistakes. Several trained eyes are more likely to pick up on a camouflaged problem than the eyes of just one person.

3

Wall, floor, roof, and ceiling systems

The subject of wall, floor, roof, and ceiling systems covers a lot of ground. These key components of a home are almost always involved in the remodeling process. Any trained carpenter knows the basics of these systems, but there is a lot more to be learned than just how to plumb a wall or frame a ceiling. This statement is never more true than when applied to remodeling.

Remodeling is challenging work. I believe that's one of the reasons I've enjoyed doing it for so many years. During my career, I've built a lot of houses, sometimes as many as 60 a year. New work is clean and easy compared to remodeling. The unknown factors of a job are much more numerous when remodeling than when building from the ground up. I've often said that, in my opinion, a good remodeler can always do new construction, but trades who are used to only new work can't always do a good job with old work. This feeling has developed over the years as I have watched people come and go in the remodeling industry.

If you are already an experienced remodeler, you have no doubt seen your share of people confused by the complexities of dealing with existing conditions. There has been the plumber who couldn't figure out how to get a 2-inch vent from a basement bath through the upstairs living space to exit the roof. You might have seen electricians dumbfounded by old knob-and-tubing wiring. And you've probably seen air-conditioning crews complaining about having nowhere to run their ducts. This is all common on remodeling jobs.

Since every remodeling job is unique, it presents new learning experiences for all the trades involved. There is no such thing as a cookie-cutter remodeling job. I've worked in townhouse projects where every fourth house was the same. After awhile, building these types of projects becomes monotonous. The walls seem to build themselves. The pieces of plumbing pipe are all cut the same, and the same amount of wire goes into every fourth unit. This gets boring very quickly, especially if you happen to be building 365 units, as I once was. No, remodeling is nothing like new work. Oh, most of the principles and practices are similar, but the on-the-job obstacles can never be compared to new work.

Whether you are a carpenter or a general remodeling contractor, you can't escape dealing with walls, floors, and ceilings. Practically every job you do will involve these elements. There will be bees living in some of the walls. You might very well find snakes or squirrels living in a ceiling, and there is no telling what you might find when you open up an old floor. Perhaps you will be staring at the business end of a skunk, or maybe you will find a cache of old money. You just never know. There is only one thing that you can be sure of, and that is that you can never be sure of anything when you're remodeling a building.

Existing walls

Existing walls make up a major part of many remodeling jobs. You might find that you have to remove these walls, or you might have to cut a new door into one of them. Maybe you will be attaching new partitions to the old walls. Even if you are only hanging kitchen cabinets, your work will be affected by the existing walls. I'm not going to waste our time telling you how to build a wall, hammer a nail, or use a level. I assume you already know the fundamentals of building and remodeling. Instead, I'm going to concentrate on issues that you might not have experienced yet. In doing this, I might be able to save you some embarrassment and some money.

Load-bearing walls

Load-bearing walls sometimes interfere with a person's remodeling plans. When this happens, the walls must often be removed. But you can't just tear down a load-bearing wall. You have to make some provisions for providing continued support to whatever the wall was carrying. You might install a steel beam, a flitch plate, or a laminated beam, but you have to do something to maintain structural integrity. Exactly what you do should be figured out by an engineer. I know a lot of remodelers make their own decisions on what to do in these circumstances, but it is wiser to place the burden of responsibility on someone else.

Since remodeling jobs often involve only interior work and many of the jobs are small, it is often assumed that an architect or engineer is not needed. This can sometimes be a false assumption. Depending upon where you work, your local code enforcement office might require plans stamped by an approved expert when structural matters are involved. Not all jurisdictions have this rule or enforce it, and this leaves remodelers free to make their own determinations. I'm not saying that you don't have the knowledge to design a suitable replacement for a bearing wall, but I wonder if you know the position you are placing yourself in by doing so.

What do you think will happen if you remove an existing support wall and replace it with a wooden header and the header doesn't hold up to the load? Well, at the least, the ceiling could sag. At the worst, part of the building could collapse, causing untold damage to property and person. Are you prepared to take on this liability? Will your insurance cover you under such circumstances, or will the adjuster say that you acted outside of your realm of knowledge and were, therefore, negligent and not covered by your policy? Have you ever thought of this possibility?

If you are involved with a job where structural issues are at question, I believe you would be wise to seek expert advice. I know that the added cost of this advice might price you out of competition, but it is better to lose a job than to create a disaster for yourself.

Partition walls

Partition walls are not as big a risk to remove as load-bearing walls. They are, after all, only dividers, but this doesn't mean you should attack them with abandon. These walls often contain electrical wires, plumbing pipes, and heating and air-conditioning ducts and pipes. If you turn a green kid loose with a sledgehammer to demo these walls, you are just asking for trouble.

Any time you plan to remove a wall, you must look several steps ahead. For instance, what is going to be done to repair the floor where the wall is removed? Will you add plywood to bring the subfloor up to an even level? What will take place with the finished floor coverings? Are they going to be replaced completely, or is a spot repair going to be attempted? Trying to match new flooring to old flooring is very difficult, to say the least. Hopefully, you have prepared your customer for this situation and worked out an agreeable solution in advance.

How do you open up a wall? A lot of contractors use reciprocating saws, and some use circular saws. I prefer a reciprocating saw, but I never start with a saw. My first work is done with a hammer. That's right, I beat my way into the wall. Why do I do this? For my own protection. Since I don't know what's in a wall, I don't want to start hacking away with an electrical saw. The blade might slice through electrical wires or water pipes. By opening access holes with a hammer, I can look into the wall cavity and see what I'm dealing with. There have been countless times when I would have been in trouble if I had started my demo work with a saw.

In addition to standard obstacles in walls, there can be some rather unpleasant surprises waiting for an unsuspecting remodeler. I was remodeling an old farmhouse once when one of the carpenters was swarmed by a huge number of bees. The bees had made their home in one of the exterior walls. As the carpenter was cutting out a section of the wall for a new window, he got a horrible surprise. Fortunately, the carpenter dropped to the floor, the rest of us made a quick exit, and no one was seriously injured. In addition to bees, I've seen bats, snakes, rats, squirrels, and even raccoons come out of the walls of homes. You have to be prepared for anything when you're remodeling.

Remodeling work frequently takes place in homes where people are living. In most cases the work area is cordoned off, to some extent, from the rest of the living space, but curious homeowners and their children still frequent the area. When you are doing your demo work, make sure you take safety precautions for yourself, the residents of the home, and other workers. I can't tell you the number of times I've gone on jobs and found studs laying around on the floor with nails sticking up out of them. This is crazy. It only takes a moment to bend the nails over, and this simple act can save someone from a lot of pain. I know this is a fundamental rule, but it is broken so often that I feel compelled to mention it.

Common obstacles

There are a few common obstacles that you should expect to encounter when removing existing walls. Interior walls are the most likely ones to be concealing plumbing, wiring, or heating materials, but outside walls can also hold these potential problems. To minimize wasted time and money, you must know how to deal with these unexpected setbacks.

Plumbing

Plumbing pipes are not found in every wall, but neither are they concentrated only in the immediate area of bathrooms and kitchens. Plumbers have to get their pipes to specific locations, and how this is done varies greatly. The paths taken by plumbers can be as unique as the plumbers themselves. Residential plumbing rarely follows any formal layout that is reflected on blueprints. Commercial jobs usually have a defined piping layout as a part of the building plans, but this is not normally done in residential construction. Since you are not likely to have a plan to work with in determining where existing plumbing is, you must do it the hard way.

Regardless of your experience in remodeling, it is impossible to predict exactly which walls contain hidden plumbing. Some walls will be more obvious as plumbing conduits than others will. For example, you can look at the roof of a home to establish the terminal points of vent pipes. You can then check in the attic to see if the vents were offset prior to penetrating the roof. An attic inspection will allow you to pinpoint walls that have vent pipes in them. This is a good start, but it is a long way from knowing where all of the plumbing is.

A trip under a home can reveal a lot about the plumbing. You can look for locations where pipes are turned up, into walls. This will provide further details that are helpful in knowing what to expect when the demolition work on walls is begun. The more you inspect visually, the less likely you are to have major changes in your plans later. But don't think for a minute that your detective work is going to keep you from running into some plumbing problems.

It is not unusual for plumbers to run pipes up one wall, through ceiling joists, and back down another wall. Many pipes might branch off of another pipe that is concealed in a wall or ceiling. These pipes can be installed in any number of places, and they are not traceable from an attic or from below a house. You must assume that every wall might be holding plumbing pipes. We will discuss plumbing more thoroughly in chapter 11.

Electrical

Electrical wires are likely to be in almost every wall you work with. Plumbing is difficult enough to predict, but electrical work is much more unpredictable. Sure, you can see switches and outlets that indicate the presence of wiring, but there is much more that cannot be seen. You pretty much have to plan on reworking existing wiring if you are going to remove any walls.

Heating
Heating and air-conditioning ducts can put a big dent in your remodeling plans. While usually movable, these ducts are large enough to cause substantial trouble for a remodeler. Fortunately, ducts for heating and air conditioning are not laced through every wall. They are typically installed below the first floor of a home. When a house has multiple stories, the ducts must extend above the first floor. This means they will be located either in walls or chases. If they happen to be in the way of what you want to do, they must be dealt with. We'll talk much more about this in chapter 10.

Other obstacles
We've just discussed the three primary types of obstacles that are encountered when removing walls, but there are other obstacles that you might have to deal with. For example, a multistory house might have a laundry chute that runs from an upper level to a lower level. Gas piping might be hidden in a wall. Small wires for telephones, door chimes, security systems, and so forth can also present some problems.

If you plan your work carefully from the start, you can avoid some of the surprises of what will be found in a wall that you have to remove. Once a decision has been made to demo a wall, move ahead slowly. Open the wall in a safe manner so that you will not destroy existing systems or harm yourself. There is very little doubt that you will encounter some unexpected obstacles on every remodeling job.

Floor systems

Floor systems in homes are not very complicated. They are made up of plates, bands, girders, joists, and sheathing. There might be some bridging, and there will be nails. Compared to some parts of a remodeling job, floor systems are actually simple. This doesn't mean, however, that they don't provide a level of risk.

If you are doing a standard interior remodel, the floor system might not have to be disturbed. In fact, it probably won't. It is not uncommon to replace some subflooring or to add some underpayment, but major alterations in a floor system are not normally part of an average remodeling job. Attic conversions are an exception to this rule, and some basement conversions require the construction of a flooring system. But on the whole, structural flooring is not a key element in remodeling.

Attic conversions

Attic conversions are one type of remodeling work where major work is usually required with a floor system. When space is designed for attic use, the structural members are not rated for live loads. For example, 2-by-6 lumber might be used in the framing of an attic floor, where 2-by-8, or larger, dimensional lumber would be required for a live load. Not only is the lumber for an attic usually smaller, it is often spaced on 24-inch centers, where spacing for habitable space is normally done on 16-inch centers. The combination of undersized lumber and extended spacing makes it necessary for substantial framing to be done before the attic can be used as living space.

Whenever you are getting involved with major structural issues, such as upgrading an attic floor for use as living space, experts should be consulted for design information. If you take it upon yourself to select the size and spacing of new floor joists, you are assuming a liability that, in my opinion, is better left to engineers and architects. My best advice to you is to seek help from qualified design professionals and then follow their instructions.

While I am not an architect or engineer, I can tell you how most of the attic conversions I've worked with have been done. Don't take these words as your excuse to bypass the help of local design professionals. Accept it as background information.

First of all, if you are going to convert an attic into living space, prepare your customers well for the events that will unfold during the conversion. For example, tell them how the existing ceiling that is attached to the structural members in the attic will be damaged. It is all but impossible to complete an attic conversion without causing some degree of damage to the ceiling below. Once the customer has been told that ceiling light fixtures should have their covers removed, that their ceilings might develop cracks and nail-pops, and that dust and dirt is likely to filter down through the ceiling, you are ready to begin the physical work.

Assuming that you are working with a stick-built roof, you will have rafters, collar ties, and bottom cords to work around. For the time being, it is the bottom cords that we are interested in. There is no reason why these pieces of lumber should have to be removed. You can simply install new floor joists around them. This simplifies the job and keeps the overall cost down.

The biggest problem with this type of work generally comes from the headroom that is lost by installing larger pieces of lumber. The loss is usually only a couple of inches of so, but it can be enough to create a short room. Moving existing collar ties up can often eliminate this problem. Another option can involve the use of engineered joists. These joists can be of a higher load-bearing capacity than a standard piece of lumber, even though the height of the special joist is lower. This, however, is something you will have to consult local professionals about.

Basement conversions

Basement conversions can call for some significant floor work. Most basements are equipped with a concrete floor. Many people install finish floor covering directly over the concrete, and this works fine in most cases. However, if the basement floor is forever damp, the moisture can damage finish flooring. One way to overcome this is to build a false floor over the concrete. Using pressure-treated lumber to frame a floor structure under such circumstances is a good idea. The pressure-treated wood is not affected greatly by the damp floor, and the air space between the concrete and the wood subflooring adds a level of protection for the finish flooring.

There are two common approaches to building a floor structure over a concrete floor. You can build a conventional floor system by attaching band boards to the basement walls and installing floor joists, on edge, as you would in conventional framing. If you need height between the concrete and wood floor to install mechanical equipment, this is a good approach to take. However, if your only goal is to install a false floor to avoid dampness and the cold that is often transferred from concrete to a finished floor, there is an easier way.

You can build a floor system out of pressure-treated 2-by-4s. Lay the lumber flat on the concrete, and attach the lumber with a powder-actuated nailing tool. This will raise the floor level by about 1½ inches, much less than if you were to install floor joists on edge. Headroom is often a consideration in basement conversions, so the less you have to raise the floor, the better. Once the screeds are nailed into place, you have an elevated wood surface to attach subflooring to. This is an economical, effective way to create a false floor in a basement.

Floor repairs

Floor repairs are sometimes necessary in remodeling jobs, especially when kitchens and bathrooms are involved. Since water often leaks through the floors of bathrooms and kitchens, damage occurs more often to the floor joists under these rooms than in any other location. I can't count the number of times I have removed old floor covering in a bathroom to find saturated, black subflooring and damaged floor joists.

If you have visual access to the floor system in the area where your work will be concentrated, you can check for damaged joists and subflooring before you ever bid a job. You should do this because many customers will be unsympathetic if you come to them after having entered into a remodeling contract and try to explain that you hadn't figured on replacing subflooring or bad joists. Your best defense against lost profits is early detection and clear communication.

Rotten subflooring is easy enough to repair. You just cut out the bad sections and install new sections. Joists, however, are not so easy to replace. But the chances are good that there is no reason to remove a damaged joist. Why bother with massive, destructive work when you don't have to? There are several ways to correct the problems caused by weakened floor joists, and these solutions don't involve the removal of any existing joists. To illustrate this, let's look at a few examples.

Assume that you are remodeling a bathroom where the toilet has been leaking for years. The two floor joists on either side of the toilet are both in bad shape. What are you going to do? First, assess how far along the joists the damage runs. It probably only extends a few feet down the structural members. If this is the case, you are in luck. Simply cut out the rotted sections of each joists. Make your cuts so that both of the joists wind up to be the same length. Now all you have to do is install a header to attach the remaining good ends of the joists to. Position your header so that the severed joists butt up against it on the face side. The ends of the header will terminate at the neighboring joists. Ultimately, your header will span between two full-length joists, the severed joists will connect to the face side of the header, and your problem will be solved. It might be necessary to add some additional blocking between the full-length joists, depending on how much of the bad joists you were forced to remove.

Let's study the above example from a different direction. Let's say that the joists are damaged for most of their entire length. This makes cutting and heading them off impractical. So what should we do? Keep in mind that you have good working conditions because the subfloor in the bathroom has been removed. Well, suppose we install new joists right alongside of the old joists? Sure, that could work. In many cases it is possible to slide new joists into place beside damaged ones. This is a lot easier than trying to remove old joists to install new ones. But suppose the joist span is too long for you to get full-length joists put into place?

If you have a situation where replacement joists are too long to get into place, just cut them in half. Slide each half of the joist into place and nail it to the damaged existing joist. Once the new lumber is where you want it, install a screw-jack post under it. You might have to create a solid base for the jack to sit on if you are working in a crawl space. A solid cinder block will accomplish this task easily. Once the jack is set up under the joist, where the two halves meet, you've got a good sturdy support.

There is a third simple way to deal with joists where only a short section of the lumber is damaged. Let's say you have a joist where the top section has rotted for a length of about 2 feet. What's the easy way to fix this? All you have to do is scab on a new section of lumber to strengthen the rotted one. It is advisable to install new lumber on each side of the damaged joist. If the damaged section is 2 feet long, the repair sections should be perhaps 6 feet long. You must make sure the repair sections attach to the existing joist where there is adequate strength for the coupling to be made. You can nail the new sections into place, or you can bolt them to the old joists. Either way, the new sections will give plenty of strength to the weakened joist.

Ceiling systems

Drywall is frequently used as a ceiling material (see Fig. 3-1). As a rule, ceiling systems don't require much attention during a remodeling job. The finished ceiling covering might (Fig. 3-2), but the support system should not require any work. One exception to this, of course, is when an attic conversion is being done. Refer to the earlier discussion in this chapter if you are planning an attic conversion. Aside from this one exception, the rest of your work with ceiling systems will normally be an elective process. For example, someone might want to go from having a flat ceiling in their living room to having a vaulted ceiling. Or the reverse could be true, and the customer might want a high ceiling lowered. This can be done with ceiling tiles (see Figs. 3-3 and 3-4).

People sometimes want to add beams to their ceilings. When the beams are only a decorative addition, there is no real structural work involved. You can buy premade beams and attach them to ceiling joists, or you can build false beams on the job. It is also possible to buy fake beams to attach to a ceiling. I would attempt to avoid installing real, full-size, full-weight beams. This involves a considerable amount of work, and the finished product is not substantially more appealing than when the ceiling is dressed out in false beams.

I've found that an easy way to give customers fake beams made from real wood is to build the beams right on site. The process is fairly easy. Start with some 1-by material, such as a 1-by-6. Screw this

Types of Drywall or Gypsum Board

Type	Thicknesses	Sizes	Uses
Regular	¼", ⅜", ½"	4 × 6 to 4 × 14	Interior walls and ceilings
Moisture resistant	½", ⅝"	4 × 6 to 4 × 16	Base for tile in bath, etc.
Fire resistance type X	½", ⅝"	4 × 6 to 4 × 16	Fiberglass and additives in core for fire hazards or high heat areas.

3-1 *Drywall types and uses.*

Probable Causes for Ceiling Defects

Cracked ceilings:
- Settlement in the building or foundation
- Vibrations in the building or foundation

Nail-pops:
- Nails pulling loose

Drywall tape coming loose:
- High humidity
- Improper installation

3-2 *Potential causes for ceiling defects.*

first board into a suitable ceiling joist. Once it is attached securely, you can build the false beam. You will need three more pieces of 1-by material. Two of these pieces will be used to for the sides of the beam. The third piece of wood will create the bottom of the beam. Building a false beam in this boxlike procedure is fast and easy. However, you might find that a lightweight, prefabricated fake beam is a better alternative for your needs.

Ceiling Tile Comparison		
Type of material	*Cost*	*Features*
Mineral-fiber	Very expensive	Noncombustible
Fiberglass	Midrange price	May be fire resistant
Wood-fiber	Inexpensive	May be fire resistant

3-3 *Ceiling tiles compared.*

Ceiling Tile Applications	
Material	*Use*
Wood-fiber	Can be applied over plaster or drywall with adhesive
Mineral-fiber	Drop-in panels which work with a grid system
Fiberglass	Drop-in panels which work with a grid system

3-4 *Uses for ceiling tiles.*

Closing in a high ceiling

Closing in a high ceiling is nothing more than simple framing. You can attach band boards to wall studs at the desired height. Once this is done, you can use metal joist hangers to support your new ceiling joists. It doesn't get much easier than this.

Opening up a low ceiling

Opening up a low ceiling to give it more of a vaulted look can be simple or nearly impossible. If you are working with a stick-built roof, the job is pretty simple. But if the house was built with a truss roof, you might just as well forget the project. Trusses are engineered for their specific purpose and shouldn't be altered in any way unless a qualified expert puts a stamp of approval on your plans.

Even when you have a stick-built roof, you should consult design professionals before you start hacking away at the ceiling joists. You might very well be able to remove the ceiling joists to allow a higher ceiling, but this is a job that should be engineered by an appropriate person. The actual work involved is not very complicated, but someone has to make decisions on how the job should be done. This individual could be opening up a can of worms if the work is not drawn out properly.

I believe strongly in keeping responsibly at a level that I am fully qualified to handle. Even if I'm sure of what an engineer is going to tell me to do, I like having the safety net of knowing that such an expert advised me professionally, and in writing, as to what actions to take. This might not keep me from getting sued someday, but it does create a chain for me to pull in when I'm forced to battle in a court of law.

Uneven ceilings

Uneven ceilings can be a problem when working with older properties, particularly if the ceilings were done with plaster. I had this problem in the first home I ever owned. It was an old two-story house, and the ceiling was far from level. To make matters worse, much of the plaster had cracked, creating an eyesore. As I worked on the house in my spare time, I finally got to the point where I had to deal with the ceiling. At that time, I had very little experience with plaster.

My first thought for repairing the ceiling was to apply a coating of filler. After thinking more about this, however, I was convinced that any coating I put on the ceiling would probably just fall off. Then I thought about putting a layer of joint compound on the ceiling and pulling it to achieve a textured ceiling. I tried this in a small area of the living room, but the results were less than satisfactory.

After coming to a conclusion that major work was going to be required in order to straighten out my ceiling, I tried to decide what to do. One of the first thoughts was to remove all the plaster and lathe, and replace it with drywall. Then I started thinking about the ceiling joists. I guessed that the lumber used to build the old house was probably not planed. To confirm this, I cut out a section of the ceiling. Sure enough, the joists were by no means uniform in their size. This meant that I would have to either fur out the old joists or build a new ceiling structure. The house had 9-foot ceilings in it, so dropping the ceiling was not going to create any hardship in terms of headroom.

Once a decision had been made to lower the ceiling height, I had to decide what method to use. My wife and I talked about using a grid system with removable tiles, but neither one of us liked what this type of ceiling would look like when used throughout the house. Ultimately, I decided to frame a new ceiling structure and hang drywall, which was later textured.

Framing the new ceiling structure was not difficult. I secured ledgers (or bands) around all the walls and hung the new ceiling joists with metal joist hangers. This not only gave me a nice level ceiling frame to work with, but it also gave me excellent access for the revisions I was making with the plumbing and electrical systems. A drop-in ceiling would have been less expensive and less time-consuming, but we preferred the look of a textured ceiling.

There are times when furring strips are an ideal, inexpensive way to get the waves out of a ceiling. Looking back, perhaps I would have been better off to have done my first plaster ceiling conversion with the strips. But I would have lost the advantage of space gained for my plumbing and electrical installations. If I had been bidding the job on a competitive basis, for only the ceiling work, I'm quite sure I would have opted for furring strips. However, I wasn't bidding the job and I was thinking ahead to the mechanical work, so I did the work the way I wanted to.

Assuming you had a job like the one I've just described, building a false ceiling might be cost prohibitive. Your plumber and electrician could cut holes in the plaster ceiling and drill the joists for their work before you furred the ceiling. Your new ceiling would conceal the holes made by the mechanical subs, and your out-of-pocket expense for lumber would be much less. When you're trying to make a living from remodeling, you have to work smart. Thinking ahead and planning around obstacles is what will keep you in business when your competitors are folding up their business tents.

Roof systems

Roof systems are not normally a part of an average remodeling job, but if your work will involve a roof, be careful during your bidding process. Roof structures are anything but cheap, and a mistake on your part can cost you more than you're making from a job. Failing to account for a rotten floor joist or a few sheets of bad subflooring is one thing. Having to swallow the costs associated with mistakes in a roof structure could choke out all of your profits, and then some.

What can go wrong with a roof structure?

What can go wrong with a roof structure? Plenty. I've seen rafters turned to sawdust by wood-infesting insects. Granted, this should not be your problem, but if you fail to do a thorough investigation before you quote a price and offer a proposal, you could wind up paying to replace a lot of roof material.

Bugs aren't the only enemy in an attic. Houses without proper attic ventilation can rot their roof structures quickly. When the attic of a home is not insulated and vented properly, condensation can form at an alarming rate. The roof sheathing will become saturated, and the rafters or trusses will begin to take on water. This type of problem usually exposes itself in the form of leaks coming through ceilings. I have seen such cases where water was literally dripping off the roof sheathing and soaking the attic insulation. It doesn't take long for this type of problem to do some extreme damage. If you happen to commit to doing a job involving such a situation, without prior knowledge of the defects, you can be in big trouble.

Most roof systems don't just deteriorate for no reason. Before major structural damage is done, there has to be some type of defect. It could be condensation or bugs, but it could also be a regular old roof leak. Of course, this type of problem isn't going to destroy an entire roof system, like bugs and condensation can. To protect yourself, you have to do a full inspection of the roof system before committing to any work involving it.

One effective way to test a roof structure is to use a probing tool. This can be a knife, a screwdriver, an awl, or any other similar item. By poking the wood with such a tool, you can tell if the lumber is solid. I have seen structural timbers that looked fine on the outside but were gutted on the inside. This was the work of wood-infesting insects. Don't count on just what you can see. Probe randomly to see that the entire system is satisfactory.

Trusses

Trusses make a good roof system, and they are economical to use. But they can give a remodeler a lot of problems. Let's say that you are giving an estimate for installing a dormer on a Cape-Cod style home. The upstairs of the house is finished, and there is no access into the knee-walls. Your customer wants a shed dormer installed so that a bathroom can be added in the upstairs hall. Since the house is of a Cape design, you assume it is framed with rafters. This is a logical assumption, but it could be an expensive mistake for you. In this particular case, the upper level of the house was done with room trusses. This is fine for the home's present use, but adding a dormer can get tricky because of the trusses.

I'm not saying it will be impossible to fulfill your contract obligation to build a shed dormer on the house, but I don't think you will make as much money as you had planned to. Since the upper level has been done with trusses, you should seek expert engineering advice on how to cut the trusses to allow for the dormer. This advice can get expensive, and since you didn't disclaim trusses, and in fact never even asked about them, the cost of engineering fees is coming out of your profits.

Trusses are great to work with when you are doing new construction, but they can be a serious threat to your bank account when remodeling around them. You should always attempt to do a visual inspection of any aspects you will be required to work with. In a case like the example I've given you, where the trusses are not visible, you should protect yourself with a disclaimer clause in your contract. For example, if you had stated in your contract that the agreement was based on the house having a stick-built roof and that additional fees would be charged if the roof was found to be built with trusses, then you'd be off the hook.

Raising a roof

Raising a roof is a big job. This is certainly the type of work where you should protect yourself with written recommendations from design experts. The occasions when most remodelers raise a roof are rare, but they do come along. Some customer decides to turn a ranch-style home into a cape-style home. A customer wants to do a major attic conversion, but insists on more headroom. Either of these situations can call for removing an existing roof and building a new one. Before you agree to get involved in this type of work, make darn sure you know what you are getting into and that you are prepared to go the distance.

Once you take a roof off of a person's house, you had better be able to get a new one back on quickly. Having a week of rain set in on a house without a roof can ruin your rating with insurance companies. Seriously though, there's a lot of preplanning needed for a roof removal. Weather is a prime concern, but it is not the only one, and it might not be the biggest one.

When it comes to raising a roof, you must first get rid of the old roof. This, in itself, is a substantial job. You must make arrangements to set up and maintain a safe perimeter to work within. You don't want to be tearing off the roof and have a huge chunk of it fall on a homeowner, child, or delivery person. Neither do you want a heavy section of roof dropping on your customer's car. Then, of course, you have to make arrangements for removing the debris from your job site. This can be done with the use of container services or a large truck. But one way or another, you have to get rid of the old roof. There is also the consideration for damage that might occur inside the home. When your crews are banging and cutting, you can bet that some of the living space will be disturbed. Expensive vases could be knocked off shelves. Light fixtures could lose their globes. Ceilings are going to be damaged, and other situations are bound to develop.

Looking past the removal of the old roof, what are you going to do once it's gone? How are you going to keep the house protected from wind, rain, and other falling precipitation? Are you going to set up some rough framing and cover it with a tarp? Should you remove the old roof in sections and replace it as you go along? All of these questions are pertinent, and as a remodeling contractor, you had better have answers for them. A slip-up at any stage of this type of work could cost you more money than you have.

As a remodeler, it is important that you think before you act. I'm sure you must have heard how it is best to measure twice and cut once. That is a good rule to live by, but as a remodeler, you have to think three times, at least, before you open your mouth. When remodelers find themselves in deep trouble, it is usually because they talked or acted before they thought through their situation. It will pay you to keep your mouth shut and your pen in your pocket until you have run through every possible scenario.

You probably know your trade very well. It might be that you are also good with people. Both of these qualities will serve you well in your remodeling business. However, until you learn to think and plan well in advance, you are going to face continual problems in the business. Whether you are tearing into a wall or ripping off a roof, you had better have a plan, a back-up plan, and hopefully, another plan. Remodeling is filled with uncertainty, and anyone who thinks it isn't is setting the stage for a big surprise.

4

Stairs

Stairs are often taken for granted. People assume that stairs can be installed where they're needed, whenever they're needed. This might be true, but functional stairs are not always feasible in all locations. While it is rare for remodelers to alter an existing set of stairs, occasions do occur when this work is required. For example, if a person is finishing off a basement, new stairs might be needed. These could be replacements for old basement stairs, or they could be the first set of stairs ever installed to allow access from the main living area into the basement. The same set of circumstances could apply to an attic conversion. So there are times when providing new stairs is necessary.

Building a set of rough steps is not a tough job, but designing an efficient layout for a difficult situation requires skill. Designing a set of stairs is often much more difficult than the actual construction of them is. Will a landing be needed? Should the stairs have a winder in them? Could a spiral staircase be used? These are just a few of the questions that might come to mind when factoring a set of stairs into a remodeling job.

Building codes regulate certain dimensions pertaining to stairs. For example, the tread width and the riser height are normally regulated. So is the amount of headroom and the width of the stairs. Provisions for handrails are also normally dealt with in local building codes. Whatever the local building requirements are, you must be aware of them and adhere to them, and this can complicate your job at times.

Local jurisdictions are empowered to modify the building codes they adopt. This means that rules for local codes might not be identical to those found in general code books. I can't tell you what the requirements for stairs are in your area, but I can give you some rule-of-thumb figures that should be close to what your local code mandates.

Primary stairs, meaning most stairs in living space, should have a minimum width of 32 inches, but 36 inches is better. There should be a minimum of 30 inches of open space when measuring between the handrails or the handrail and the wall. A maximum riser height should not exceed 7½ inches. All treads should have a minimum width of 9 inches. Minimum head clearance should be set at 80 inches. When a landing is installed, it should have a minimum depth of 36 inches. Handrails are usually installed so that they are between 30 and 33 inches above the walking surface. You can normally get by with just one handrail with a closed staircase, but some areas might require two.

Secondary steps are often subject to less stringent code requirements. But this is not always the case, so check with your local building inspector. When secondary steps are identified, they are usually steps going into an unfinished basement or attic. While these steps might not have to conform to requirements for primary stairs when they are used with unfinished space, remodeling the space into living space can trigger a rule where the stairs must be upgraded to meet code requirements for primary stairs. Again, these numbers are not necessarily what is required by your local code, so check on the local level before planning or building stairs.

Exterior stairs

Exterior stairs or steps are sometimes a part of remodeling projects. If you build a deck for a customer, you will probably have to build steps for it. The same could apply to the construction of a screened porch. Complex designs are not normally incorporated into exterior stairs. The most complicated design typically encountered involves a platform so that the stair can offset at a 90-degree angle. There is no real challenge here. Stringers come off the upper landing and go straight to the platform. From there, another set of steps descends straight down to the ground. Some outside construction might get a little more involved, but most outdoor stairs are simple to figure.

In addition to decks and porches, outside steps might be used to access a remodeled room over a garage. Some houses might have exterior steps leading up to space created in an attic conversion. Computing the rise and location of these more extensive stairs can become more difficult. But the same basic principles used to calculate interior stairs apply when working with exterior stairs. Since most work with stairs will be done inside a home, let's concentrate our time on them.

Interior stairs

Interior stairs can be built in a number of configurations. Most, however, are either straight runs or have a winder or platform in them.

More exotic versions might be built with a sweeping arc. Some stairs are spiral in design and require minimum space for installation. There are open-tread stairs and closed-tread stairs. Some stairways are enclosed with walls on each side. Others have a wall on one side and a railing on the other. A few have railings on both sides and no walls. Each type of stairway has it good points, but they all have their bad points, too. It will be up to you and your customers to figure out what type of stairs will work best.

The two most common occurrences that will require you to build or upgrade stairs will be the conversion of a basement or attic. Most other interior remodeling work will not affect existing stairs. There might be, from time to time, a desire to have an existing staircase relocated, but in 20 years of remodeling, I can't ever recall this job coming up.

A basement conversion

A basement conversion can require you to upgrade existing basement steps or build a complete set of stairs. If you are upgrading an existing set of stairs, the work will be self-explanatory once you are sure of your local code requirements. You might have to add an extra stringer. There will probably be a need for additional railing and pickets. It might be that the rise or headroom cannot meet code requirements for a primary stairway. In this case, you might as well start from scratch. In fact, I have found that it is usually prudent to remove rickety old basement stairs and build new ones right from the start. If customers are going to spend major money to finish off a basement, they might as well have decent stairs leading into the space. Besides, it can take longer to tinker with old stairs than it would to build new ones.

I have seen many jobs where the existing basement stairs were in the way. Their placement made it impossible to get maximum use of the available space. Sometimes the stairs have been in the only feasible place they could be, but I've seen many jobs where the basement steps could be relocated. Whether you are moving the stair location completely or modifying the way in which the stairs are installed, you can enhance some basement conversions with this type of work. This will make the customer happy, and if you play up your ideas during the bidding and selling process, your input on the stairs could be enough to win you the job. Let me expand on this for a moment.

Let's say that you've been called out to give an estimate on a basement conversion. The homeowners escort you into the basement and point their plans out to you. As you look around, you see that the existing stairs are built so that the end of them restricts the size of a new family room the couple wants. Other contractors have already been on the job, and they took the customer's recommendations at face value, never mentioning other options. You, on the other hand, speak up with ideas on how the basement could be more spacious with a different stair location. Well, the homeowners look at you with big eyes and wide smiles. You are the first person to show them a way to get a bigger family room, which happens to be their main reason for converting the basement space. By using your knowledge of stair designs, you have just gained a competitive advantage over all the other contractors. Little sales maneuvers like this can boost your sales and your income.

When you are looking at a basement conversion, you should investigate all options for the stairs leading into the space. If existing stairs are in place, obviously it will be easier to use that same location. However, easier is not always better. If the stairs come down in the middle of the basement, your customer might prefer to have new steps built that could come down a side wall and not take up so much valuable space. Even just adding a landing and a 90-degree turn near the bottom of the steps could open up enough room for a hallway. It is always best to approach remodeling with an open mind. The more you study the circumstances, the more likely you are to find better ways of accomplishing your goal.

Attic conversions

Attic conversions require the building of new steps. In some cases there might be a set of secondary steps installed to the attic for access, but these steps will generally have to be upgraded. A lot of attics have only scuttle holes or pull-down stairs for access. Under these conditions, you must find a place for a full-size set of stairs. This can be a bit of a challenge. It is fairly easy to work in a set of access stairs, but to install formal stairs that are accessible from public areas is a whole other matter.

When faced with tight quarters for installing a conventional stairway, many remodelers turn to spiral stairs. These units do take up a minimum of room, but they also have some drawbacks. Spiral stairs are difficult for some people to climb. The shape and size of a spiral stairway makes it very difficult, if not impossible, to move furniture up and down them. The seemingly vertical climb up a spiral stairway is another strike against this type of unit. I'm not suggesting that you should never use spiral units, but you and your customer had better think through all angles of the proposition before proceeding. In fact, let me tell you a couple of quick stories about two different jobs where spiral stairs were on the list of things to do.

The first job I'm going to tell you about involved a friend of mine. He and his wife had a new home built for them many years ago. I wasn't building houses at that time. I was concentrating on remodeling. Anyway, the house was built with a full, walk-out basement. My friend wanted a spiral stairway installed between the basement and his living room. One of his reasons for wanting this was so that he could carry wood up from the basement for the stove in his living room. Another friend of mine was the carpenter on this job. He built the house and the stairs to the specifications provided by the owner. Everything went well through the summer months. Well, almost everything.

The new house had laundry facilities in the basement. The new homeowners soon discovered that toting laundry baskets up and down the spiral stairs was no fun. The narrow stairs made it difficult to navigate with a basket full of laundry, and the steep climb was tiring on the way up. As if this were not bad enough, things got worse in the winter.

A month or so into the heating season, my friend called and asked me to come over at my first opportunity. He didn't say anything about his stairs or about anything else that was related to work. I assumed I was being invited over for a social call. The following Saturday found me sitting in my friend's living room. It was toasty warm and there was a substantial pile of wood near the stove.

As I admired my friend's new home, I couldn't help noticing pieces of bark and wood debris between the wood pile and the sliding-glass door from the deck. This seemed strange to me, since the wood was stored in the basement. Why would anyone go out onto an icy deck, down exterior steps, and lug wood up from a basement when they could use interior stairs? I questioned my buddy on this.

I was told that the spiral stairs were just too difficult to climb with an armload of wood. The conversation continued and revolved around the spiral stairs. It turned out that one of the main reasons I had been invited out was to give some free professional advice on what other stair options were available. We talked for a good while, and I offered some suggestions. A few weeks later, my crew was working on replacing the spiral stairs with a conventional stairway. My friend threw away a good deal of money by not thinking his plan through all the way in the first place.

Moving onto another job, I can tell you about a customer who was saved from the type of pain described in the last example. This person wanted to convert the attic over his garage into office space. His idea was to use a spiral stairway to gain access to the office. He thought it would look nice for his clients, and he liked the fact that the unit wouldn't deprive him of much space in his garage. When I arrived on the job to give an estimate, the stairs were quickly a topic of conversation.

As we talked, I learned of the homeowner's plan to use the new space for an office. I inquired as to whether there would be desks in the office. He looked at me with a strange stare, and confirmed that there would be desks in the office. I stopped him right there by asking how he planned to get the desks into the office. It was as if I had hit the man with a baseball bat. His face went blank. He looked up at the garage ceiling and then back at me. After rustling through some papers in a folder he was holding, he produced specifications for the spiral stairs he had almost ordered. It only took a few moments for the man to realize how bad he would have felt if the spiral stairs had been installed. You see, the stairs he had in mind were much too small to allow free passage of a desk.

In my opinion, spiral stairs should be used for decorative effects and secondary steps, but not as primary steps. They are fine if you just want occasional access to a room that will not contain large furniture, but if the stairs will see daily use, then spiral units are probably not the best choice.

Open or closed

When you are consulting homeowners on the types of stairs to have installed, you will have to address the issue of whether the stairs should be open or closed. Of course, existing conditions will have something to do with the final decision. There are advantages and disadvantages to both types of stairs.

Closed stairs are, in my opinion, a little safer when used by children and elderly persons. Kids love to slide down banisters, and this can be a dangerous pastime. Children also try to make open stairs into their own personal playground. Balusters are not monkey bars, and they can break away and allow a child to fall. If an adult slips on the stairs, and this happens frequently, the momentum of their fall could cause the railing and balusters to break. This might result in a much more nasty fall. For these reasons, I prefer a closed stairway under certain circumstances.

Closed stairs are not as attractive as open stairs. They don't allow light to flood the stairs, and the closed-in effect can be confining. It is also true that an open stairway tends to make a home appear larger. Anytime an open concept is used, rooms seem to look bigger. From an image point of view, I prefer an open stairway. Yet I like the functional qualities of a closed staircase.

Since much of the debate over open and closed stairs hinges on personal preference, the outcome is subject to an individual's own preferences. As a remodeling contractor, you should consult your customers on the pros and cons of each type of stairway. Let the customers make their own decisions, but give them enough information so that they can make an informed choice.

Planning

Planning is the key to success when it comes to stairs. You should explore all options before making a firm commitment on how to build a particular set of stairs. For example, if your customers are advancing in age, it might be wise to build their stairs with multiple landings installed. This will give them a place to stop and rest along their climb. You might have an occasion when an oversized width would make negotiating stairs easier for your customer. Every job will have its own set of circumstances to work around. It's your job to keep trying out different ideas on paper until you arrive at an ideal solution for your stair installation.

5

Windows and skylights

Windows and skylights are the eyes of a home. Many remodeling jobs involve the installation of new windows and the replacement of existing windows, and almost any home can benefit from the addition of windows and skylights. The more natural light a house has, the bigger it looks. Also, bright rooms are more appealing rooms to be in. This, along with other reasons, is what makes the use of new and replacement windows so popular.

Windows are such big business in the remodeling field that there are contractors who specialize in them. Some contractors spend nearly all of their time working with windows. If your company is not getting a big piece of this action, you are missing out on some money. But whether you specialize in replacement windows or just work with windows as part of your routine remodeling, there is money to be made from them. To capture some of this capital, you have to know how to sell and install windows in a way that will make your customers happy.

Confusion

Confusion runs high with consumers who try to sort out their window options without the expert guidance of a professional contractor. Sales associates in supply houses inundate consumers with literature and sales hype. Much of this only serves to make matters worse for the average person. The confusion starts with U-factors and runs a long gamut. You can take advantage of this situation. If you can assist your customers in sorting out which windows will be best for them, you are more likely to win their confidence and job.

For you to be able to consult efficiently with your customers, you have to have a depth of knowledge of the subject being covered. If you were given a test on windows, do you think you would pass with flying colors? If you take windows and skylights for granted, you are short-changing your income. There is enough money to be made in windows to warrant a little extra time being invested to upgrade your knowledge. With this in mind, let's begin our lesson on windows and skylights.

Types of windows

How many types of windows are there? (See Fig. 5-1.) A lot. There are more than enough variations in windows to make anyone happy. Almost everyone thinks of a double-hung window when asked to visualize a window. Is this what you would think of? Hey, let's play a little game. Take a moment to think of six types of windows. Don't take too long on this. You should be able to name at least six or eight types of windows right off the top of your head. Did you come up with six different types of windows? Well, let's compare your answers with the following descriptions of different types of windows. If you didn't do well on this exercise, you need to hone your knowledge of windows.

Residential Window Unit Types

Double-hung	Awnings	Bay
Casement	Sliding	Bow
Fixed		

5-1 *Types of residential windows.*

Double-hung windows

Double-hung windows are probably the most well-known windows in use. They are quite common and very popular. I would guess that there are more double-hung windows in use than all other types of windows combined. What makes these windows so favorable? Part of their popularity is cost. Double-hung windows are affordable. Tradition probably plays a part in the choice of double-hung windows. I suspect that the main reason double-hung windows are so prolific is that they are the type of window that most contractors push on their customers. This is not said to demean contractors. My point is that few contractors offer their customers a full range of window choices.

Single-hung windows

Single-hung windows look like double-hung windows. The difference between the two is that both sashes move in a double-hung window and only one sash, usually the bottom one, moves with a single-hung window. Single-hung windows are a little less expensive than double-hung windows, but I don't think the savings is enough to offset the popularity of double-hung windows.

There is something ironic about the comparison of double- and single-hung windows. Many people shun single-hung windows as being cheap products. As I've already said, the primary difference between single- and double-hung windows is that only one sash moves with a single-hung window. Now, a double-hung window can have only one sash fully open at a time. There is more control available when double-hung windows are used. The lower sash can be raised, and the upper sash can be lowered. I know there must be people who use this option to their advantage, but most people always raise the lower sash. If this is going to be the case, why not just use single-hung windows? I'm not saying that you should convince your customers to go with single-hung windows, but it does seem that with the habits of most homeowners, single-hung windows would work just as well as double-hung windows.

Casement windows

Casement windows are more expensive than single- and double-hung windows. But they also offer advantages that the other windows can't. For example, a double-hung window can never have more than half of its total size open. Not true with a casement window. Since casement windows are hinged on the side and crank out, it is possible to get full air flow through the entire size of a casement unit. This can be a big advantage. Additionally, casement windows are typically more energy efficient than double-hung windows. While casement windows cost more to buy, they can save their purchaser money in utility bills over future years. This savings can more than pay for the extra acquisition cost.

There is another big advantage to casement windows that a lot of people never think about. How many times have you struggled to push open a double-hung window? Can you imagine how difficult raising a double-hung sash is for people with limited strength or physical disadvantages? Think about it. Opening a double-hung window can be a major chore for some people. When compared with how easy it is to crank open a casement window, double-hung windows might not be suitable for elderly residents, children, or people with physical limitations. Keep this in mind when talking with your customers. Since good windows are a long-term investment, you will do well to look into the future for customers who might grow into a stage where operating double-hung windows will be a struggle.

Awning windows

I'll bet you didn't think of awning windows when you were compiling your mental list. These windows are what I consider special-purpose windows. They are not the type of window that would normally be installed throughout a house. Awning windows do, however, have their strengths.

Since awning windows are hinged at the top and open upward, they can be left open in many rains without having water come through the window opening. A blowing rain can still invade living space, but if the precipitation is falling straight down, an awning window will allow ventilation while blocking out the foul weather.

Privacy can be maintained when awning windows are used. These windows can be installed high on a wall and still be opened easily. This provides light and ventilation at a height that is high enough not to encroach on someone's privacy, such as in a bathroom. Another good place for awning windows is in a sun room. If you are remodeling a room to be used for a spa enclosure, awning windows will allow moisture from the spa to escape while maintaining privacy. These windows should be used sparingly, but there are definitely times when they should be used.

Sliding windows

Sliding windows were popular years ago, but they are not in such good standing today. Sliders are typically considered to be cheap windows that don't offer good energy efficiency. While it is still possible to find some sliding windows being installed, they don't rate high on the list of desirable windows for many people.

Bay and bow windows

Bay and bow windows can change both the interior and exterior appearance of a home. It is also possible to increase the square footage of living space with a bay window. You must, however, consider the additional cost of foundation work, framing, and finish work that goes into the building of a bay window. Nail-on bay windows brighten up a room dramatically, and they enhance the overall appearance of a house. Both of these window units run on the expensive side, but there are times when their cost is justified. One example of this might be when remodeling an eat-in kitchen. The construction and installation of a bay window can create a nice nook for a breakfast table. This isn't a cheap proposition, but on the other hand, it will not cost a fortune.

Garden windows

Garden windows can be used anywhere, but they are particularly popular in kitchens. These expansive windows let in a lot of light, and their design allows plants or other items to be set in them. Garden windows come in various styles, so you will have to shop around to see all of the features you can offer your customers.

Fixed-glass panels

Fixed-glass panels don't show up as often as I think they should. I've used fixed glass in countless jobs. It is an inexpensive way to let huge amounts of light flood into a home. The low cost of fixed-glass panels make them desirable in sun rooms and other rooms where ventilation is not your goal. These panels can also be used in conjunction with operable windows. By doing this, you get a wall of windows for a much lower cost. Any good glass company can provide you with a variety of glass panels.

Skylights

Skylights provide tremendous opportunities for remodelers. If you are fighting a dark room, skylights can be the answer. Of course, you must have a direct path to a roof before you can make use of a skylight. It is not mandatory that you have a vaulted ceiling to work with. If there is attic space over the location where you wish to install a skylight, you can frame in a light box. Just as there are a number of window choices available, so are there a lot of skylights to work with.

Plastic bubbles

Plastic bubbles are the least expensive type of skylights. These domes come in various shapes to accommodate nearly every need. Some of these units have a flange that is installed directly under roof shingles.

Other models are made to be curb mounted. Both types are pretty easy to install, and the units themselves are very inexpensive.

There are drawbacks to these low-cost skylights. One of the biggest disadvantages is the lack of energy efficiency. Being made of plastic-type material, the insulating quality of a bubble skylight is poor. Not only do these skylights cause heat loss, but they also tend to condensate badly at times. This factor alone can be enough to disqualify the units from consideration. When skylights condensate, the light boxes that accommodate the units suffer from water stains. Flooring below the skylight can become damaged from dripping water. If your customers insist on using uninuslated skylights of any type, be sure to protect yourself from upcoming complaints of condensation.

If your customers are seeking skylights to help exhaust summer heat from their home, plastic bubbles are not going to get the job done. These units are fixed. They do not open. Skylights can be very effective in venting summer heat from a house, but these fixed units are no good for this purpose.

Plastic bubbles are available in clear colors and in tinted colors. I have always favored a bronze tint when using these skylights, but that is mostly a personal preference. The installation of skylights can cause carpeting and furniture to fade, due to direct sunlight. This is something you should point out to your customers. Clear skylights might cause the fading process to accelerate.

Fixed glass

Fixed-glass skylights come in various degrees of quality. These skylights also come in many different sizes. Skylights with stationary glass panels can range from the very cheap to the very expensive. Their quality can rival that of any other skylight. The only major drawback to skylights with fixed glass is their inability to provide any ventilation or exhaust potential.

Operable units

Operable units offer the most flexibility in the selection of skylights. These units can be opened to remove summer heat, and they can catch some breezes when mounted in steep roof pitches. I just finished building a new house for myself, and I installed an operable skylight in my office. It is equipped with a screen and is designed to be opened with a pole. This can be done manually or with an automatic opener. In my particular case, the skylight is mounted low enough in the roof that I can reach it and open it by hand. I should also say that I installed two skylights in my great room. These are fixed units. Operable units are very nice, but they are also expensive.

Roof windows

Roof windows provide a reasonable alternative to building small dormers where the only real purpose of the dormer is to allow the installation of a window. Roof windows can let in more light than a window in a dormer, and they eliminate the need for such extensive framing. If I were remodeling a Cape-style house for myself, I might use dormers to give the building a traditional architectural look, but otherwise, I would rely on roof windows for my light and ventilation. Roof windows are available with screens, built-in blinds, and other options. These units are expensive, but they are a cost-effective alternative to building dormers.

Installing windows

Installing windows is not normally a difficult task. There are times, however, when unexpected circumstances can throw you a curve. For example, a customer might want to replace an existing kitchen window with a new garden window. Since the garden window will probably be larger than the existing window, you must plan on framing a new rough opening. If you've been in the remodeling business for long, this part of the job won't present any problems for you. However, what happens if the plumbing vent for the kitchen sink is installed in the stud bay next to the existing window? The new garden window will need to occupy this space, but there is a pipe in it. What would you do?

If a vent pipe is running up in an area that will interfere with a window installation, you must have it relocated. This usually isn't a big job, but plumber's aren't cheap, and even small jobs can have big price tags. A plumber will probably offset the vent into the next clear stud bay and then tie back into the existing vent before it exits the roof. It might, however, be necessary to invest more time in the job. Your plumber might have to get under the kitchen sink and reroute the vent, and drain, from below the floor level. This will run your cost up somewhat. Relocating the plumbing won't take long and even if you hadn't counted on the expense, you won't have to hock your truck to pay for it. But it is always best to avoid unexpected expenses. In this case, you could do that with a clause in your contract that protects you if unforeseen obstacles are found within the wall.

Electrical wires might very well present some trouble for you when installing new windows. Most good electricians run their wires low enough or high enough so they will not interfere with future windows, but not all electricians are so thoughtful. You could open up a wall and find a string of wires running right through the proposed window location. The wires can be moved, but again, you are incurring additional expense. This is why it is good business to have certain clauses in your contract to give you a way to recover your expenses in dealing with unexpected costs.

Check and double-check

Check and double-check the required rough-opening measurements before you start cutting into the siding on a customer's home. There are few things more embarrassing that cutting a hole in the side of someone's home that is too big for the new window being installed. It's easy to make holes larger, but it's tough to shrink them. When you are measuring for rough openings, don't take anything for granted. I've seen carpenters measure one or two windows and assume that all the remaining windows were the same. People don't always choose windows with identical measurements, so an assumption like this can put you in hot water. You should measure and research each individual window before you take any action for it.

Look on both sides

Before you start cutting in a new window, look on both sides of the wall where the window will be installed. I know this sounds stupid, since any professional remodeler should have the common sense to do this, but not all of them do. Walking around the interior of a home with the homeowner showing you where windows are desired can distract you from outside obstacles. If you fail to think ahead and investigate what's on the other side of the wall, all kinds of things can happen. At the least, you could have an irate customer on your hands when you inform the homeowner that a window placed in an agreed-upon location will not work. Worse yet, you might even start cutting in the window, from the inside, without realizing that you are going to run into a roadblock. Taking a walk around the exterior of the home will allow you to avoid this problem.

What types of outside obstacles might get in the way of a new window? A bulkhead door can be a problem, and so can an attached tool shed. You'd feel pretty funny cutting a new window into a dining room only to get a view of the inside of a tool shed, wouldn't you?

If a home depends on fuel oil for its heating system, the fill and vent pipes for the oil tank, or even the oil tank itself, could block the installation of a window. All of these situations are easy to spot if you watch for them, but you have to take the first step and look for them.

Watch out for hidden masonry walls

When you are quoting a price to install new windows, you should watch out for hidden masonry walls. I had a friend, who is a remodeler, run into this problem just a few months ago. The contractor took on a major remodeling job. He was converting a building from two-family use into four-family use. The job required extensive interior work, and the property owner wanted all new windows. In addition to replacing existing windows, a lot of new windows were to be added due to the expansion of rental units. My friend has a lot of experience in remodeling, but he goofed on this job. When he gave the property owner a price for the work, he had no idea of what was waiting for him inside the exterior walls.

It turned out that the building being remodeled was built long ago, when attacks from hostile groups were not uncommon. As protection from bullets and arrows, the original builders constructed the exterior walls with brick, and a lot of it. Over the course of time, various remodeling efforts had been made on the property, and it was covered with wood siding on the exterior and plaster on the interior by the time my buddy got involved with it. He saw the clapboard siding and the plaster and assumed he was bidding a typical old job. But when he went to cut in the first window, he hit a brick wall, quite literally.

I went to the job site to meet my friend for lunch one day, and I saw the brick work. The number of windows being installed escapes me at the moment, but I know there were a lot of them. Can you imagine having your job go from a simple one to this type of nightmare? I can't even begin to guess how much money my friend could have lost on the job. Fortunately, the property owner had deep pockets and a kind heart. Rather than hold my friend to his written quote, the property owner agreed to pay extra for the window installation. In 20 years of remodeling, this was the first job I had ever seen where brick had been covered up with wood siding, but I promise you, it was. This just goes to show that even veteran remodelers can run into big problems without ever seeing them coming. But a good contract that excludes liability for such hidden expenses can help to protect you.

Working with skylights

Working with skylights can lead to some interesting experiences. Most skylight installations go off without a hitch, but there are times when existing conditions make the work something of an adventure. Any time you are working with old houses, you can run into strange and unusual circumstances. For instance, you might find that the roof structure is not made of typical rafters or trusses. It could be made up of old beams. If this is the case, you are going to have some extra framing work to do before you can install a skylight.

Roofs on older homes can look pretty good and be in horrible shape. If you don't get up on the roof before you quote a price for installing a skylight, you could be making a big mistake. Suppose the existing roof is too brittle to work with? What will you do if the house has a slate roof and you have failed to notice this fact until after you have committed to a price for installing two skylights? Have you ever considered that the front roof on a house could be protected with asphalt shingles while tin covered the bathroom roof? It can happen. You can't afford to take anything for granted when you are a remodeling contractor. Hey, I've even seen houses where parts of the roof were covered with old metal signs. Yes, signs. In fact, there is a house, here in Maine, not more than 30 miles from where I live that has its entire roof covered with old signs. How do you flash a skylight into a rusted old metal sign?

Skylight installations can be easy or hard. The type of roof covering you are working with certainly plays a part in which way the job will go. The rafter configuration is another element to be considered. In addition, the condition of an attic can affect the speed with which you can install a skylight. Insulation can get in your way. Puny bottom cords can make walking around in the attic treacherous. You have to investigate all existing conditions carefully before you start throwing figures around.

Once you have covered all the bases where problems might pop up from existing conditions, you can go about your work in an efficient way. The actual installation of a skylight, under normal conditions, is not difficult. Jobs that require long light boxes get a little tricky, but they don't offer much trouble to an experienced carpenter. Flashing the skylights properly is one of the most important parts of an installation. As long as you follow the installation instructions provided by the manufacturer, you are not likely to encounter any problems. But some contractors think they know it all and don't need instructions. This is silly. Not all skylights are alike. If you fail to read and follow the instructions packed with a skylight, you could be setting yourself up for trouble down the road.

Helping your customers

Helping your customers determine what type and style of windows they should buy is a big responsibility. So is helping them sift through sales hype and technical jargon, but it is a part of your job. If you don't handle this side of your job well, you might not have any work to do. Let's spend the remainder of this chapter discussing the many ways for you to assist your customers in making decisions on windows and skylights.

Light

Additional light is always one benefit derived from adding new windows and skylights. Surveys have shown that home buyers like rooms that are bright and cheerful. This makes adding natural light to a room a good investment, within reason. You can point out to your customers what rooms in their home will benefit the most from various types of windows and skylights. For example, a skylight installed over a new whirlpool tub can provide some nice evenings of star gazing while relaxing. Skylights in a kitchen can brighten the work area and make the room more comfortable to be in. A garden window can also add more light to a kitchen.

Appearance

Appearance is always important when considering home improvements. Adding a new window can balance the exterior elevation of a home. Architectural enhancements can come in the form of bay and bow windows. Windows with arched transoms above them can set a house apart from the rest of the homes in a given area. When you are thinking about, and selling, new windows, you have to consider all of your options.

Necessity

Some windows are installed out of necessity. For example, if you are creating a new bedroom, you might have to install a new window to meet egress requirements in the building code. Attic conversions typically require the installation of new windows, and roof windows are a good option in these cases. If a customer is being forced to add new windows, you should offer a wide selection of options for consideration.

Ventilation

Ventilation is, of course, a primary reason for having windows in a home. When this is the impetus behind installing new windows, you should describe how different windows work in a way that your customer will understand. For example, you should point out that casement windows allow full air flow while double-hung windows are restricted to one-half of their size in air flow. Awning windows also give complete air flow, so lay out all of the options and explain them to your customers.

Skylights can also be used as ventilation tools, assuming that they are capable of being opened. A house equipped with high ceilings, reversible-rotation ceiling fans, and operable skylights can provide many ventilation options.

Floor space

If only a little floor space is needed to tweak a room into prime condition, the construction of a bay window might be just the ticket. You can control the size of the unit and the floor space achieved. It might be wise to use a combination of fixed glass and operable panels to make a cost-effective bay window.

Sun rooms

Sun rooms are very popular additions to homes. When I was working in Virginia, it seemed that we were constantly building sun rooms. Casement windows, fixed glass, and awning windows all work well together in this type of remodeling project. A lot of sun rooms are done with sliding-glass doors, but ventilation is limited when this approach is taken. The use of casement and awning windows eliminates the restrictions associated with sliders, whether they be sliding doors or sliding windows.

Energy efficiency

Energy efficiency has become a big issue with windows. Most homeowners don't know how to judge the efficiency of a window they are considering. One factor is, of course, the U-factor of the glass. You can point out to homeowners how to assess the insulating quality of glass by its U-factor. Most homeowners are familiar with R-factors, but many have never even heard of U-factors. Since U-factor ratings work in basically the opposite direction of R-factors, many inexperienced people buy poor quality windows, thinking that they have done well. When discussing energy efficiency, you must educate your customers on window design and construction. Show them why a casement window is usually a better value, in terms of energy efficiency, than a double-hung window. I recommend taking cutaway sections of various windows to the job during the bidding process. It is much easier for people to understand information you are providing if they can see examples of what you are talking about.

Maintenance

Maintenance is another factor to be dealt with when talking about windows. Does your customer want a clad window that requires minimum maintenance or a wood-frame window that is cheaper but needs routine painting? If you are not confident of your knowledge in this, or any other, area of windows, talk to your suppliers. Manufacturers will be more than happy to supply you with sales brochures and technical information. When you are in a selling mode, your product knowledge might be all you need to take a job away from a lower bidder.

Organize your material

Organize your material well. A solid sales presentation always benefits from a well-organized proposal. Good organization of your material will also make it easier for your customers to follow you through your presentation. If you are going to talk about Low-E glass or Argon gas, have supporting documentation available to hand out to your customers. This will not only give them something tangible to assess, but it will also get them involved in your presentation. This is a key to making sales.

You can both benefit

When you are discussing windows with your customers, you can both benefit from knowledge that you have gained. Your customers will receive honest, usable information to make a buying decision. You will reap the rewards of a good presentation in the form of a signed contract. Take whatever time you need to get up to speed on the many various window options. You owe it to yourself, and your customers, to be the best that you can be.

6

Siding and exterior trim

Siding and exterior trim is a field of remodeling where a contractor can set up shop as a specialist. Many do, and these specialists are hard to compete against if you are a general remodeler. It stands to reason that if you do the same type of work day in and day out, you should get very good at it. This is usually the case with siding specialists. Since they are set up only for siding and exterior trim, and that is the only work they do, they are fast. Being fast translates into either increased profits or lower bids, depending on the approach you choose to take. This is why it's tough for a general practitioner in remodeling to compete with any type of remodeling specialist.

Whether you're up against a replacement-window company, a full-time roofing contractor, or a siding specialist, your prices will probably be higher than theirs. Certainly, low prices are not always the deciding point in who wins a bidding contest, but price is always a factor. It often pays to be a specialist. As a specialist, you can create a certain image that will allow you to make more money than your competitors, or you can work cheaper and still make the same amount of money as nonspecialists. The decision is yours.

I specialized in kitchen and bathroom remodeling for many of my first years in remodeling. The reasons for this were simple. I'm a master plumber, and I found kitchen and bathroom remodeling to be both in demand and profitable. Oh, I built my share of additions, sun rooms, decks, and garages, but I generally made the most money when working in kitchens and baths. To this day, I find these same two categories to be very nice to me. But I know other remodelers who make their highest profits from siding. Still, there are others who do best with additions. For obvious reasons, there is more money to be made with large jobs, such as additions, but on a percentage basis, some of the best-paid remodelers claim the money is in smaller jobs like windows and siding.

I've done siding jobs successfully, but I've never seemed to grab the golden ring with them. This, of course, has been my own fault. My company is geared up for kitchens and baths, not siding. This is not to say that the people I work with are not competent in the installation of siding, but I have yet to find a way to beat the contractors who do nothing but siding. I have the same problem with roofing.

When I worked in Virginia, there were siding crews who would show up on the job at dawn and work until dark. They were incredibly fast, and their endurance was something to be admired. Siding a complete house in a day was commonplace. Every move these crews made was synchronized. My crews were not so well adapted to siding installations. We did fine on custom homes and high-priced remodeling jobs, but when it got down and dirty on starter homes and average retrofits, I couldn't compete profitably.

I have given you this brief bit of my history to let you know that siding might be an area of remodeling to avoid, unless you want to commit to it on a big scale. If you are doing a new addition and the siding to go with it, you will probably do all right. But if you are aiming at straight siding jobs, where no other work is required, I doubt if you will enjoy maximum profits, unless you are a specialist. Siding is, however, a field where you can specialize and make a better-than-average living. The options that are available to you are numerous.

Should you specialize?

Should you specialize in siding installations? Maybe. If you like siding work, live in an area with a decent amount of aging homes, are set up for siding, and can find fast mechanics to work with you, siding is a viable specialization. If any of these conditions are not met, you might not do so well in a siding business.

Siding is a very competitive field. Since licensing requirements in this area of remodeling are typically lax, there is a lot of competition. Much of it is easy to overcome, but then you have those dedicated crews that work from dawn to dusk, like I encountered in Virginia. Siding can generate a huge profit, in terms of percentages, but the actual cash value of a siding job is nothing to compare with an attic conversion or a room addition. Are you willing to give up the big scores to get a lot of little jobs? Depending on your personal situation, you might actually be better off with a lot of little jobs. There are more of them, but you don't have to be accountable for as many people on small jobs. A siding crew of just three people can be very productive. Compared to the number of people involved in a major conversion or addition project, three people are much easier to keep tabs on.

Based on my past personal experience, I would not attempt to bid low-range to midrange siding jobs unless I was set up as a specialist in the field. My experience has proven the bidding activity to be a waste of time. You might not find the same to be true for you, but I do know several contractors who have run into the same circumstances that I have faced.

Siding is so simple

Some contractors believe siding is so simple to install that there is nothing major that can go wrong during this phase of construction. I say that this line of thinking is nonsense. True, siding is not as complicated or as perilous as removing a complete roof structure and building a second-story addition. But there is still plenty that can go wrong on a siding job. Let's discuss some of the problems that might crop up on a siding job.

Pump jacks

When you or your crews are installing siding, do you use pump jacks or staging? One or the other of these types of elevated platforms is needed, and either one of them can damage a lawn. How do you protect a person's grass when you are setting up? Do you put blocks of wood under your staging to level it? How often do you use wide boards under your equipment to distribute weight more evenly? You might not have run into a really picky customer yet, but if you stay in the remodeling business long enough, you are bound to encounter some customer who will make your life miserable. The catalyst to fire up this nasty customer could be the marks your scaffolding leaves in a lawn.

How can you hedge your odds against upsetting a customer with depressions in the lawn? Putting wide boards or plywood under the supports of your work platform will help. At the least, they will prevent deep holes from being punched into the earth. But the boards might kill any grass that is beneath them. As long as you don't keep the boards in one place for more than a day, the grass should recover. But if you set up and leave your equipment in the same place for several days, the customer's lawn might turn brown in the spots where you had your boards. Since there is a level of risk here, you should talk to your customers before doing any work and describe the potential problems associated with installing new siding. This little chat won't stop bad things from happening, but it can make your customers more forgiving.

Broken windows

Broken windows are more common than you might think on siding jobs. A cross bar from a section of staging can swing loose, when being disassembled, and break the glass out of a window. Careless workers sometimes ram cross bars, jack poles, and even siding into windows. There is also the occasional hammer that is dropped onto the work platform, which then bounces into a window and breaks it. Accidents happen, but they seem to happen much more frequently with some contractors than with others. You can't really prepare a customer to accept a broken window because there is no legitimate excuse for such a thing to happen.

Inside breakage

Inside breakage of personal belongings is common on siding jobs. Too many contractors fail to tell their customers what to expect when old siding is removed and new siding is installed. The banging done on exterior walls is enough to make picture frames fall. It is also plenty of force to make knick-knack shelves drop to the floor. A broken picture frame might not seem like a big deal to you, but it can be to a customer. Let me tell you a short story of such a case.

I met an elderly lady last year when she wanted some work done in her home. As I walked through the house, I noticed an extensive collection of decorative plates, the kind sold in gift shops. The plates were from all over the country. In addition to the plates, there were numerous empty holders on the shelves, and a few of the plates had obviously been glued together after having broken. As small talk, I inquired about the background of all the plates.

The lady told me that she and her late husband had traveled all over the country, and they had collected plates as they went along. With her husband being recently deceased, the plates were all she had left to remind her of those happy times out on the road. The way this woman talked about those plates, you would think they were her grandchildren. It was very obvious that each and every plate on those shelve was dear to her.

As I learned the history of each plate, one by one, I found out why there were so many empty holders on the shelves. I also learned how the damaged plates that remained in the collection had come to be broken. A siding contractor had been hired to replace the lady's existing siding with vinyl siding. During the work, the contractor's crew had created enough disturbance on the outside of the home that the missing plates had been knocked out of their resting places. A good number of the plates were destroyed beyond repair. Needless to say, the lady was heartbroken to see pieces of her best memories go into the trash. Even if the contractor had been remorseful, which she said he wasn't, there would have been no way to undo the damage.

If the contractor had advised this lady of the potential for the plates being broken, I'm sure she would have removed them from their shelves until all of the work was done. The contractor's negligence cost the lady a lot, in terms of emotional loss. He also didn't do himself any favors in getting new job referrals. You can bet the homeowner would not be quick to recommend such a contractor to friends.

If you've been doing siding work for awhile, you know what's likely to happen on most jobs. Tell your customers what to expect. I've heard contractors say that they don't inform their customers of what might happen because they are afraid of losing the job. I doubt that you will ever lose a job by being honest and helpful with your customers, but if you do, you probably wouldn't have wanted the job anyway.

Bats, rats, and things

When you are removing siding from a house, you might discover bats, rats, and all sorts of other things. The exterior walls of houses can be home to a multitude of wild creatures. Snakes, squirrels, bats, mice, bees, and other living creatures often take up shelter in the walls of homes. Pulling a piece of siding off of a high gable and coming face to face with startled creatures can make you a little weak in the knees. If a swarm of angry hornets comes flying out fast to see who just destroyed the side of their nest, which was attached to the back of a piece of siding, a siding installer can get quite a scare. Being perched some 20 feet above the ground on a small walk board is not a good place to be when a bunch of mean hornets are looking for something to attack.

Depending on where you work, you might never run into any of the wild things that I've just told you about. But I assure you it can happen because it has happened to me. I grew up in the country, and when I started working in the trades, many of the jobs were associated with old houses. Many of these houses were out on some acreage, and it was not at all uncommon to find all sorts of living things in the homes. I've been nose to nose with snakes, and I've been dropped low by fleeing bats. Bees have attacked me, and rats, big Norway rats, have given me the creeps. Squirrels have scampered by me, and raccoons have stared out of walls and ceilings at me. Believe me when I tell you that almost anything can be waiting for you on the other side of that siding you are removing. Of course, more modern homes don't offer the same risks, since they have more consistent sheathing between wall cavities, attics, and siding.

If you are working with exterior trim and have to remove a section of soffit, be careful. This is a favorite hangout for bees. It is also a place where snakes might seek refuge. Can you imagine yourself pulling down a section of soffit only to have a large, lively snake fall into your face? It could happen, so be careful.

Nails

I would like to assume that all siding installers know what types of nails to use, but I know this just isn't the case. How many houses have you seen where siding was installed with the wrong nails, and the nails caused rust streaks to run down the siding? I've seen several over the years, and there is no excuse for this type of problem. The right nails cost more than the wrong nails, but the difference is a small price to pay in order to preserve the siding. I always insist on stainless-steel nails when working with wood siding, and I hope that you are knowledgeable and responsible enough to use the proper nails on your jobs.

Electrical wires

It should go without saying when talking to professional remodelers, but I'm inclined to mention power lines. Every siding job will involve some work around power lines. If a home is served by overhead power, the siding around the weatherhead can make working conditions dangerous. Respect electricity and the damage it can do. Before you set up near an electrical service, have the utility company come out and wrap the lines to reduce your risk of injury or death.

Types of siding

What types of siding do you offer your customers? (See Figs. 6-1 and 6-2.) Are you a full-line installer, or do you only work with vinyl? Is wood siding the only type that you will install? Are you willing to install any type of siding a customer requests? There are only a few types of siding that make up most of the market, but in addition to these standards, there are other types of siding available. You might get requests for any type of siding.

Siding Compared

Material	Care	Life, yr	Cost
Aluminum	None	30	Medium
Hardboard	Paint	30	Low
	Stain		
Horizontal wood	Paint	50+	Medium to high
	Stain		
	None		
Plywood	Paint	20	Low
	Stain		
Shingles	Stain	50+	High
	None		
Stucco	None	50+	Low to medium
Vertical wood	Paint	50+	Medium
	Stain		
	None		
Vinyl	None	30	Low

6-1 *Comparison of various types of siding.*

Cedar siding

Cedar siding is very popular, especially in new construction. The cost of cedar is one of its few disadvantages to a homeowner. Cedar looks good, it can be used on almost any type of house with desirable results, and it lasts for a long time. However, it should be sealed or stained promptly to prevent discoloring. I've seen a lot of homes where cedar siding was not treated promptly, and the siding turned gray. Some people like this weathered look, but don't

Siding Advantages/Disadvantages

Material	Advantages	Disadvantages
Aluminum	Ease of installation over existing sidings Fire resistant	Susceptibility to denting, rattling in wind
Hardboard	Low cost Fast installation	Susceptibility to moisture in some
Horizontal wood	Good looks if of high quality	Slow installation Moisture/paint problems
Plywood	Low cost Fast installation	Short life Susceptibility to moisture in some
Shingles	Good looks Long life Low maintenance	Slow installation
Stucco	Long life Good looks in SW Low maintenance	Susceptibility to moisture
Vertical wood	Fast installation	Barn look if not of highest quality Moisture/paint problems
Vinyl	Low cost Ease of installation over existing siding	Fading of bright colors No fire resistance

6-2 *Pros and cons of various types of siding.*

count on your customers liking it. You should advise your customers that cedar will discolor if it is not sealed within a reasonable time. Then, if the siding discolors, the customer can't plead ignorance.

Pine siding

Pine siding is one of my favorites. It is easy to work with, it's wood, it can be stained or painted, and it gives a good finished appearance. Pine is substantially less expensive than cedar, and once it is installed and stained or painted, it is hard to tell that it is not cedar. Some people don't like the knots found in most pine siding, but I think they add to the character of a home.

I've used pine siding for many years, and I've never been disappointed with it. I do make a point of having it stained, or painted, quickly. Pine siding that is left in its raw condition and exposed to rain will turn black. It doesn't take long for the discoloration to set in. I recently discovered a supplier who has a machine that stains the siding before it is delivered to a job site. When I built my new home, I gave this prestained siding a chance. It worked out great. The fee charged by the supplier to stain the siding was less than what my painters were quoting for the work, and the siding arrived in good shape. Since it was already stained, there was no opportunity for the wood to discolor. By using this procedure, I saved a little money on my staining costs, and I saved a good bit of time on the job. If you have not experienced this type of arrangement, you should check with your local suppliers to see if they can offer the same service.

Aluminum siding

Aluminum siding is not used very much anymore. There was a time when it was very popular, but that time has passed. Vinyl siding has, in my opinion, made aluminum siding a thing of the past.

Vinyl siding

Vinyl siding gets mixed reviews, depending on who you're talking to. Some people swear by it, and others swear at it. I like some of the attributes of vinyl siding, but on the whole, I am not thrilled by it. My experience has shown that real estate appraisers are not too keen on vinyl siding either. This is a big factor to a builder who is working to get the most appraised value possible for every dollar spent. But if you're not concerned with a maximum appraisal and you're installing what a customer wants, vinyl is fine.

One of the biggest selling points associated with vinyl siding is that it is said to be maintenance free. While vinyl siding never needs painting, it sometimes does require a power washing. Damp locations can cause mold and mildew to form on vinyl siding. When this happens, a power washing is needed to clean the siding. This is less expensive than painting, but it is a form of maintenance.

Overall, vinyl offers a lot to homeowners. The fact that the color is a part of the vinyl is a big advantage. Since the color won't chip or peel, it lasts for a very long time, and it never needs to be painted. A house that is equipped with vinyl-clad windows, vinyl siding, and wrapped trim is about as maintenance free as it can get. Another advantage to vinyl siding is that it can often be installed over existing siding, reducing the expense incurred by a property owner. All of these factors combine to make an attractive sales package.

Other types of siding

Other types of siding exist and are used, but the ones we have just covered are, by far, used most often. Some customers might want another type of siding, such as T-1-11, but these cases will be rare. Homeowners with expensive taste might seek a board-and-batten siding, but again, there will not be a lot of call for this. Cedar shakes might account for a very small percentage of siding requests. If you're prepared to work with cedar, pine, and vinyl, you should be in the hunt for the majority of siding work to come your way on a residential level.

Asbestos

Siding that contains asbestos can present some health and financial problems for you. If you're going to remove this type of siding from a home, you will most likely have to hire contractors who are licensed to do asbestos abatement work. This can get very expensive, so you cannot afford to overlook this potential cost. This is another situation where a clause in your contract can save you a lot of money. The clause should discuss what will happen if the siding is found to contain asbestos. If the homeowner is willing, you can check the siding before you commit to a price to remove it. If it contains asbestos, you can make financial arrangements for its removal before you enter into an agreement.

Before you sign

Before you sign a contract to install siding, you should do a complete inspection of the property to be sided. You might discover that the walls are way out of plumb and that some compromises must be made during the installation. It is much better to discover this before the job is started. The same goes for an asbestos situation.

As with any type of remodeling work, you should sit down with your customers and discuss the job thoroughly before you sign a formal proposal or contract. There will be many details that must be worked out. For example, how will the old siding be removed from the job? Will this be your responsibility or that of the homeowner? Getting rid of a large load of siding can get expensive, so you should establish if this cost will be in your bid or not. If you just lump the removal costs into your price, without advising the customer of the expense, you might be presenting a proposal that is much more expensive than those of your competitors who did not address the issue of removal. As long as you educate your customers in the expenses to be expected, they can compare bids fairly. If they are not sure if your competitors are assuming responsibility for removal work, a few quick phone calls to the other contractors will provide the answer. These calls should be made by the potential customer.

Siding a home is fairly simple work. It's not the trade-related work that you have to worry about. It's the risk of unexpected problems that should concern you. These problems can be avoided with proper planning, a thorough inspection, and clear communication with your customers.

7
Roofing materials

Roofing materials are pretty standard, in terms of what is commonly used to cover the roof structure of a home. Asphalt shingles are certainly the most commonly used roofing material on residential properties. Fiberglass shingles are, however, making a move to outsell asphalt, and they might be reaching their goal in some areas. Other types of roofing, such as cedar shakes, tiles, and slate are not installed on many new houses in today's construction and remodeling market. But there are houses with these roofs on them that remodelers have to work with. If you have never worked with a slate roof, you might be surprised at how different this roofing material is from other types that you might have dealt with. The same can be true of working with a tile roof. A shake roof is different from an asphalt roof, but shakes are easier to work with than tile or slate is.

Remodelers are generally subjected to tougher working conditions on roofs than are contractors who concentrate on new construction. It is much easier to roof a new home that is under construction than it is to piece together roofing on remodeling jobs. Trying to get a skylight installed in a slate roof is not easy. Neither is it simple to install a skylight on a tile roof. Your working conditions on a roof can present numerous problems.

Roofing, like siding, is another phase of remodeling where it can be difficult to compete with specialists. Companies who do nothing but roofing are usually lean and mean when it comes to bidding wars. If your remodeling company is geared towards general work, you might not be very successful in bidding jobs where the only work is roofing work. This is something you will have to experiment with to determine on your own. I know that I've never been able to compete with roofing companies when bidding jobs where roofing was the only work needed.

Even if you don't want to be known as a roofing contractor, you will likely become involved with a good deal of roofing work.

Whether you are building an addition on a home, installing a skylight, or adding attic ventilation, you will be working with roofing materials. Many of the roofs you work with will not be in great shape. Some of them might not even be safe to walk on. Your knowledge of roofing has to include much more than just knowing how to snap a chalk line and lay out shingles. (See Figs. 7-1 and 7-2.) Assessing existing roofing conditions will be important in your remodeling career. Not only will you need a depth of knowledge in this area, you will also need a good working knowledge of the various options available in roof coverings. Let me give you a quick example of how knowing about materials and their performance can be an asset to you.

Potential Life Spans for Various Types of Roofing Materials

Material	Expected life span
Asphalt shingles	15 to 30 years
Fiberglass shingles	20 to 30 years
Wood shingles	20 years
Wood shakes	50 years
Slate	Indefinite
Clay tiles	Indefinite
Copper	In excess of 35 years
Aluminum	35 years
Built-up roofing	5 to 20 years

All estimated life spans depend on installation procedure, maintenance, and climatic conditions.

7-1 *Life spans of roofing materials.*

I live in Maine. The winter temperatures in this state get cold, very cold. Climatic conditions can have an effect on roofing materials. For example, fiberglass shingles might develop problems in extremely cold temperatures. (See Fig. 7-3.) I have found this to be true

Minimum Roof Live Loads

Roof slope	Load, psf
Less than 4/12	20
4/12 to less than 12/12	16
12/12 or greater	12

7-2 *Minimum roof live loads.*

Roofs bear wind and snow loads which vary widely—check local codes.	
Northern states	40 lbs./sq. ft.
Central states	30 lbs./sq. ft.
Southern states	20 lbs./sq. ft.

7-3 *Sample regional roof loads.*

in Maine. My experience has been mirrored with other contractors. Local suppliers have commented to me on the number of warranty calls they receive on fiberglass shingles. My talks with local contractors and suppliers have proven what my experience has shown. Fiberglass shingles can give contractors problems in cold weather.

Fiberglass shingles installed in my area have a history of cracking and blowing off. I assume this is due to the cold temperature. However, I cannot say with certainty that temperature is what causes the shingles to crack. The professionals I have spoken with concur with my opinion that cold temperature is the primary cause for fiberglass shingles failing.

Two of the big selling features of fiberglass shingles is their reported insulating qualities and fire resistance. I considered using fiberglass shingles on my new home, but I decided against it. My choice was asphalt shingles. To this day, I have never installed fiberglass shingles on a job. This is not because they are a bad product or that people don't like them. It's just a matter of my never having a request for them. I don't doubt that fiberglass shingles are very good. My biggest concern with using them in Maine is the cold temperature experienced in winter. Your region of the country might not be affected by these extreme temperatures, and fiberglass shingles might very well be in great demand. A lot of them are sold and installed here in Maine, and I don't want to give an impression that you shouldn't use them. On the other hand, I want you to be aware of the problems I noticed with these shingles in Maine. Since I've already jumped into a discussion on fiberglass shingles, let's continue along this line with additional information.

Asphalt shingles

Asphalt shingles (Fig. 7-4) have long been an industry standard in residential roofing. They have been installed for years, and they are still the industry leader in residential roofing materials. I've worked with asphalt shingles throughout my 20-year career, and I've never been disappointed by them. In my opinion, these shingles make an ideal roof, and they are easy to work with.

Roofing Materials Lowest Permissible Slope

Asphalt or fiberglass shingle	4 in 12 slope
Roll roofing with exposed nails	3 in 12 slope
Roll roofing with concealed nails 3" head lap	2 in 12 slope
Double coverage half lap	1 in 12 slope
Lower slope. Treat as flat roof. Use continuous membrane system, either built-up felt/asphalt with crushed stone, or metal system with sealed or soldered seams. Wood shingles may be applied on slopes as low as 3 in 12.	

7-4 *Recommended slope minimums for various roofing materials.*

Many of your customers will probably ask you what type of roofing material you will recommend. This might depend on the roof pitch (Fig. 7-5). Each job can have its own set of circumstances, but I suspect that you will either suggest asphalt or fiberglass shingles. When you make a recommendation, you should back up your opinion with facts. Have some manufacturer brochures available to give to your customers. Take some time to go over the brochures with your

Roof Pitches	
Traditional	*Metric*
2/12	50/300
4/12	100/300
6/12	150/300
8/12	200/300
10/12	250/300
12/12	300/300

7-5 *Conversion table for roof pitches.*

customers. Your opinion is very valuable to a homeowner, but I recommend that you let the customers make their own decisions. If you push a particular type of roofing on a customer, the sale might backfire on you. For example, if I were a big proponent of fiberglass shingles and sold them on all of my jobs, I might be confronted with some unhappy customers down the road. If you go out on a limb by making specific recommendations, you might find that you will be held liable, in some form, before you are done dealing with your customers.

Wood

Wood shingles and shakes are a viable roof for some types of homes. (See Fig. 7-6.) These roofs are, however, something of a fire risk unless they are treated to increase their fire resistance. Wood roofs are expensive, and they are not normally used in most modern construction. This doesn't mean that you won't have occasions to work with wood. Some existing homes will have wood-covered roofs. As you go about your remodeling work, you will find times when you have to work with wood shingles and shakes.

Tile

Tile roofs are not common in most regions. This doesn't mean that there are not thousands of tile roofs out there, just waiting for a remodeling contractor. Moving around on a tile roof is tricky. The tiles

Roofing Materials

Roofing type	Minimum slope	Life years	Relative cost	Weight, Pounds/100 sq ft
Asphalt shingle	4	15–20	Low	200–300
Slate	5	100	High	750–4,000
Wood shake	3	50	High	300
Wood shingle	3	25	Medium	150

7-6 *Comparison of various roofing materials.*

can be slippery, and they can break easily. Few customers will have tile roofs or request a tile roof, but you might find a job here and there where tile is used.

Slate

Slate was a popular roofing material years ago. While I have not had much experience with tile roofs, I have worked with numerous slate roofs. I can tell you from experience that slate roofs can be very slippery. It is not unusual for moss-type vegetation to grow on a slate roof. This makes footing even more treacherous. Slate is also very heavy, and brittle. (See Fig. 7-7.) Working with slate effectively requires experience, caution, and patience.

I haven't seen a new house roofed with slate for years. Before I left Virginia, slate was being used on some high-scale homes, but even then it was a rare circumstance. I don't recall ever seeing a slate roof in Maine. Slate was a dominant roofing material in some sections of Virginia where I worked. If slate roofs are present in your area, you should build a base of knowledge about them. Sooner or later, you are going to run into a job where you are required to work with slate.

Existing conditions

Existing roof conditions can have a lot to do with what you do and how much money you make. Roofs that look pretty good from the ground can be in bad shape. Roof sheathing that is not investigated can be rotted. Existing valleys can be leaking and yet undiscovered.

Weights of Building Materials

Component	Material	Load, psf
Roofing	Softwood, per inch	3
	Plywood, per inch	3
	Foam insulation, per inch	0.2
	Asphalt shingle	3
	Asphalt roll roofing	1
	Asphalt, built up	6
	Wood shingle	3
	Copper	1
	Steel	2
	Slate, ⅜"	12
	Roman tile	12
	Spanish tile	19

7-7 *Roofing material weights.*

Flashing in areas where your work will take place might be defective. Even though this isn't technically your problem, you might get blamed for it. If you are planning to install a new roof over an existing one, you had better check to see how many layers of existing roofing are already on the roof. You might bid the job with an intent of applying a new layer of shingles over existing ones only to find that you have to strip the roof before you can do any replacement work. There are many little problems that can pop up around roofing work, and there are also some bigger troubles possible. I've just given you some examples of what to look out for, but let's look over some other examples of how you can wind up in a mess.

It was about to fall in

I went out on an estimate call a couple of years ago to discuss doing an attic conversion, but when I inspected the roof, it appeared that it was about to fall in. My first suspicions were triggered when I pulled into the driveway. The roof line of the house was sagging badly. When I walked into the house, I quickly spotted signs of water damage in the ceilings. Then I moved up into the attic. This was the worst attic that I had ever been in. To tell you the truth, I was afraid the roof might collapse on me before I could get out of the house. One of my carpenters was with me. We looked at each other and retreated quickly from the attic.

When I got back into the main part of the house, I explained to the homeowner what I had seen in the attic. We talked briefly, but I had no interest in taking on this job. The homeowner was planning on creating living space in an attic where the roof was going to come down soon. When I suggested removing the existing roof structure as part of the project, I was told that other contractors had looked at the job and hadn't been concerned about remodeling the existing attic. Who these contractors were is a mystery to me, but I know I wouldn't set foot in an attic like that to work. I left the job with no further interest in pursuing it.

I know this chapter is not about attic conversions. It's about roofing, but this story does pertain to roofing. I think that any roofing contractor with experience would have noticed the sag in the roof. This should be enough of a red flag to make a seasoned contractor look for more information. However, I don't doubt that some roofing contractors might take on a job like this one. My best guess is that if anyone went on a roof like the one I've just told you about, they would probably fall right through. This story should show you that it is important to look before you leap.

Don't get blamed for what you didn't do

As a contractor, it is important that you protect yourself and don't get blamed for what you didn't do. As soon as you do any work on a roof, you might be opening yourself up for problems that you didn't cause. This can be the case with flashing or valleys that are leaking. Even if they are leaking before you set your ladder up, you might get blamed for the leaks. This is another reason why it pays to inspect attics closely before committing to any roofing contract.

I handled a remodeling job once where there was an existing leak around the flashing for a chimney. The living-room ceiling was discolored from water damage. I noticed this immediately and questioned the homeowners about the leak. They indicated that they were aware of it and that they would like us to fix it while we were remodeling the living room, bathroom, and basement. I started to tell the customers that I didn't want to get involved in the roof work. It was such a small job that there was not any real profit in doing it, but there was some risk. The work we were doing for them was priced at more than 20,000 dollars, so how could I turn them down? Anyway, I had our people take care of the flashing, or so I thought.

After the major remodeling was done and we had finished the punch list, the customers were ecstatic. They loved their newly remodeled space. It was not until several months later that I learned the leak my people had fixed wasn't really fixed. It was still leaking. The people were very nice about the continued leaking. The leak was finally fixed for good, and life went on. But doing this little favor for the customers set us up to lose money. I admit, we made enough profit from the big work to give them the repair work, but still, nobody likes to throw away money. The point is this, doing little jobs can cost you more than you make.

In the example I've just given you, we were at fault for the leak. My people had attempted to fix it and failed the first time. But suppose we had been doing some other type of work on the roof and still got blamed for this existing leak? It could have happened that way. Even if you are innocent, it can cost more to prove your innocence in court than it would to fix the problem. If you notice an existing problem on a job that you are pricing out, make a note of what you suspect. Detail the potential problem on paper and have the customer sign in acknowledgement. This will help protect you.

Two types of roofing

Some houses have two, or more, types of roofing on them. You could pull up to a house and see asphalt shingles on the front and find the back roof to be covered with tin. This situation is not common, but I have seen it happen. Bathrooms in older homes are famous for this type of problem. You see, older homes didn't have inside plumbing when they were built. When bathrooms were added, the roofs on them sometimes didn't match the existing roof. This type of situation is not rare, but neither is it common. As long as you do a complete inspection of properties before you make remodeling and roofing commitments, you can avoid problems like this.

Multiple layers

It is not unusual for older homes to have multiple layers of roofing. As you probably know, it is not wise to pile layer after layer of roofing on top of itself. It is generally acceptable to leave one layer of old roofing in place when installing a new roof, but putting a new roof over several layers of old roofing is not such a good idea. If you have an experienced eye, you won't have any trouble seeing when a roof is covered with multiple layers. On the other hand, it never hurts to protect yourself with a clear, concise clause in your remodeling contract. If for some reason you wind up having to strip off old roofing and remove it from the premises without getting paid for it, you are going to lose money. Don't let this happen to you.

Watch out below

When you are working on a roof, it is important that you and your crew watch out below. It's easy for tools and materials to slip away and go sliding off a roof. If someone happens to be under the falling object, you are in a world of trouble. Whether it is a roll of felt, a hammer, or some shingles, anything falling from a roof can cause serious damage. You, or your company, can be held accountable for this type of accident. Whenever it is possible, you should make sure that no one will be under your work area.

I sat in my work truck one day and watched a roofer walk right off a roof. He was rolling felt out on a townhouse. For some reason, he was rolling the felt out by walking backwards on the roof. As my helper and I sat there watching, the roofer backed right off the roof of a two-story townhouse. Fortunately, a large pile of snow broke the roofer's fall. The man was still injured, but the aches and pains were nothing like they would have been if the snow pile hadn't been there.

In addition to watching a roofer walk off a roof, I've seen all sorts of potential roofing disasters develop. I've seen hammers come sliding off of roofs, and I've watched rolls of felt get away from their handlers. Any of these situations could result in major lawsuits. You have to be careful at all times when you are involved with roofing.

8

Interior and exterior doors

There are few major remodeling jobs that don't involve doors of some type. You might be installing new doors, where doors have never been before. Your job might require replacing a standard entry door with a sliding-glass door. A French door might be on your list of things to do. Doors are a part of most big remodeling jobs.

Compared to other aspects of remodeling, the installation of doors is not real high on the list of complex tasks to undertake. However, installing a door can involve a lot more than you anticipate. This is especially true if you are installing a replacement door of a size different than that of the existing unit. There is, of course, more to doors than just the physical installation of them. As a professional remodeler, you are also the property owner's consultant. When asked for recommendations on types of doors, you are expected to have some quality information to offer. This is, perhaps, one of the weak points of many remodelers.

As we progress in this chapter, we are going to discuss different types of doors. We will also talk about common problems that sometimes arise around door installations. But to get us started, we're going to test your thought process. For the sake of this exercise, assume that I'm a homeowner and that you are a remodeling contractor who is talking with me about some work I want done. I will give you a few scenarios to respond to, and we will assess your performance at the end of each example.

Sliders versus gliders

This first story will cover the issue of sliders versus gliders. In this situation, I am an elderly person who wants to replace my old single entry door with a much larger, primarily glass door. As part of this project, you will be required to build an exterior sun deck for the new door to open onto. Our conversation has just turned to doors, so let's see what you will recommend.

I'm advancing in age, and I have limited arm strength. My goal is to have a new door installed that will let in a lot of light. I want a door that will provide adequate energy efficiency, but it must be easy for my arthritic hands to open. I don't do well with regular round door handles. After doing some personal research, I've come to the conclusion that I probably want a vinyl-clad, high-quality, sliding-glass door. One with a screen, of course. What are your feelings on this issue?

As a professional remodeler, you have a certain obligation, in my opinion, to help this customer with what can be a difficult decision. Consider the circumstances surrounding the customer for a moment. What recommendations would you make under these conditions? Would you take the easy route and go along with what the customer has expressed an interest in? Should you make the customer aware of additional options that might better suit the needs of a slightly restricted, elderly person? I believe this is a time to make the customer aware of gliding doors.

Gliding doors look like sliding-glass doors. The appearance of a glider will satisfy the look that the customer is after. Not only will the gliding door meet the requirements for style and appearance, it will be easier for the customer to open and close. The handle on a glider or slider will be sufficient for someone with stiff fingers to use, but you might have to install a second handle on the side of the door where only a finger groove is provided. This is a minor point to anyone who is not afflicted with some type of disability, but it can be a big advantage to someone who suffers from arthritis. Gliding doors open and close with much less effort than that required to move a sliding-glass door. This is an advantage for everyone, but especially for someone with limited arm strength.

Since energy efficiency is a concern of the customer, you might offer information on terrace doors. The look of these doors is not the same as a slider or glider, but a lot of light is available with this design. Installing a lever-type handle on the door will overcome the problem this customer has in dealing with round knobs, and efficiency should be better with a terrace door.

Can you see from this example how there is more to the installation of doors than just carpentry work? Any good carpenter can install a door, but it takes a thoughtful and experienced remodeler to make contributions to customers that are above and beyond the normal level.

Six-panel doors

In this example, I am a customer who has my heart set on installing all new, six-panel interior doors. This work will be done in conjunction with other interior remodeling work, which will require the replacement of existing interior trim. I'm an average homeowner, so money is a factor, but it's not the only motivator in my decision-making process. What type of door would you recommend?

As this remodeler, you have two types of doors to offer me. You can sell me pine doors or molded doors. Which one are you going to work with me on? Ah, you need more information, don't you? Your first question to the homeowner in this example should be in regards to whether the doors will be painted or stained. If the doors are to be stained, pine doors are the logical choice. When painting is planned, either door will be suitable for the job, and molded doors will be less expensive, while providing the same basic appearance.

Sometimes you have to ask questions before you can give customers good answers. Let's assume that the homeowner in this story was willing to accept molded doors, but you just assumed that pine doors were what the customer would want. You would bid the job with pine doors. Now, what would happen if a second contractor came along behind you and talked more extensively with the homeowner. This contractor might discover that molded doors are fine with the property owner. When the second contractor puts in a bid for the same basic work that you gave a price for, your price is going to be high, assuming that the price of the doors in the estimate are the only variable. If you don't take the time to discuss jobs thoroughly with your customers, you might be doing them a disservice, as well as yourself.

Closet doors

Our next story has to do with closet doors. You have a customer who is remodeling extensively, and the work will require the replacement of all existing closet doors. There will also be some new closets built that will need doors. Your customer has always been used to sliding closet doors and doesn't consider any other possibilities. You are given a set of plans and specifications for the job, and it clearly states the installation of sliding doors for all closets. What are you going to do?

In a situation like the one just described, most contractors will bid a job as per plans and specs. You can do this without any guilt, but you might be able to improve your odds of a sale if you voice your opinion. What's wrong with installing sliding doors on a closet? You should know the answer to this question without even thinking about it. When sliding doors are used, only one-half of the closet is accessible at any one time. A set of bifold doors will allow full access to the closet, so why not use them? This is the question I would pose to the customer.

When you step out of the crowd and show customers your knowledge and your concern for their well being, you are well on your way to becoming a more successful remodeler. Something as simple as pointing out the good points of bifold doors can be all it takes to knock your competition out of the running. Remember this. You are a remodeling contractor, not a professional salesperson, but without sales, there is no remodeling work to do.

Traffic pattern

This story has to do with a homeowner who is worried about the traffic pattern around the kitchen, living room, and dining room. You are building a new addition on the home that will serve as a dining room. Since the house has never had a formal dining room, all meals were prepared in the kitchen and served at an eat-in location. The new dining room will be located in such a way that a brief journey through the living room will be required to get to it. Both homeowners are concerned about the new door being installed between the kitchen and the living room. They don't want a cased opening because they don't want guests to have a clear view of the kitchen when they are seated in the living room. However, they are concerned that a door will cause problems, due to its swing. If the door swings in, it will block the appliances in the kitchen. A door that swings out, into the living room, will be cumbersome. What can you recommend?

A simple, cost-effective solution to this problem would be a set of swinging doors, the types depicted in old saloons. These doors, strategically placed, would block direct vision of the kitchen counter and work area. While dirty dishes and such would be obscured from view, the swinging doors would allow a flowing, open look to the home's design. This could certainly be the ideal solution, but suppose the customer wanted something a bit more formal? What would you suggest at this point? How about a six-panel pocket door?

The installation of a pocket door will not create a problem like a swinging door would. The pocket door will store in the recess of a wall when opened, and the six-panel door will look elegant when closed. A pocket door will also serve to block all view of the kitchen. If a swinging door is not right, a pocket door should do the trick.

By now, you should be getting an idea of how the use of different door styles can accommodate the various needs and desires of your customers. What works for one customer might not suit another. (See Fig. 8-1.) Once you have a full arsenal of door products to offer, you can fill every void and niche. With this in mind, let's move onto the different types of doors available.

Widths of Passageways

Passageway	Recommended	Minimum
Stairs	40"	36"
Landings	40"	36"
Main hall	48"	36"
Minor hall	36"	30"
Interior door	32"	28"
Exterior door	36"	36"

8-1 *Recommended passageway widths.*

Exterior doors

Exterior doors come in all shapes and sizes. They are also available in a variety of materials. Matching the right door to your customer's need is the first step in a successful installation. We have looked at some examples of how this type of matching might be done, but we haven't explored the many options available for you to offer your customers. Let's do that now.

Standard entry doors

We often hear people talk about standard entry doors, but what is a standard entry door? There are so many types of doors available for use as an entry door, it hardly seems possible to correctly term any one door as a standard entry door. In general, a standard entry door, in my opinion, is a solid door that has a width of 3 feet. Even after making this stipulation, there are a multitude of doors that fit the mold of a standard entry door. To clear this up, let's dig a little deeper.

Wood doors

Wood doors have long been installed in homes. There was a time when they were an industry standard for residential construction. They are, however, losing some ground in today's construction market. While not as popular as they once were, wood doors still command their share of attention. This attention can come at a substantial price.

Wood doors are often attractive, and they can be quite ornate. The doors can be painted or stained, and this advantage alone sometimes sells them. With the variety of styles available for wood doors, it's easy for your mind to become boggled. All you have to do is skim through a supplier's catalog to see the pages after pages of doors offered in wood construction. Certainly, this wide selection is another selling feature for wood doors. But as good as wood doors can be, they harbor their downsides.

It is not uncommon for a wood door to swell when it becomes damp. I've seen wood doors swell to a point where they could not be opened, even with somewhat excessive force. This, of course, is not the type of situation most people want to encounter when they're late for work or their house is on fire. So I have to say that swelling is a strike against wood doors.

How do wood doors stack up in the security department? They are unquestionably more secure than a glass door, but not as dependable as a steel door. This might or might not be a factor when offering a type of door to your customer, but it's an issue you should at least keep in mind.

Will a wood door rot? Of course it will if it's not protected properly. When you compare the longevity of a wood door to a steel door, you are going to have a difficult time showing any advantage for the wood unit. This factor might influence a customer's buying decision.

Can a wood door be stained? Yes, and this is one of its stronger selling points. Steel doors are good in many respects, but they're worthless to the homeowner who wants to have a stained door. Wood doors don't own the domain of stained doors, but they certainly take a lion's share of this market.

Where does a wood door stack up in a review of energy efficiency? Again, wood is a better insulator than glass, but a wood door cannot compete with an insulated steel door. From an insulating point of view, wood doors are okay, but they're nothing to rave about.

Price is often a consideration in the purchase of a door. Wood doors range widely in price, but they tend to be affordable. By affordable, I mean that a wood door is not so expensive that it can be installed only in upper-crust homes, but neither is it the most competitive type of door when it comes to a price war.

When should a wood door be used as an entry door? Anytime a customer is willing to pay for one. Now really, you should take a more serious approach to the question of when to use a wood door. One founded reason would be if the door is to be stained. However, a fiberglass door might be a better alternative. I think appearance is the major factor to focus on when evaluating a wood door. If your customer is seeking a certain look, wood might be the best way to satisfy the customer's desire. In my opinion, appearance and staining are the two most logical reasons to opt for a wood door.

Fiberglass doors

Fiberglass doors are relatively new on the market. These innovative doors, however, bring much to the bargaining table. Some of them can be stained to achieve similar results as you would with a wood door. A fiberglass door will not swell, and it should have a better insulating value than a wood door. Security is good with a fiberglass door, and about the only real drawback I can think of is the price you might pay for such a door. I must admit, I've never installed a fiberglass door. My experience has included shopping these doors for customers who wanted a stainable alternative to wood, but the cost scared my customers away. From everything that I've learned about them, fiberglass doors do seem to offer many features worth considering.

Steel doors

Insulated steel doors are the mainstay of my business when it comes to main entry doors. Six-panel, embossed steel doors are both very affordable and quite popular. Their insulating qualities are good, and they don't swell up like a wood door can. Just the fact that they're made of steel imparts a sense of security, and customers seem drawn to them. Their low cost doesn't hurt their appeal, either. As long as a customer is willing to live with a painted door, I think a steel, insulated door is hard to beat.

Glass

A main entry door that contains glass can be a security risk. It is certainly a place for some heat loss, but this is not as big of a deal

as some people make it out to be. How many houses have you
seen that didn't have windows? If the glass in windows is acceptable from a heat-loss perspective, why shouldn't the glass in doors
fall under the same guidelines? The security issue is somewhat different. A door with a lot of glass in it, or even just a little glass near
the locking arrangements, is a liability when compared to a solid
door. There is no good defense around this issue. But what is to
stop a criminal from breaking out a window if access is wanted
through a glass obstacle? Let's face it. If a burglar wants into a
house bad enough, there are very few feasible security measures
that will prevent entry.

Some people feel more secure when an entry door has some
glass in it. The glass allows them to see who is on the other side of
the door. Sidelights are often used for this purpose, but they too can
pose some security risks. If a key-operated dead-bolt lock is installed
on a door, a small pane of glass broken out is not enough to allow
entry to an intruder. Regardless of your personal feelings, or mine,
there are customers who demand entry doors that contain glass.
When this is the case, there is a lot to offer a customer.

I don't want to lump glass doors all together here. There are so
many types of doors that consist mainly of glass that I would prefer
to discuss them individually. For the sake of this section, let's limit
glass doors to be those that include lookout glass. An example could
be a door with a fan-shaped glass top.

Aside from seeing who is on the other side of a door, there is
another valid reason for installing an entry door that contains glass.
The reason is natural light. Doors that have glass in them brighten
up a foyer or home. The same is true of transoms installed over
doors. Architecturally, glass-filled doors and glass transoms can do
a lot to set a house apart from others in the neighborhood. There
are certainly some good reasons for installing doors that contain
glass.

Nine-lite doors

Nine-lite doors, doors with nine glass panes in the upper half of
them, are very popular for side and back entrances. This particular
type of door is well received when it joins a kitchen to the exterior of
a home. The construction material of a nine-lite door can vary, but it's
the bright natural light offered from this type of door that attracts customers. Due to the design of this type of entry door, security is sacri-
ficed for appearance and the functional use of natural light. Still,
these doors rank high in customer popularity.

Sliding-glass doors

Sliding-glass doors are frequently used an entry doors to specialized portions of homes. If a house is equipped with a deck, there is a good chance the door leading from the home to the outside play space will be a sliding-glass door. These doors are used in sun rooms, off of breakfast areas, and sometimes in master bedrooms. Sliding-glass doors can't be beat if the goal is to brighten up a room, but there are trade-offs.

Many sliding-glass doors rate poorly in energy efficiency. Much of this has to do with the volume of glass involved in the door's construction. But there are many inexpensive doors that don't fit up well, therefore allowing heat to escape and cold air to infiltrate. Cheap sliders often condensate terribly. This can lead to moisture problems in carpeting, and it's not unusual for these doors to frost up in winter. The mere act of opening or closing a cheap slider can be more than some people can handle. Security is another issue. It is impossible to create a good sense of security with a sliding-glass door. Special devices that wedge the door shut protect against some unauthorized entries, but since the door is made almost entirely of glass, there is no protection from a criminal with a hammer.

Even with the many troubles surrounding them, sliding-glass doors remain relatively popular. If you are going to sell a customer a cheap slider, make sure the customer is aware of what the trade-offs for the low-priced model are. My experience has shown that stock sliders can range from less than $300 to well over $1,200. This is quite a price span, and there are some good reasons for it. You should take the time to explain the features and benefits of various doors to your customers. Point out why some doors cost more than others, and let the customer decide what features are worth paying for.

Gliding doors

As we've already seen in one of the earlier examples, gliding doors mirror sliding-glass doors in appearance and general function. The biggest advantage to a glider is the ease with which it can be opened and closed. Depending on the physical condition of your customer, this can be a big benefit in itself.

Terrace doors

If sliding-glass doors have been threatened in the marketplace, it has been largely due to terrace doors. These hinged doors provide a quantity of light similar to that of a slider, but they do so in a more energy-efficient package. They are also easier to operate. Terrace doors have one fixed panel and one panel that swings open. They can be filled with glass, but unlike a slider, terrace doors will accept slip-in mullions that give the appearance of individual panes of glass. This is often considered to be an upgrade over a solid glass panel.

Since terrace doors operate much like any other entry door, they can be fitted with dead-bolt locks, and their weatherstripping is often more effective than that of a sliding door. Terrace doors are not perfect for all remodeling jobs, but they do seem to command a lot of favorable attention.

French doors

French doors are not used too often as entry doors, but they can be. These doors tend to be very expensive. Their primary appeal is that both panels of the double door open, unlike those of a terrace door, where only one side opens. French doors usually have individual panes of glass that run from the top of the door to the bottom. Security is obviously difficult with a French door, and so is protection against heat loss. These doors see more use as interior dividers than they do as exterior doors.

Interior doors

When you are ready to discuss interior doors with your customers, the list of options will not be as long as the one associated with exterior doors. This, however, is not to say that there is not a lot to consider. Construction material will not be as much of an issue, and neither will energy efficiency. Security risks will diminish, and so will some of the glass options. But this still leaves wood doors, molded doors, bifold doors, pocket doors, sliding doors, and so forth. The doors you guide your customers to for the interiors of their homes can affect the appraised value of their remodeling efforts. If for no other reason, this is reason enough to take door selection seriously.

Molded or wood

One of the first questions you might be faced with is a customer who can't decide whether to go with a molded or wood door. There is one quick test that might put this discussion to a quick end. Molded doors will not take stain effectively. If your customer wants stained doors, molded doors should be dropped from consideration. When the doors will be painted, your debate must continue.

Price might very well be the second criterion to use when trying to decide between molded and wood doors. Pine doors can cost twice what a molded door costs. I'm speaking of six-panel doors. Molded doors, when painted, give a good showing for themselves. In my opinion, a molded door that has been painted is every bit as attractive as a wood door that has been painted. I've used molded doors on my jobs for years, and I've used them in the various homes I've built for myself. Through all of this use, I've never found anything to complain about.

There is a segment of the buying population who feels they only get their money's worth with wood doors. I disagree with this, but I admit that there are times when it's senseless to argue the issue. If the old saying about customers always being right is true, you are sure to paint some wood doors in your remodeling career. To me, this seems like a waste of money, but it does pay to give your customers what they want.

Luan doors

Up to now I've been discussing six-panel doors, but what about luan doors? These flat, hollow-core doors will accept stain, and they're inexpensive. I've installed them in numerous starter homes and in remodeling jobs were budgets were tight. They are a very plain type of door, but there is no question that they're serviceable, and they do allow the option of staining. From a personal point of view, I prefer six-panel doors, but flat luan doors do have their place.

Sliding doors

Interior sliding doors are normally used in conjunction with closets. These are typically flat-surfaced, hollow-core doors. They are inexpensive and effective. The biggest complaint I'm familiar with surrounding these doors is that only one-half of a closet can be accessed at any one time when they're installed. This is a reasonable grievance. I can't remember ever installing any of these doors.

Bifold doors

Bifold doors are generally considered to be head and shoulders above sliders when used for pantries, laundry nooks, and closets. The big advantage to bifold doors is that when they're open, the space behind them is nearly 100 percent accessible. These doors are so well accepted that I rarely bother with any other type that might be a competitor.

Pocket doors

Pocket doors are special-use doors. I have installed them for bathrooms, kitchens, studies, and probably some other uses that are not coming to mind. These doors store in a wall when not in use, and since they don't swing open, they never interfere with the use of a room. Pocket doors are not practical for all uses, but they certainly do a nice job under special circumstances. I should mention that these doors are available in a six-panel configuration.

The actual work

The actual work involved with replacing or installing a door is not much of a problem for experienced carpenters. There are, however, a few little problems that can pop up. It is also possible to save some time on the job by purchasing the right types of doors. We will finish out this chapter by talking about potential problems and time-saving techniques.

Prehung doors

Prehung doors are, in my opinion, the only way to go. Why would you ever buy a door and build the complete door unit on site? Sure, there might be a rare occasion when a custom-made door unit's needed, but nine times out of ten, a prehung door will do just fine. Think of all the time that is saved with a prehung door. They cost a little more than a slab door and the components needed to make a complete unit, but the time saved in labor more than offsets the cost. It is beyond me why any contractor would prefer to work harder instead of smarter, but there are people in the trades who would. I recently encountered two of them, and it cost me some money.

In addition to being a remodeler, I'm also a home builder. I recently built a new house for myself. The carpentry crew I used was one that I had used on two other houses, but we were not as accustomed to working together as some of my crews and I have been. When it came time to order my interior doors and trim, a big mistake was made. Some of the fault, okay—all of the fault, rests on my shoulders as a lack of good communication. As the general contractor, whatever goes wrong on a job is your fault, and this means that I must assume full responsibility for the stupidity revolving around the ordering of my interior doors.

I ordered prehung, molded, six-panel doors that were pre-trimmed with split jambs. This is one of my standard types of interior doors. Unfortunately, I was using my new house as a testing ground for this particular carpentry crew. I wanted to see if they had the ability to be a stand-alone, independent representative for my company. They didn't pass the test, in more ways than one. Anyway, I asked the crew leader to give me a takeoff for the interior doors and trim. Being pressed for time in many areas, I failed to do my own takeoff. This is where my stupidly rears its ugly head. My crew leader provided an itemized takeoff, as requested, and I ordered the material. It never occurred to me that anyone would order prehung doors that were not fitted with pretrimmed split jambs. My guy did.

When the casing was delivered to my job, I went to work painting it furiously. The casing just happened to be the first part of the trim that Kimberley, my wife, and I painted. By the end of the weekend, we had most of the trim painted. A day or so later, the doors arrived. My crew leader took one look at the doors and got an expression on his face that told me something was wrong. Guess what happened?

My carpenter, who has built a good number of houses, had ordered enough casing stock to trim the doors on site. He never considered that I was going to order pretrimmed doors. I never thought about anyone planning to install this type of door in any other way. The result was my having special-ordered doors that were pretrimmed and a garage full of painted casing, much of which wouldn't be needed. Kimberley and I were more than a little upset. If you've priced Colonial casing lately, you will understand why we were not happy.

I've told you this story not only to show you that I'm human, but also to illustrate that not all builders and carpenters think alike. I can't imagine wanting to spend the time needed to trim each door individually when doors can be ordered with prefab trim packages. Obviously, not all carpenters share my opinions. I stick by my guns though. There is no more cost-effective way to order doors than to have them shipped prehung and pretrimmed.

New doors

Installing new doors in rough openings that you have created is not much of a job. Any experienced carpenter can handle this work. But remodelers are often faced with circumstances that are less than perfect. Someone who is installing new doors on a new construction job or a new addition shouldn't run into any major trouble. Take this same task and associate it with remodeling and cutting new doors into old walls, and you have potential for problems.

It is common to use shims when installing doors under the best of conditions. The shims are usually thin and provide minor modifications of a rough opening to ensure a good door installation. But what happens when a standard shim isn't enough? Many old homes have shifted and settled to a point where finding a plumb wall is nearly impossible. I've seen jobs where the existing framing was so far off that the carpenters had to use some substantial lumber as shims, of a sort. When this has happened, the carpenters fumed and fussed about the walls. They worked for quite a while to bring existing studs into an acceptable condition. Personally, I never understood why they went to so much trouble working with old framing. Is there an alternative? Yes.

If you open up a wall to install a new door, you are going to have to do some framing. The wall is going to need repair before the job is done, and time is money. What would you do under these conditions? Well, as I said, I've seen carpenters take detailed measurements and trim lumber meticulously to make a plumb opening. This, in my opinion, is a waste of time. Why not just install new studs to create the opening, even if it means removing one or two old studs? This approach will generally prove to be faster and easier than trying to salvage the use of old studs.

Enlarged openings

Remodelers frequently have to replace existing doors with larger doors or different types of doors, and this normally means making enlarged openings. (See Fig. 8-2.) The work here is simple enough, until some obstacle is encountered. You might find that a plumber ran a vent or drain pipe up the wall in an area where you now have to install a door. There is a good chance that electrical wires will be in your way. Either of these situations will require the services of a licensed trade, and your cost on the job will go up. If you will be enlarging existing door openings, budget some money for relocation work associated with licensed trades.

Staying out of trouble

Staying out of trouble is not difficult if you look ahead and plan your work, and hanging new doors will not be troublesome if your rough framing has been done properly. Assuming that the opening is the right size and that it's plumb, putting in a new door will not take long. Most contractors lose time installing doors because they, or their predecessor, did not frame the rough openings properly. It is a very good idea to check all openings before drywall is hung. If you catch a framing problem before the walls are covered, changes will not be especially difficult to make. If you wait until the job is nearly done and you are in the process of hanging new doors to discover an error in framing, your finish work can take a lot longer than you planned for.

Doors—Typical Dimensions

Exterior		
Thickness	*Width*	*Height*
1¾"	2'8" to 3'0"	6' to 8' residential 7'0" commercial

Interior		
1⅜"	2'6" min. bedroom 2'0" min. bath, closet	6'8"
Doorknob	36" above floor	
Door hinges	11" above floor and 7" down from top of door Optional 3rd hinge ½ way between other 2	
Door clearance (interior doors)	1/16" at top and latch side ½2" at hinge side ⅜" at bottom	

8-2 *Typical door dimensions.*

9

Insulation

Working around insulation can be an aggravating experience. Many people find insulation to be very irritating to their skin, and some contractors have trouble breathing normally when working with insulation. Yet insulation is a part of every modern construction job. This means that you will come into contact with it at some time in your work. Not all remodeling jobs put contractors face to face with insulation, but some do. Even if you aren't involved in the installation of new insulation, you are very likely to have to put up with insulation in one form or another.

Have you ever removed a ceiling and had old insulation rain down on you? If you have, you know how uncomfortable the rest of the work day can be. Getting insulation in your face, in your clothes, and all over you can make finishing out the day a real struggle. Even if you are wise enough to check above a ceiling before you open it, you might not be able to avoid old insulation. When this is the case, the best you can do is prepare to work around it.

Installing new insulation is not a very technical type of work. Almost anyone can learn quickly how to install most forms of insulation. As a contractor, you can have one of your laborers or trainees do the dirty work for you, but this might not prove to be profitable. It is one thing to be able to install insulation. It is quite another thing to be competent enough to install it profitably.

Insulation is one phase of remodeling work that I've never enjoyed. Try as I have, there seems to be no way to escape working with it. I have used helpers to do installations, but I've never made much money working in this manner. My experience has proven that, for me at least, more money can be made by hiring specialized insulation companies to do the installation work for me. I don't know how the companies make money. You see, I've found that aggressive insulators will provide the labor and material to insulate a job for about what I have to pay just for the insulation. This essentially means that I am getting the installation for free.

Unless you are working on an extremely tight budget, and doing most work with your own two hands, there is little justification in doing your own insulation work. A good crew from a professional insulating company can get the job done much faster than you can, and the cost will probably not be much more than what you would spend on materials. Your time can be put to better, and more profitable, use. Go out and sell another job. That's where the real money is.

Types of insulation

There are many types of insulation available. Some types are better suited for certain types of jobs than others. The R-values of insulation vary. While most contractors have standard procedures for their insulation installations, it can pay to know what all of your options are. As with any other aspect of your business, the better informed you are, the better off you are.

Regardless of whether you install your own insulation or sub the work out, you have to know enough about the various products to satisfy your customers. You might go for months, or even years, without having a customer ask for a detailed comparison of the types of insulation available. However, if this question comes up during a meeting between a prospective customer and yourself, you could lose a lot of credibility if you are unprepared to answer it. Let me give you a quick example of what I mean.

Let's say that you are a remodeling contractor and that I'm your potential customer. You are in my home, pitching me on the virtues of your company. During the presentation of your proposal, I notice that the quote is ambiguous on the issue of insulation. The clause in the proposal states that the job will be insulated in compliance with local codes, but it doesn't give me the kinds of details I want. After reading your entire proposal, I sit back and start asking for clarification on certain areas of the agreement, one of which has to do with insulation.

My first question pertains to the attic insulation you will be installing. Will it be in batts, or will it be loose-fill insulation? You tell me that it will be loose-fill. Then I ask if the insulation will be blown into place or installed by hand. You stumble over words, trying to think while you talk. It appears to me that you have not considered the method of installation. This concerns me. Since you don't know how the insulation will be installed, how do you know how much to charge me? Have you just pulled your prices out of thin air?

My next question requires you to describe the type of loose-fill material that will be used. Will it be a glass-fiber product, mineral wool, or cellulose? You are again at a loss for words, and this makes my impression of your professionalism dwindle. It is becoming obvious to me that you don't know much about the insulating work that will be done for me.

Even though I'm guessing that you are not up to speed on insulation, I ask you to explain the pros and cons of mineral wool insulation. I go on to ask for a detailed evaluation of how glass-fiber insulation stacks up against cellulose. Your lack of skilled responses is really starting to worry me. Should I eliminate you from consideration simply because you are not fluent in insulation details? I probably shouldn't, but I might. You could be the best remodeling contractor in the area, but if you impress me as someone who doesn't take technical issues seriously, I might not trust you to see my job through to a successful completion. By not knowing the answers to my questions pertaining to insulation, you could lose the entire job. The fact that you rely on professional insulation contractors to advise you on what types of insulation to use could be lost on me. If these professionals were present to answer my questions, there wouldn't be any problem. But since you are alone and unable to give solid responses to my questions, I'm definitely going to lose some confidence in you. This is something no contractor can afford to have happen. To avoid getting boxed into a corner, you need enough knowledge of insulation to carry on a competent conversation. Now that we have established a need for you to know more about insulation, let's examine the various types available and what their prime uses are.

Glass-fiber insulation

Glass-fiber insulation is, by far, the most widely used type of residential insulation. It is installed in crawl spaces, exterior walls, and attics. The insulation is available in various forms. You can buy loose-fill material, faced batts, unfaced batts, and so forth. R-values vary, based on the thickness of the insulation. As well known and popular as glass-fiber insulation is, it is also one of the more difficult types to work with if you have sensitive skin. Glass-fiber insulation makes a lot of people itch. This condition is usually worse in hot weather, but it can occur at any time of the year. Aside from the irritating nature of glass-fiber insulation, the remainder of its features and benefits are basically good.

Batts

Batts and blankets of glass-fiber insulation are used in attics and exterior wall cavities. Gaining access to an attic to install batts and blankets is usually easy, but to insulate a wall with this type of material, the entire wall with have to be opened up. In some remodeling jobs this isn't a problem, since the structure might be having all of the interior wall coverings removed from exterior walls. If destroying wall coverings will be a problem, you can still use glass-fiber insulation.

Loose-fill

Glass-fiber insulation is available in a loose-fill form. This type of insulation can be spread around an attic by hand, or it can be blown into attics and exterior walls. Unlike batts, where entire walls have to be opened for installation, loose-fill material can be blown into wall cavities through small holes. The holes are much easier and less expensive to repair than a complete rip-out of the wall coverings.

Rigid boards

You might not expect to find glass-fiber insulation in the form of rigid boards, but you can. These boards are used to add insulating value to exterior walls that are being constructed. The rigid boards are also used to insulate basements walls, both inside and out. They can even be used to help insulate vaulted ceilings, where there is no attic. In terms of rigid insulation, glass-fiber doesn't stack up well against its competitors, polystyrene and urethane.

Mineral wool

In many ways, mineral wool is similar to glass-fiber insulation. This insulation is available in batts, blankets, and loose-fill. It's R-value, per inch of insulation, is the same as that of glass-fiber insulation. Mineral wool is by no means a poor insulator, but if you don't like to itch and you want a slightly higher R-value, cellulose might be worth considering.

Cellulose

Cellulose insulation is limited in its use. Since the product is available only as a loose-fill insulator, it is not practical to install cellulose in the stud bays of new construction. If you will be blowing insulation into existing walls, cellulose is a worthy contender. It's R-value rating is slightly better than mineral wool and glass-fiber insulation. There are both good and bad points to assess with cellulose.

If cellulose insulation gets wet, it loses much of its insulating quality. Not only this, untreated cellulose is a considerable fire hazard. When you plan to install cellulose insulation, make sure that it has been treated to be fire resistant. Old paper is the prime ingredient in cellulose insulation. Knowing the properties of paper, you can imagine how cellulose insulation performs when it is subjected to extended moisture, insects, rodents, and so forth. It doesn't fare well.

The strong points to cellulose are that it is affordable and will not normally cause irritations for installers. There is also the fact that recycled paper is what cellulose is made of, so there is little to worry about in terms of odor emissions or health threats.

Polystyrene

Polystyrene is used in the construction of rigid insulation boards. The insulating quality of polystyrene is very good. The downside to this insulator is its cost and the fact that it can be flammable. The R-value for polystyrene is the same as that of glass-fiber insulation and mineral wool. All of these insulation materials share a rating of R-3.5 for every inch of insulation installed.

Urethane

Urethane is one of the most effective insulators available, but it is illegal to use in some locations. If you consider that most insulation materials have a value of around R-3.5 and urethane has a rating of R-5.5, it is easy to see why urethane is known as the leader of R-values. Unfortunately, urethane is also known to produce cyanide gas if it burns. This, of course, is a deadly gas. Due to the potential risk of creating a poisonous gas, urethane insulation has been banned in a number of locations.

Urethane is available in the form of rigid boards and as a foam. The foam version was extremely popular for old homes made of brick and block. If allowed by local codes, urethane is far and away the most effective insulation material you can use, in terms of R-values. But you aren't likely to fill the stud bays of a new addition with foam. You have to plot your work in accordance with your personal circumstances.

R-values

R-values are a unit of measurement intended to establish the resistance of a certain material. The higher the resistance level is, the better insulating quality the material has. For example, insulation with a rating of R-19 is not as good as an R-30 insulation. Most homeowners are familiar with R-values, so you shouldn't be forced to educate many people on what R-values are or how they work. However, you might get some questions pertaining to existing building materials and their R-values.

Do you know what the average R-value of a single-glazed window is? I know that windows are normally rated with U-values, where the lower the rating the better the window, but windows can be rated with "U" or "R" values. The R-value of an uninsulated window is about R-1. (See Fig. 9-1.)

R-Values for Insulation

Material	*R-value per inch of insulation*
Fiberglass batts	3
Fiberglass blankets	3.1
Fiberglass loose-fill	3.1 to 3.3 (when poured); 2.8 to 3.8 (when blown)
Rock-Wool batts	3
Rock-Wool blankets	3
Rock-Wool loose-fill	3 to 3.3 (when poured); 2.8 to 3.8 (when blown)
Cellulose loose-fill	3.7 to 4 (when poured); 3.1 to 4 (when blown)
Vermiculite loose-fill	2 to 2.6
Perlite loose-fill	2 to 2.7
Polystyrene rigid	4 to 5.4
Polyurethane rigid	6.7 to 8
Polyisocyanurate rigid	8

9-1 *Insulation R-values.*

A double-glazed window should have a rating in the neighborhood of R-2. What would you guess the R-value of an average older door to be? If you guessed R-1, you should be in the ballpark. Storm doors can raise the rating to R-2.

When customers are talking with you about adding new insulation, they might want an idea of what their existing building components are doing for them in terms of R-value. In a wood-frame house, a typical exterior wall that's covered with wood siding will carry a rating of around R-5. If an insulating sheathing has been installed beneath the siding, this rating could go up to R-7. If a home has an 8-inch brick wall, the R-value will probably be around R-4.

Ceilings that are made of drywall normally carry an R-value of 4. If there is an attic, this rating is subject to the attic conditions over the drywall ceiling. It is not unreasonable to assume an R-value of eight in some circumstances. You can't arrive at an accurate R-value unless you know what all of the existing materials are and the circumstances surrounding them.

Floors made of wood might carry a rating of R-4. If carpeting is installed over the floor, this rating might hit R-6. Most houses, even old ones, will have some insulation in them. Attics and crawl spaces are the most likely areas to find this insulation in. Since access is better for an attic or floor than it is for an exterior wall, these locations usually get top billing when it comes to doing an energy upgrade. To evaluate the R-value of insulation, you must have some means of measurement. This is typically done by measuring the depth of the insulation and converting the depth to an R-value. To do this conversion, you need some numbers to plug in. They are given in Table 9-1. (All R-values are based on 1 inch of insulation.)

Table 9-1.
Converting depth of
insulation to an R-value

Glass-fiber	R-3.5
Mineral wool	R-3.5
Cellulose	R-3.6
Vermiculite	R-2.2
Perlite	R-2.4
Polystyrene	R-3.5
Urethane foam	R-5.5

Vapor barriers

Vapor barriers are needed when installing insulation. Without them, moisture can build up in wall cavities and cause wood products to rot. Mildew is another potential side effect. There are several ways to create a vapor barrier. Many manufacturers offer both faced and unfaced batts of insulation. The facing on a batt of insulation serves as a vapor barrier. Insulation contractors frequently install unfaced insulation and then cover it with plastic. This also creates a vapor barrier.

Condensation can be a big problem in some houses. When condensation forms, moisture is present. This moisture can cause a house to deteriorate before its time. If a proper vapor barrier is not installed, condensation can rot wood structural members and reduce the efficiency of insulation to half of its normal R-value rating. This damage generally occurs over a number of years and is not normally found until significant structural damage has been done. As a remodeler, you are in a prime position to discover this type of problem. If you are called in to install a new window or to replace some drywall, you might find that condensation has wrecked a wall. Be on the lookout for this.

Towards the heated space

Vapor barriers should be installed towards the heated space of a home. If you are using faced insulation, the facing should be visible from the living space of the house, prior to being covered with drywall. Installing insulation backwards, and I've seen jobs where this has been done, will result in some serious moisture problems.

I remember an article in a newspaper showing how an nearly new house had rotted because the vapor barriers on the outside walls had been installed backwards. Instead of repelling moisture back into the house, these backwards barriers trapped water and caused it to saturate the insulation. The result was ruined insulation, rotted wood, and a very, very unhappy customer.

From personal experience, I've found that most mistakes with vapor barriers occur in crawl spaces. This is the one location where I have personally encountered insulation installed with the vapor barrier upside down. Whether these installations were done by professional contractors or homeowners I don't know, but I do know that the jobs had been done incorrectly.

Ventilation

Ventilation is needed in a home, and installing insulation and vapor barriers can reduce ventilation to a point where air inside the home might not be healthy. The current construction field has undergone numerous changes over the years. Some have proven to be good, and others have not enjoyed such enviable track records. One mistake learned during this time is that it is possible to make a house too tight. If air is not allowed to come and go in a house, big problems can crop up. As a contractor, you should be aware of these potential problems.

People want to conserve energy and money, so they hire people like you to tighten up their homes. Weatherstripping is added, replacement windows are installed, caulking is done, and insulation and vapor barriers are installed. If you carry this work to extremes, you might be creating a very dangerous situation. You might think you are giving your customer a perfect home, when in reality you might be creating a nightmare of physical complications for the residents.

Are you aware the carpeting and furniture can emit dangerous substances? Do you know what Radon is and how it affects people? How much do you know about the vapors and fumes that might accumulate during an average day's cooking in a kitchen? Going to an extreme, how long can a person breathe stale air before the oxygen levels are depleted? All of these questions pertain to what we're talking about. If a house is sealed up too tightly, any of the issues we have just touched on can grow in magnitude.

How many houses get wrapped before they get sided? A lot. Would you assume that most newer houses are filled with insulation and secured with plastic vapor barriers? I would. Are today's windows and doors tighter than the ones that were in your grandparent's home when you were a toddler? They certainly are. With all the fuss to create a more efficient home, some builders have created monsters. The houses they built are too tight. Don't allow yourself to fall into this same trap. Give your customers a good job, but don't seal them in so tightly that they will suffer from the potential consequences.

10

Heating and air conditioning

Heating and air conditioning are often standard equipment in the homes of today. While there are still houses where air conditioning is not needed or is not present, there are very few homes without heat in them. Most houses have central heating systems, though some are still being heated by only wood stoves and space heaters. Heating and air conditioning, for the most part, are considered mandatory equipment in a home.

As a remodeling contractor, you are not likely to get called to replace a furnace or to install a new air-conditioning system. You are, however, very likely to get caught up in this type of work when it is being done in conjunction with other remodeling efforts. Since most remodeling contractors assume the role of a general contractor, you will bear some burden of responsibility in the area of heating and air conditioning. Are you prepared to accept this role? If not, you need to hone your skills in talking intelligently about heat pumps, forced-air furnaces, hot-water heating units, and so forth. Fortunately, this chapter is going to give you all the information you need to deal with customers on these issues.

Evaluating existing systems

When you are forced into working with heating and air conditioning, you are going to find yourself evaluating existing systems. Unless you have a lot of experience in this field, you should take an expert with you when inspecting existing units. A boiler that looks perfectly fine might have a cracked section. The heat exchanger on a heating system can be bad and very difficult for untrained eyes to detect. If you are adding space to a house, you will have to determine if existing

111

heating and cooling systems can be tapped into. They might not be large enough to handle the increased demand of extra living space. If you forget to factor in a new heating system when doing your cost estimates, you might lose a lot of sleep trying to figure out how to worm your way out of the mistake. It is definitely in your best interest to take a professional along with you on routine inspections of existing systems.

I've talked to a lot of homeowners over the last 20 years. When I meet with people to discuss work they want done, I like to do a little probing. My conversations start off on the subject of work at hand, usually veers off to what other contractors have said, and then my approach moves into a more friendly position. This is when I ask about children and grandchildren. During my visits for estimating, I attempt to gain as much background information as possible. This helps me make sales. One topic that almost always comes is the subject of other contractors who are bidding the job. I don't normally come right out and ask how many bidders I'm up against, and I rarely try to get the names of my competitors. What I want to know is what have previous contractors told these potential customers?

Some contractors will say just about anything to get work. Others are just ignorant enough to make statements that put qualified contractors up against a wall. Let me give you an example of what I'm talking about. Let's say that you are estimating an attic conversion. As part of your estimate, you are concerned about getting heat to the upstairs living space. You're not comfortable that the forced hot-air furnace and existing duct work will be adequate. On top of this, the customer wants you to install a new air-conditioning unit and tie it into the existing duct work that is used by the furnace. After listening to the customer, you express your concerns about the existing equipment not being suitable for the job. You recommend installing a one-piece heat pump in the attic, since it will be all one big room, used as a studio.

After making your feelings known, the customer replies by saying that two other contractors didn't have any problem with doing the job the way it was specified. The homeowner starts to question your knowledge and ability. In reality, you are right and the other contractors are wrong, but the homeowner is choosing to side with the previous contractors. This might be because two independent contractors didn't raise the same concerns that you have, or it could be that the customer doesn't like to be wrong. Either way, you're in the hot seat.

Now that you have your potential customer questioning your experience, what are you going to do? If you're right, and in this case you are, you should stand your ground. This might cost you a sale, but it is better to lose the sale than to take it and wind up in a big mess. If you had an expert with you who knew heating and air conditioning as well as you know general remodeling, you could sway the customer. While it's true that two remodelers didn't voice concerns over the mechanical equipment, having an expert back you up could be all it would take to win this job. You are in a difficult position. If you tell the customer that the job requires more than a simple mechanical tie-in, you could lose the job. It's possible that you are being too cautious, but it's better to be safe than sorry. If you throw in with the other two contractors and bid the job against your better judgment, you could be setting yourself up for a lawsuit when the systems don't perform properly. What are you going to do?

In this position, I would suggest that the homeowner either allow me to return with one of my experts, or that some expert be contacted by the homeowner directly. I would explain my concerns and the repercussions of putting too many demands on an undersized system. If the homeowner chose to argue with me after this type of educational explanation, I would decline any interest in bidding the job.

Does this story sound a little farfetched? Well, it's not. I've run into circumstances similar to those in the story. My background gives me a broader knowledge of mechanical equipment than what most remodelers have. This advantage has proven useful over the years. There have been several times when customers have told me that contractors had assured them that existing ducts for their heating systems could be used to convey cool air from a new air conditioner. This is rarely the case. Oh, the air will find its way through the ducts, but cooling will not be efficient. Duct sizes are larger for air conditioners than they are for furnaces. A forced-air furnace could be tied into ducts serving an air conditioner, but the reverse is rarely true.

The size of duct work is not the only potential problem that remodelers run into. There are many times when an existing heating or cooling system will be adequate to tap into, but there are also plenty of times when they won't be. How can you tell if an existing system is suitable for expanded use? The best way is to have a couple of experts check the system out. They will have to do a heat-gain, heat-loss work sheet to determine accurately what size system will be needed. Experienced heating-and-cooling mechanics can often make very educated guesses, but be careful not to accept these guesstimates as gospel. I know that many good contractors can eyeball a system and tell if it is capable of taking on extra duty. But if you don't want to wind up in a bind, get the experts to do a full-blown work sheet on the job and ask for their recommendations in writing. This type of action will help keep you off the hook if things don't work out just the way you would like for them to.

There is no rule-of-thumb method used for sizing heating and cooling systems. Some contractors size them with tight limits. This is especially true in tract housing, where every dime counts. A lot of contractors, like myself, install systems that are a little larger than they need to be. This provides a margin of error to compensate for any miscalculations. These oversized systems can often handle some extra load, but don't expect any existing system to be substantial enough to take on a large addition or an attic conversion. It is possible that an existing system can manage these types of improvements, but the occasions will be rare.

I've seen contractors push heating and cooling systems to the max. This isn't a good idea. If you overload a system, there is going to come a time when the system doesn't work to its expected performance. When this happens, some angry homeowner is going to be calling you with complaints. This problem can be avoided by simply doing the job right the first time. If you have to go back at your own expense to do a retrofit, your profit will be out the window.

It is common for homeowners to put remodelers in tough spots. How many times have you gone out to look at a job and had the homeowners ask you for a guess on what the estimate will amount to? Is it feasible for a contractor to give someone an off-the-cuff price for a basement conversion, an attic conversion, a complete kitchen remodel, or any other type of major work? No, it isn't. Yet a lot of contractors do it. Why do they feel compelled to make rash comments? I don't know, but I've seen a lot of contractors do it.

There is a big difference between making a rough estimate on the spot and having a preplanned price in mind. Some types of home improvements can be sold right on the spot. Decks, for example, can be figured on a square-footage basis with enough accuracy to make selling one right on the spot feasible. Room additions can even be figured out in advance, but you have no way of knowing what to expect from a heating or cooling system until you see it. If your company uses a per-square-foot price for room additions, it must be based on being able to tie into existing mechanical systems. If you quote a price for an addition and then find that the existing mechanical systems won't handle it, who do you think is going to be forced into paying for a new system? Probably your company.

Duct work

Duct work will be one of the first considerations when evaluating an air-conditioning system or a forced hot-air heating system. Someone is going to have to determine if the existing ducts can be tied into effectively to serve new living space. This someone should be an expert, and preferably the one who is giving you a firm quote for doing the work. Don't attempt to evaluate duct work on your own, unless you have a much higher level of knowledge about such systems than an average remodeling contractor.

There are some basics about duct work that you can look for. When duct work leaves a plenum (this is the duct work located in the immediate area of the furnace), it will normally leave as either a trunk line or as individual ducts. If the ducts coming off the plenum are small, you are looking at individual supply ducts. More likely, you will see a large, rectangular duct extending for some distance. Smaller ducts will take off from this main trunk. As the trunk line becomes longer, it should also become smaller. To maintain a proper air flow, the size of a trunk line has to be reduced as it becomes longer in length. If you see a trunk line that is not reduced as it runs most of the length of a home, you can expect to have air-flow problems. It would seem that this problem would be rare, but it is not all that uncommon.

I recently rented a house while building my new home. The house I rented suffered from an oversized trunk line. Whoever installed the duct work did a poor job. Since the trunk line was not reduced progressively, rooms at the far end of the main duct were never heated as well as rooms closer to the origination point of the trunk line. Because the duct was too big, there was no opportunity for a volume and pressure of air to exhaust through the heat registers. This resulted in cold rooms. To get the cold rooms warm, the thermostat had to be set so high that other rooms in the house were too hot. If you ran into a house like the one I had rented, and added to the existing trunk line, your new installation would not perform well.

The customer might accept its performance, since some of the other parts of the home would probably be affected similarly, but you shouldn't set yourself up for the risk. If you see a major trunk line that is running full size for a long length, call in an expert to evaluate the needs for making the job right, and discuss the problem with your customer before any work is done.

The main trunk line is the only portion of duct work that should have an effect on any new work that you do. However, if the seams on the trunk line are not sealed properly, air can escape. This reduces the air flow and the effectiveness of the trunk line. Ultimately, it can affect your new tie-ins. They will not receive the amount of air that they should. If you see gaps at seams in the trunk line, discuss the problem with your customer before you accept the job, and detail a release of liability for the potential problems associated with existing conditions.

We've talked previously about how duct work for an air-conditioning system is usually larger than that used for a heating system. This is, perhaps, one of the most likely traps for a remodeler to fall into. If a customer wants you to tie a new air-conditioning system into existing ducts, have the size of the ducts evaluated by an expert. Taking a job on face value, without accurate sizing data to go by, can result in major problems for you.

The main unit

The main unit of a heating or air-conditioning system is an expensive component. While you should not be responsible for the overall condition of this unit, you could be held accountable for not knowing or notifying the customer that the existing unit is inadequate for the additional load you are creating for it. This is, again, a time to call in an expert. Whether the main unit is a boiler, a furnace, or a heat pump, you should have a qualified professional evaluate it. Even if you are making only modest increases in living space, you could be setting yourself up for big trouble if you don't document that the existing unit can handle the new load.

Radiators

Depending on where you work, radiators might still be very much in use. Older houses frequently depend on radiators for their heat. If you are estimating a job where the customer wants radiators installed by you, be careful. Radiators are sometimes hard to come by, and they are never cheap. Before you make any commitment for installing radiators, confirm their price and availability.

Electric heat

Electric heat is simple enough to understand. It's so simple, in fact, that some remodelers find themselves in trouble because of it. Let's say that you are doing an estimate for a basement conversion. All of the upper level of the home is heated with electric baseboard heat. You've discussed heating options with the customer, and they are willing to stick with electric heat for the new living space. Your job seems simple. Hang a few baseboard units, run a little wire, and bingo, the heat work is done. This might be true, but don't count on it. Suppose the main electrical service is full and will not accept any new circuits? Who is going to pay for adding a new setup for the additional heat? If you take the job before discovering that the box is filled to capacity, you might very well be eating the cost of an additional service. Check the panel box to make sure there is room to grow before you commit to installing new electric heat.

Options

What are your options for heating or cooling new living space? Is planning for an addition the same as planning for an attic conversion? Does a basement conversion offer challenges that other types of living space don't? How are you going to heat and cool the room you are building over that garage? Designing and planning heating and cooling systems for new living space is a job that should be left to experts. If you are a general remodeling contractor, you are not likely to possess the skills needed to create a near-perfect design. But you are the person who most homeowners will talk to about their options, and this means you must prepare yourself for their questions. It is best to leave detailed technical questions for the experts, but you should be able to make some general recommendations on your own. To prepare you for this, let's look at some common questions you might be asked.

My basement

I want to finish off my basement. Can you tell me what the best way to heat it is? This is a loaded question. Finding a best method for heating a basement might depend heavily on the customer's personal opinion of what "best" is. Is cheap installation cost best, or is inexpensive operating cost best? Either could be, depending on the circumstances. For example, if someone is finishing off a basement as a game room that will be used only on weekends, the heating requirements during the week are minimal. It could make a lot of sense to install electric baseboard heat for this room, since electric heat is the cheapest of all types to install. Electric heat can be very expensive to operate, but if it is only called upon once or twice a week, the high operation cost, on a per-hour basis, might not create a problem. Before you can tell a customer what's best, you have to know what the customer is trying to achieve. This means that for every question you are asked, you have to ask some yourself.

Basement conversions offer a few challenges that other types of rooms don't normally present. For one thing, the floor of a basement makes it extremely difficult to route heating pipes or ducts through or under it. Some basements have low ceilings to begin with, and dropping the ceiling height farther to accommodate duct work can present a real problem. If the exterior walls of a basement are furred out with thin material, putting heating ducts or pipes in them can be nearly impossible. Plus, the cold produced around a buried masonry wall can have an adverse effect on heating equipment.

One advantage to a basement is that the main heating unit for the whole house will probably be located in the basement. This makes access to the unit easier than it would be if an attic conversion were being done. It might very well be possible to run individual ducts through joist bays and down interior partition walls. Since there is often a girder somewhere near the center of a basement, it might be that a trunk line is already chasing along the beam. Since the beam will probably be boxed in during the conversion process, it would make sense to run duct work along the beam and enclose it in the same box.

Electric heat is an inexpensive option to install. Assuming that the electrical box is adequate for new baseboard heating units, electric heat is simple and cost-effective to install. However, paying for the operation costs of running electric heat can get very expensive. The long-term effect of electric heat might prove that its low initial cost is overshadowed by its high cost of operation.

When you are sitting down with customers in an attempt to work through plans and design issues, it is important to look at all angles. It is unreasonable to assume that any one person is an authority on all subjects. This certainly applies to a remodeling contractor. If you are a carpenter by trade, it is unfair to expect your knowledge of heating and air conditioning to be on par with that of a person who has developed in the HVAC trade. This doesn't mean that you shouldn't have a cursory understanding of the trade. You should. It will pay dividends throughout your career to know as much about all of the trades as you can.

How will you get them up there?

I need to have new heating and air-conditioning ducts run into my attic. How will you get them up there? This questions often arises around attic conversions. Duct work is cumbersome in its size. Unlike small plumbing pipes and electrical wire, ducts can be difficult to route through a finished home. The most common method for getting new ducts into an attic is the use of chases. Sometimes the chase is built in the corner of a room. They are often built inside of closets. It is common for chases to be used to disguise the location of duct work.

I want a new family room

I want a new family room built onto my house, but I don't think my existing heat pump is large enough to handle it. This is a statement that you might run into. If the existing heat pump is too small to heat and cool the addition, you could offer to install a one-piece heat pump that would serve only the addition. This would be less expensive than replacing the existing heat pump with a larger one.

I have forced hot-air heat

I have forced hot-air heat in my home, but I don't like the dust associated with it. This statement is not uncommon among homeowners. Forced-air systems do displace a lot of dust. If you are in the middle of a major remodeling job, the homeowner might be considering a replacement heating system. What would you recommend?

If a customer is dead against any type of duct work and forced-air system, you can offer a hot-water system. Hot-water baseboard heat is very popular in areas where winter temperatures are extremely cold. These systems are not inexpensive, but they are very good at combating cold, and they don't blow dust all around. Electric heat is another option to consider, but its operating cost might be prohibitive, depending on the geographical location of the home. A house is Florida might do very well with electric heat, where a house in Maine would cost a small fortune to heat with electricity.

Rely on licensed professionals

It is always best to rely on licensed professionals when dealing with HVAC issues. These contractors should know their trade better than you do. However, calling in a mechanical contractor is not the end of your responsibility. As the general contractor, it will be up to you to coordinate the planning and installation of heating and air-conditioning systems. For example, if a chase is going to be needed to hide duct work, you have to know about it and plan for it. It is essential that you have good communication and a close working relationship with all of your subcontractors. When one trade is working outside of the communication circle, plenty can go wrong. Call in experts for your HVAC needs, but stay informed and keep a watchful eye on the job. Remember, the customer is going to hold you responsible for the work done by your subcontractors.

11

Plumbing

Plumbing is one area of work where a lot of remodelers lose money. Existing conditions apply to almost all types of work, but they might apply more to plumbing and carpentry than any other types. Many remodeling contractors begin their careers as carpenters. As they learn their trade, they venture out on their own, taking with them a good working knowledge of carpentry.

While being prepared to deal with a multitude of potential problems in their established fields, these contractors are far from prepared to deal with plumbing systems. They've seen them and they know something about them, but they don't know enough to keep themselves out of trouble. This can also be true of electrical wiring and other existing conditions. But plumbing seems to be the number-one downfall for most remodelers who are bidding jobs without the assistance of individual experts. Part of this problem might be that plumbing can seem simple, when in reality the codes pertaining to plumbing are quite complex.

I've seen jobs where remodelers grossly underestimated the costs involved for new plumbing. Many of these situations could be caused by a lack of knowledge on the remodeler's part. If these contractors had called in a competent plumber before signing a contract with a homeowner, most of the losses could have been avoided. But for some reason, many contractors wait until they have been awarded a job to call in a plumber. By this time, if there is a problem, the contractor must absorb the financial loss. Whenever plumbing is involved in a remodeling job, the price of the work can go way up, so don't allow yourself to get caught on a bad financial updraft.

How can you avoid problems with plumbing? You can't always avoid the problems, but you can shelter yourself from them. You can do this by having experts look over existing conditions and future plans. You can further protect yourself with liability clauses in your contracts. Another way to reduce your risk is to learn everything you can about plumbing and the codes that govern its installation. This is advisable even if you do rely on outside professionals for all your plumbing needs.

Since plumbing is a licensed trade, not just anyone can legally install plumbing. This means that you will most likely be calling in plumbing contractors for your jobs. Some large remodeling firms have their own in-house plumbers on payroll, but this option is too expensive for most contractors. Subcontractors are typically the most cost-effective way to get your plumbing done.

When you go out to price a job, do you take your entire stable of subcontractors with you? Most contractors don't. Taking a representative of each trade with you on estimate calls is impractical. It's a good idea, but one that doesn't work well in the real world. A better approach is to make the first estimate call on your own, and then bring in the specialized trades to look over areas of the job where you are not comfortable with your own assessment. This should, however, be done before any estimate or quote is given to the customer.

The plumbing code

The plumbing code is a complicated thing to understand. Many professional plumbers don't understand it, and some who do only understand portions of it that apply most to what they do. So if plumbers have trouble with the code, how can you expect to understand it? Well, the code does consist of some cryptic language, but most of it can be broken down into readable text. I learned the plumbing code by reading the book on my lunch break. When I had questions about the code, I asked people who would know the answers to explain them to me. In doing this, I learned the entire code in a relatively short period of time. You might find that reading a code book in your off hours is no fun, but it can make you a more profitable remodeler.

If I know little about their field, I always feel vulnerable when hiring people to work for me. As a contractor, it used to bother me to hire electricians and other subcontractors who worked in trades that I was not familiar with. Oh, I'd seen plenty of electrical work being done, but I didn't know why it was being done the way it was. The same was true of HVAC work and other trades. If I hired a contractor to paint a house, I wanted to know about how long the job should take and what types of materials should be used. This was the only way I could think of to keep my subs honest. In feeling this way, I worked hard to learn a lot about all of the trades. I know some of them better than others, but I know all of them well enough to know when a subcontractor is trying to put something over on me. I strongly recommend that you follow my lead in this matter. Surviving for years as a contractor is difficult enough, but doing it when you don't know what you're doing is much harder. You owe it to yourself to get acquainted with all of the trades.

Plumbing is a good trade to start your new learning cycle with. I'm not saying that you should strive to get a license to install plumbing, but you should learn the basics. If you don't know the difference between a gate valve and a stop-and-waste valve, you could make a mistake in figuring the cost of installing a water heater. A much bigger problem could arise if the house you are about to add a bathroom in has a sewer that is rated for only two toilets, both of which are already installed. Digging up and replacing a sewer is not a cheap proposition. There are a number of potential disasters waiting for you in the plumbing phase of your work as a remodeler. Let's talk about some of them.

In the kitchens

A lot of remodeling goes on in the kitchens of homes. Kitchens are traditionally one of the most profitable rooms for a homeowner to remodel, so they get a lot of attention. There are magazines available where the primary topic throughout the entire publication is kitchen remodeling. With this public display, kitchen remodeling is a booming business. If you are not already doing a lot of this type of work, you might find yourself doing it soon. When is a kitchen remodeled and some plumbing is not altered? Not very often. Nearly all kitchen jobs involve plumbing. And whenever plumbing is involved, problems might be looming in the background.

Let's put ourselves on a hypothetical job site. We are there to estimate a complete kitchen remodeling. The job calls for the existing sink location to be moved 4 feet down the exterior wall. A new island cabinet will be installed, and it will contain a sink for washing vegetables. This island sink is in addition to the standard, double-bowl sink in the main counter. A garbage disposal is wanted, and so is an ice-maker connection. The area under the kitchen is a crawl space, so access is reasonably good. This is a two-story home, and there is a bedroom over the kitchen.

The first thing you do is open the doors on the sink base to inspect the existing plumbing. There are copper water pipes and plastic drainage fittings. You feel comfortable knowing that the materials are modern. In fact, you see no real problem at all. There is access below the floor, the materials are modern, and the work seems innocent enough. What could go wrong? Well, you are about to find out.

To point out the potential problems surrounding this job, let's take the information we've gained and examine it one line at a time. The first order of business is the relocation of the existing sink location. Did you check to see that the existing sink was vented properly? No, you didn't. When you relocate a fixture, a permit is required. It is also standard procedure for all major work, such as a fixture relocation, to trigger compliance with current codes. The old sink might not be vented or maybe it was vented with a mechanical vent. While this would not have been a problem if all you were doing was changing sinks, the fact that you are changing the sink location makes all the difference in the world. All of a sudden, you might have to extend a vent from the sink to a point outside the roof of the home. This would obviously require some work that you would not normally plan on in a simple kitchen remodel. But this is not the only potential problem waiting for you.

The customer wants a new island sink installed. Do you know how to vent an island sink? Are you aware of the pipe size that is required for this type of combination drain and vent work? Did you even know that the sink is required to be vented? If you want to survive as a contractor, you'd better know information like this. Island sinks are complicated to vent. They require access to a vent that either penetrates a roof or that is tied into a vent that does. This might be the existing vent in the kitchen, if there is one. But the pipe size could still get you. Your plumber might have to go way back under the house to find a drain large enough to tap into for the island sink. This, of course, will require running new, larger piping to the sink location. You probably thought that the new sink could be tied into the pipe under the flow that serves the present sink, but this might not be the case. See how your losses are building? And we're not done yet.

Do you remember the request for a garbage disposal? Did you give that much thought? I'm sure you probably figured it would be a simple installation, since the piping was all so modern. Well, the hookup would be simple, but can the customer have a disposal? Ah, you hadn't thought of this, had you? Some plumbing codes prohibit the installation of a garbage disposal where the drain will empty into a septic tank. This is not a universal rule, but it does apply in many places. If the house you are working up an estimate for is served by a private waste-disposal system, you might not be allowed, by code, to have a garbage disposal installed. If this is the case, you should make the customers aware of it promptly.

There is another catch in the code that could make your cost for installing a disposal more than you expect it to be. Depending on what your local plumbing code requires, your plumber might have to upgrade the drainage pipe for the disposal to a larger size. Most jurisdictions require a kitchen drain that will serve a disposal to be larger in diameter than what is required just for a sink drain. Again, more money is lost.

Now, what about the icemaker? Well, the icemaker is innocent enough. Your plumber should have no trouble tapping into the cold-water pipe under the house. This will provide a water source for the icemaker, and running the tubing in a crawl space should not present any unusual difficulties. So out of four plumbing items, three of them carry potential risk beyond what most remodelers would think of. There is still one more potential problem that we have not discussed.

Plumbing codes regulate the number of fixtures which can be served by various sizes of pipes. Typically, no more than two fixtures can be served with hot and cold water from a ½-inch pipe. When you looked under the sink to check out the piping, you noticed that the pipes were copper, and we will assume they were ½-inch pipes, since they are so common under kitchen sinks. What you didn't do is trace the pipes to see if other fixtures were being served by them. If any other existing fixture is getting its water from these pipes, installing the island sink will require upgrading the supply pipes to ¾-inch material. Can you see how some simple plumbing can turn your profit picture into a nightmare?

Adding a new bathroom

Adding a new bathroom to a home can become very involved and quite expensive. The job might entail substantially more work that what you would first assume. In the following examples, we will talk only about issues pertaining to plumbing. There is, of course, a lot more to adding a bathroom than just plumbing, but we should stay focused on the issue at hand.

A basement bath

What's involved with installing a basement bath? A lot of people want one, and there's good money to be made by installing them. But there are some red flags that should go up when you begin your estimating process. If you already know what these indicators are, you are ahead of the pack. For those who don't know what they are getting into with a basement bath, let's look at an example.

Whenever a basement bath is added, the concrete floor must be broken up, unless the bathroom was roughed-in during the home's construction. This should come as no surprise to you. But what are the details involved with the drainage and vent system for a basement bath? Let's assume that you have been called out to figure a job where a full bath is wanted in the basement. You inspect the job and see that the sewer for the home leaves the basement at a height of about 3 feet above the finished floor level. This means there are no drains in the floor that are suitable for connecting the bathroom to. You now know that a pump system will be required. This evaluation should be easy enough for any experienced remodeler to read. But what is involved with a pump system?

The floor will have to be broken up to accept a sump basin. The size of the basin will vary, but it will usually be about 30 inches deep and about 18 inches in diameter. Once the basin is in place, drains will run under the concrete floor to the various fixture locations. This will require cutting the concrete and trenching the ground. This is pretty simple with the use of a jackhammer, unless you find something you didn't expect. This is a point that you should cover in your contract. I got burned on a job once because I didn't address underground obstacles.

Years ago, we were installing a basement bath in a home in Virginia. When we broke the floor up and started to dig through the crushed stone, we found water. I'm not talking about a little puddle of groundwater. We hit an underground stream. The water moved so rapidly that it was washing away the stones that we had disturbed. Pumping the water was out of the question. It was coming in faster than we could pump it. Our plumbing trenches were flooded. As you can imagine, glue joints on plastic pipe don't set up well when they're submerged in water. With no other option, we had to pipe the drains with cast-iron pipe. This allowed us to get the job done, but the cost for doing this work was much more, both in labor and material, than what it would have been if the job had been done with plastic, as I had planned. These little unforeseen adventures can erode your profit quickly.

Assuming that existing conditions don't throw you any curves, a basement bath is pretty straightforward. As long as you realize up front that a pump station is needed, you've got a good head start. But suppose the sewer is too small? Most plumbing codes will not allow more than two toilets to be installed on a single 3-inch drain. To keep the construction cost down, many tract houses have plumbing with 3-inch sewers, to keep the construction cost down. A good number of the houses already have two toilets, so no others can be added to the sewer. If you come into one of these homes and agree to install a full bath, you could be in a world of trouble. Before you give anyone a price for installing a new bathroom, check the size of their sewer and the local code requirements. If the sewer has a 4-inch diameter, you're safe, but beware of 3-inch sewers.

Attic bathrooms

Attic bathrooms don't require pump systems, but they can still be affected by the size of the building sewer. Always check the diameter of the building sewer before you commit to installing a new toilet. The biggest problem with an attic bath is usually hinged on getting pipes up to the attic. Some plumbers, in some houses, can do this without any destruction to existing wall coverings. Most jobs, however, will require either the opening of walls or the building of chases for the pipes to be installed. This is something that you should be aware of from a budget point of view, and it is an issue you should cover with customers before they walk into their home and see a plumber hacking away at their fine wallpaper.

Another problem that you are likely to encounter with an attic bath is the floor level. Plumbing pipes have to be graded for adequate drainage. This grade is usually set at ¼ inch per foot of pipe. In other words, if you have a pipe running 20 feet in length, one end of the pipe will be 5 inches higher than the other end. This can give you some trouble in an attic, where headroom is at a premium to begin with. Make sure that you and your plumber plan the installation to avoid running out of room for the pipe grade. There is one other thing along this line that I should mention. When you are figuring the rise of a pipe for a toilet, don't forget to add height for the turn-up and the closet flange. A 3-inch elbow and a street flange can consume a lot of space, and this height is in addition to the drain pipe.

Slipping in a half bath

Slipping in a half bath somewhere in a house is a common remodeling project. The powder room might be placed under a set of stairs, or a closet might be converted to accommodate it. Either way, a 2-inch vent is going to be needed for the plumbing. This vent must either rise to a level 6 inches above the flood-level rim and tie into another vent, or it must extend through the roof of the home. This can be a big deal if you haven't allowed for the extra work in your cost projections.

Additions

Additions sometimes contain plumbing. The installation might be a wet bar or a full bath, but either way, the plumbing will need a water supply and a drainage outlet. This can be quite difficult in some cases. Water pipes are more flexible in their installation than drains are, so most of your big problems will be with the drains. Some additions are built in a way that makes tying into an existing drainage system nearly impossible. For these jobs, plumbers often run the drain from the addition underground until it intercepts with the sewer for the property. This can be effective, but it also tears up a customer's lawn. If you anticipate doing this, you had better prepare the customer for the trauma. You had also better figure in the cost of excavating equipment and landscaping repairs because these items can amount to substantial money.

Not all additions require extensive outside plumbing work. Some of them are built so that the drains can run under the addition, penetrate the home's existing foundation wall, and tie into the existing building drain. This is something that you will have to evaluate on each job. If outside work is required, you can't afford to overlook the cost.

Old plumbing

Old plumbing can present a lot of problems for remodelers. For instance, old galvanized steel pipe tends to clog up with rust and other deposits. (See Fig. 11-1.) This happens whether it has been used to convey potable water or drainage. Anytime you authorize your plumber to tie into existing galvanized pipes, you could be setting yourself up for callbacks. My experience has shown that all galvanized pipe should be replaced with modern plumbing materials. The up-front savings of tying into old steel pipes is generally lost in unbillable time for callbacks. And this doesn't even take into account the frustration of homeowners who have just paid handsomely for quality remodeling work that doesn't function properly. My advice is this. If you see galvanized pipe on a job, talk the customer into replacing it. (See Fig. 11-2.)

To illustrate how you can become responsible for existing piping problems, let me share some of my experiences. I've done a lot of kitchen remodeling. Many of the jobs have entailed the addition of garbage disposals. In my earlier years, I used to work right from the trap arm (the pipe that sticks out under the kitchen sink). If the trap arm was galvanized, I would have my people connect to it. It didn't take more than a couple of jobs for me to change my philosophy on this issue.

Where to Look for Causes of Water-Pressure Problems

	No water pressure	No water pressure at fixture	Low-water pressure to fixture
Street water main	X		X
Curb stop	X		X
Water service	X		X
Branches			X
Valves		X	X
Stems, washers (hot & cold)		X	X
Aerator		X	X
Water meter	X	X	X

11-1 *Suggestions for locating problems with water pressure.*

I discovered that old galvanized drains that would adequately drain a sink full of water would not necessarily take on the discharge of a garbage disposal. This experience came at a high price. The sinks would test out okay when they were installed because only water was going down the drain. But as customers used their disposals, the drains would begin to clog up. Snaking the drains would punch holes in the clogs and get the drainage running again, but the repairs didn't last long. Invariably, the galvanized pipe had to be cut out and replaced with plastic pipe. This, of course, frequently involved cutting into walls and messing up brand-new remodeling jobs. Customers don't appreciate this type of action. Anyway, I learned quickly to have all galvanized drains replaced, even if it had to be done at my own expense. It was cheaper to replace them during the remodeling work than it was after, and the customers never got mad under these conditions.

Some other types of old drainage pipes that you are likely to run across are DWV copper and cast iron. Both of these materials make good drains, and they last for a very long time. Unless circumstances are unusual, there will be no need to replace either of these types of drains.

Common Minimum Fixture-Supply Sizes

Fixture	Minimum supply size
Bathtub	½"
Bidet	⅜"
Shower	½"
Toilet	⅜"
Lavatory	⅜"
Kitchen sink	½"
Dishwasher	½"
Laundry tub	½"
Hose bibb	½"

11-2 *Common minimum fixture supply sizes.*

Lead pipe is not found in a lot of homes today, but it still turns up from time to time. The most common locations are near the traps of bathtubs and the bends under toilets. If you notice any lead pipe, plan on replacing it. This material is soft and does not adapt well to remodeling work. Vibrations from cutting out floors, building new walls, and so forth are likely to make the old lead joints leak. Even the lead itself is likely to crack and leak. Count on replacing any lead you find.

Brass pipe was used to convey potable water in years past. This pipe is not all bad, but it is not as desirable as modern materials. I won't say that you have to replace all brass pipe that you find, but if you have to tap into a brass system, you should be prepared for some problems. The screw joints along the system might develop leaks as you monkey around with fitting in new tees. If I saw brass pipe on a job, I would make sure that the customer was not going to hold me responsible for stress leaks down the line.

Galvanized steel pipe that is used for water pipe is just about as bad as the same pipe used for drains. I've seen galvanized water lines clog up with so much debris, such as rust, that water would only trickle out of the end of it. If you plan to ask your plumber to work with old galvanized water piping, be prepared to pay a steep price.

Old cutoff valves can complicate your plumber's life. If the main cutoff valve in a house won't stop the flow of water, your plumber might be forced to cut the water off at the street. This usually isn't a big deal, but it can add up a little in labor. If you know that you will have to tap into existing water lines, you can test the main cutoff while you are doing your estimate inspection. Finding out ahead of time that a valve is defective can save you money and save your plumber some time and trouble.

Used materials

Not many homeowners request contractors to install used materials, but occasions arise where this is the case. I've had homeowners who wanted my company to install plumbing fixtures that they had purchased at yard sales and such. In my time in the trades, I've had requests to install just about every type of used residential fixture in remodeling jobs. I don't have a blanket policy against doing this, but I don't like it, and I don't do it very often.

Used fixtures can be trouble just waiting for a place to happen. If you have your plumber install some of them, you might be the lucky one to win the honor of being the place where the trouble surfaces. Old toilets can have hairline cracks that can't be seen easily, but that can leak profusely. Sinks offer the same risks. Used water heaters can leak, be full of sediment, have burned-out elements, and a host of other problems. Bathtubs and showers can also harbor unseen defects. If you want to be safe, refuse to install used plumbing fixtures.

Claw-foot tubs are one type of used fixture that seems to be very popular in some remodeling jobs. A case can be made for installing these units, since they are not common. I urge you, however, to use care when approaching any job where used fixtures are requested. Write a liability waiver that limits your exposure to the connections made to the fixture. By doing this, if the fixture itself is defective, you and your plumber won't be under the gun.

Keep your eyes open

When you are estimating a job where plumbing work will be needed, keep your eyes open. If copper pipe is stained green, beware. The pipe might be on the verge of rupturing due to too much acid in the water. When your plumber tries to cut into the pipe, an entire section might have to be replaced. If the building sewer is too small, you could lose all of your profit installing a new one. Whenever major work is done on a system, most codes require that the entire system be brought into compliance with current codes. This can get extremely expensive. A 40-gallon water heater might be doing just fine under existing conditions, but if you are building an in-law addition, where additional people will be putting demands on the water heater, the heater might not meet the demands.

You should always involve experts in your estimating process before you give any firm prices to customers. It is possible for you to spot some obvious trouble spots with plumbing systems, but you need a seasoned plumber, one who has worked in remodeling for awhile, to make sure that you stay out of hot water. It might be a little inconvenient to have your plumber tag along with you on estimates, but it can save you a lot of money and embarrassment.

12

Electrical work

In many ways, electrical work is very similar to plumbing. It's not that the work itself is the same, but the risks for remodelers are closely related. Many remodeling jobs involve plumbing, but almost every remodeling job involves some form of electrical work. This is a phase of work that is hard to avoid.

Electricians are required to be licensed in order to practice their trade. This licensing requirement prohibits average people, like most remodeling contractors, from doing their own electrical wiring. This puts pressure on you to find good subcontractors in the electrical field. How can you tell if your potential electrician is any good? References from other jobs help, and the fact that the trade is licensed doesn't hurt. But the best way to tell is to know something about the trade. I told you in the last chapter how I felt about hiring people to do work that I have no solid understanding of. My feelings then are the same now. I feel strongly that it pays to put yourself in the shoes of each trade you will be dealing with. If you don't, telling the difference between a good subcontractor and a bad one is much more difficult.

There are very few remodeling jobs that you can take on that don't involve some electrical work. The work might be as simple as adding a ground-fault outlet or as complicated as wiring a new addition. In either case, you are going to have to rely on a licensed electrician. It is also likely that homeowners will ask you some pointed questions on the subject of electricity before you complete your estimate inspection. What kinds of questions are you likely to face? Well, let's see.

Electrical concerns

Electrical concerns are likely to come up in just about any discussion of major remodeling. Customers will want to know what their upgraded electrical needs will be. Some of the most important questions might never be asked. Why is this? Simply because consumers are not tuned into electrical codes, so they don't know what questions to ask. They might assume many things that are not correct. It is your job, and that of your electrician, to educate these people. Let's start this discussion with some of the questions I've been asked most frequently by customers.

How hard is it to change?

How hard is it to change my electrical service from fuses to circuit breakers? This is a common question when working with old houses. While updating an electrical service should take less than a day, the job is expensive. It is also usually very worthwhile, and in some cases, it is mandatory for the remodeling scheduled to be done. A good electrician can swap out a service without much disruption to the homeowner. The power will be off for several hours, but the job will not take more than a day to complete.

Can I use electric heat in my new space?

Customers who are price-conscious on their initial cost of remodeling frequently explore using electric heat, since it is the cheapest heating option normally available. Electric heat requires a lot of electricity. Houses that have old 60-amp fuse boxes cannot have electric heat installed unless the electrical service is upgraded. Homes with 100-amp services and circuit breakers are limited in what amount of electric heat, if any, they can support. Standard procedure calls for a 200-amp electrical service and circuit breakers to be used in conjunction with electric baseboard heat. Many new houses have 200-amp services, but there are an awful lot of houses being lived in that don't have adequate electrical services to work with electric heat.

What are these ground-fault things?

What are these ground-fault things that I've heard about? People have heard about ground-fault interceptors (GFI), but most folks don't know what these devices are, when they are needed, or how they work. I assume that you are aware of what GFI devices are, but let me expand on this subject.

GFI devices can be in the form of circuit breakers or individual outlets. The outlets are much cheaper. These devices are installed in "wet" areas. The purpose of a GFI device is to protect people from hazardous electrical shocks. Since water and electricity don't make a good match in terms of personal safety, GFI breakers or outlets are required in certain locations. These locations typically include the following:

- Bathrooms
- Kitchens
- Outside outlet locations
- Darkrooms
- Laundry rooms (where a sink is installed)
- Garages

Basically, a GFI protection device should be installed in any location where a person might be in contact with water and electricity at the same time. For example, a whirlpool bathtub should be wired into a GFI protected circuit. This would be done with a GFI circuit breaker. Breakers can be used for all GFI circuit locations, but GFI outlets are a less expensive option. By having the first outlet in the circuit be a GFI outlet, all remaining outlets on the circuit are GFI protected. The electrical code requires GFI protection in locations like those just mentioned, so GFI protection can't be considered an option. It is a necessity.

How will you get the wires up there?

When people are considering attic conversions, they often ask how you will get the wires up there. It might be possible to fish the wires through existing walls, but this cannot be counted on. Since most attic conversions require heat and plumbing, it is sensible to assume that some chase ways will have to be made or that some existing walls will have to be opened up. This provides a path for electrical wires as well.

The unasked questions

The unasked questions pertaining to electrical work are often more important than the ones that are asked. Most homeowners don't know enough about electrical systems to understand what questions to pose. This is where your knowledge and expertise shines. If you can point out key issues to potential customers before they are even aware that such issues exist, you have a much better chance of making a sale. With this in mind, let's peruse some of the unasked questions that you can capitalize on.

Is your electrical service adequate?

Is your electrical service adequate for all of these changes? This is a question you should ask whenever a customer is requesting the addition of new circuits. A garbage disposal or dishwasher might seem innocent enough, but if there is no room left in the panel box for a new circuit, an easy job can turn into an expensive mistake. You should always check the electrical panel before you make any firm commitments to provide additional circuits. (See Fig. 12-1.)

Appliance	Amps	Volts
Clothes dryer	30	120/240
Clothes washer	20	120
Dishwasher	20	120
Kitchen range	50	120/240
Water heater	30	240

12-1 *Common amp and voltage loads.*

Are you aware of the code requirements?

Are you aware of the code requirements pertaining to the work you want done? This question should always be asked. Honest homeowners will almost always say that they are not aware of code requirements. This is your chance to show off a little and impress the homeowner. For instance, you can quote the need for GFI protection. This can be followed with code requirements on outlet spacing. Essentially, wall outlets cannot be more than 12 feet apart. The code requires a light or appliance with a 6-foot electrical cord to be placed in any location along a wall without having to use an extension cord to reach an outlet. Along kitchen counters, the spacing is reduced to 4 feet. These types of statistics impress people, and if you can impress them, you can sell them. However, don't take the code regulations that I'm giving you here for gospel. Check your local code for current requirements.

Have you thought about your switch locations?

Have you thought about your switch locations and which switches will control which lights? This question can be very important during the planning stage of a job. By showing people how they can specify the location of switches, within reason, and how they can suggest what lights the switches operate, you can give the customer a better job. People pick up on these types of questions, and they identify them with caring and concern on your part. This is a big step towards closing a sale.

Have you set a budget?

Have you set a budget for your light fixtures? Most electricians bid their jobs without including the price of light fixtures. They will typically detail a fixture allowance in their bid, but their price might not include any allowance for fixtures. If you forget to mention this fact to your customers, they might have to come up with hundreds of dollars that they hadn't planned on. One fixture, such as a dining room chandelier, can cost several hundred dollars. It is also possible to buy fixtures for less than 10 dollars. Before you can bid a job successfully, you must establish a lighting allowance with your customer.

This list of questions could continue for several more pages, but you should be getting the idea of what I'm telling you. Don't wait for your potential customers to ask all of the questions. It is not fair for you to expect them to know what questions to ask. You should prompt them with questions that are pertinent to the job. In doing this, you head off problems before they develop, you win more jobs, and you have happier customers.

Existing conditions

With electrical remodeling, existing conditions don't normally create as many problems for a remodeler as plumbing can. This is not to say that existing electrical systems can't cause trouble for you. The primary concern for contractors in most remodeling jobs, pertaining to electrical work, is the electrical service. If the panel box is in compliance with code requirements, has adequate room for any additional circuits being created, and is in satisfactory condition, the remainder of existing wiring does not necessarily affect you. Unlike plumbing, where old pipes are being tapped into, old wiring is left alone during remodeling. By this, I mean that new circuits are not tied into existing circuits. Naturally, your electrician might have to reroute existing wires. This can get you involved in existing conditions. But if you are doing an attic conversion, a basement conversion, or building an addition, you should not have any reason to work with old wiring. All of your work will be focused on running new wires to the existing panel box.

Since the panel box is so crucial, this is one of the first things that you should look at during your estimate inspection. If the service is a fuse box, you can expect some trouble. When the box is a 100-amp circuit-breaker box, you should still expect some trouble. With today's houses, a 100-amp electrical service is considered small. If you are doing any significant additional wiring, a 100-amp box might not be sufficient. A 200-amp service will generally be large enough to avoid major electrical upgrades in the service panel, but you can't just assume this. If a house is large or has a number of separate circuits, even a 200-amp panel can become full quickly. If you look in a panel box and see that it is full, or nearly full, you should be aware that costly modification to the electrical service for the home might be needed before your work can be completed. This is a good time to have your electrician look over the job to give you firm price quotes.

I don't want to give you the impression that the electrical service is the only place where existing electrical conditions can affect you. It is not. For example, you might be replacing an existing water heater as a part of your remodeling job. This is certainly not unusual. Neither is it unusual for older electric water heaters to be connected to wires that are, by present code requirements, too small. It was common for years to run 12-gauge wire to a water heater. Under today's code requirements, the wire must be no less than 10 gauge. The current code also requires an independent disconnect box to be located near the water heater. This has not always been the case. So if you stumble onto a water heater that is wired with 12-gauge wire and no disconnect box, your cost to replace the heater will have to include upgrading the wire and installing the disconnect. A job like this can get expensive, and it can eat away at your anticipated profit.

Kitchens

Are you aware that major kitchen appliances are required to have their own electrical circuit? Well, they are, and many older homes were not wired in this manner. If you are doing extensive kitchen remodeling, there are several code upgrades that might be needed. Your electrician might have to run a whole new circuit for kitchen outlets. Kitchen outlets are required to be installed on two separate circuits. GFI protection will be required in the kitchen, and appliance wiring might have to be reworked to provide individual circuits. All these new circuits can fill a small panel box quickly, so you have to be able to evaluate these existing conditions during your estimate phase.

Bathrooms

Let's talk about bathrooms for a moment. If you are gutting and redoing a bathroom, there are a couple of electrical issues to be aware of. A bathroom is required to have GFI protection. Many old bathrooms don't have this, so you will have to plan on the expense to provide it. If the bathroom does not have an operable window, a ventilation fan will be required. This will cause you to run new wiring, buy and install the fixture, and extend a vent hose for the fan. Finding a way to vent a fan that is located in a bathroom can be tricky. If the bathroom doesn't have attic space above it or isn't built on an outside wall, getting the vent to open air space can require extensive work. If you fail to pick up on this during your estimate, the cost for doing the job might come out of your pocket.

When you remodel a bathroom, your work might very well include the installation of a whirlpool tub. If it does, you will need to wire the motor for this fixture with a GFI circuit. This isn't particularly difficult, but a GFI breaker costs about 10 times what a regular breaker does, and then there is the cost for more wire than you might have thought would be needed. On top of this, there is the labor for a licensed electrician to run the wire and install the breaker. These are both little jobs that you might not have figured on. All in all, not knowing that a whirlpool needs to be GFI protected can cost you a few hundred dollars.

New installations

When you become involved with new installations of electrical wiring and fixtures, the work will be subject to local code requirements. (See Figs. 12-2A, 12-2B, and 12-2C.) This should not cause you any specific trouble. A qualified electrician should bid all jobs so that the work will comply with local code requirements. There are aspects of new electrical installations that you should discuss with your customers to avoid conflict and confusion later on. Let me give you some examples.

Conductors Allowed Per Box

Box shape	Outside dimension inches	Wire size #6	Wire size #8	Wire size #10	Wire size #12	Wire size #14
Square	4 × 1¼		6	7	8	9
	4 × 1½	4	7	8	9	10
	4 × 2⅛	6	10	12	13	15
	4¹¹⁄₁₆ × 1¼	5	8	10	11	12
	4¹¹⁄₁₆ × 1½	5	9	11	13	14

12-2A *Conductors allowed in square electrical boxes.*

Conductors Allowed Per Box

Box shape	Outside dimension inches	Wire size #6	Wire size #8	Wire size #10	Wire size #12	Wire size #14
Round & octagonal	4 × 1¼		4	5	5	6
	4 × 1½		5	6	6	7
	4 × 2⅛	4	7	8	9	10

12-2B *Conductors allowed in round and octagonal boxes.*

Conductors Allowed Per Box

Box shape	Outside dimension inches	Wire size #6	Wire size #8	Wire size #10	Wire size #12	Wire size #14
Rectangular	2 × 3 × 2¼		3	4	4	5
	2 × 3 × 2½		4	5	5	6
	2 × 3 × 2¾		4	5	6	7
	2 × 3 × 3½	3	6	7	8	9

12-2C *Conductors allowed in rectangular boxes.*

A ceiling fan

A ceiling fan is a popular add-on during remodeling jobs. Ceiling fans can be purchased at very affordable prices, but the cost to install them can escalate quickly. Let's say, for example, that you have been hired to build a sun room. The sun room will connect to an existing living room. As part of this improvement, the customer wants to have a ceiling fan installed in the living room. The living room has a vaulted ceiling, and a ceiling fan will add to the appearance and function of the room. You are doing your estimate for the sun room when the homeowner comes out of left field with the request for a ceiling fan in the living room. You jot down the request in your notes and nod your head affirmatively. Now what happens?

You might have just put yourself into a bind. How are you going to get a support bar and box installed in the living room ceiling without damaging the ceiling? You aren't going to. The ceiling will have to be cut to allow the box and bar to be installed properly. Now, who's going to assume responsibility for patching and painting the damaged area? Is the new paint going to match the paint on the rest of the ceiling? If it doesn't, are you going to pay to have the entire ceiling painted? How are you going to wire the switch for the fan, without damaging the living room wall? Remember that you are working with a vaulted ceiling where there is no attic. This means that routing the wires will be most difficult. Can you see now how a little add-on can make your life miserable?

In the example you've just been given, you are lucky. Since the sun room is being built so that it adjoins with the living room, you have some latitude to move about that you would not have if the sun room wasn't being built. The common wall between the sun room and the living room gives you an opportunity to route your wires without destroying the living room wall. Even with the benefit of having open walls to work with in the sun room, adding this simple, inexpensive ceiling fan can wind up costing you hundreds of dollars.

Ceiling fans are not the only new fixtures that can cause trouble similar to what we just discussed. Fans installed with support bars are more difficult to deal with than simple light fixtures, but adding any new fixture can create difficulties for an electrician. Before you agree to do any new installations for a customer, you should check for potential problems carefully. Ideally, you should have your electrician available to make judgment calls on potential complications.

Access

Access for new wiring is not usually a big problem. Most homes have attics, basements, or crawl spaces where wires can be installed. Some of these locations are easier than others to work in. For example, a basement provides much better working conditions than a crawl space. An electrician can work faster in a basement than in a crawl space. If your electrician can work faster, the cost of labor should be less. Conversely, if you spot areas where access will be difficult, you should plan on higher labor costs. This applies not only to electrical work, but to all types of work.

People often assume that electrical wires can be pulled through existing walls without damaging the finish on the walls. This is, indeed, true in many cases, but not in all. If a wall has fire blocking installed in it, getting a wire up or down the wall without opening the wall will not be possible. If you assure a customer that your electrician can snake wires through a wall, you'd better hope that the wall doesn't contain obstructions that prohibit the pulling of wires. I feel that you should refrain from telling customers information that you cannot be sure of. If you turn out to be incorrect in your information, you will lose credibility, and you might have some angry customers on your hands.

Garbage disposals

Garbage disposals and dishwashers are common appliances added during kitchen remodeling. Wiring these appliances is not normally a big deal. An electrician can usually gain access to a panel box, insert a breaker, snake a wire under the house, and run the wire to the location of the new appliance. Even when a house is built on a slab foundation, the electrician can usually run wires through an attic to get them to the location of a new appliance. But this simple type of wiring is not always possible. If the kitchen has an exposed-beam ceiling with no attic and is sitting on a concrete slab, fishing a wire to a new disposal or dishwasher can be much more difficult. You have to look for these types of obstacles before you can commit to a price for a customer.

All new installations can involve access problems. In my opinion, access and existing electrical services are the two most crucial aspects for a remodeler to look for when doing an estimate that involves electrical work. I've mentioned throughout this book that you should consult with experts on any issues that you are not absolutely sure of. This advice is crucial to your success as a remodeling contractor.

13

Wells and septic systems

Remodelers who work in cities have little reason to work with or around wells and septic systems. Rural remodelers, however, come into contact with wells and septic systems on a regular basis. You might be thinking that a well or septic system has very little to do with a remodeling contractor. In metropolitan areas this can be true, but it is far from accurate for contractors who work in rural areas.

Many contractors don't give a second thought to wells and septic systems. This is often a mistake. You might not think that adding two bedrooms in the attic of a home has anything to do with a septic system, but it does. Now whether or not you have any direct responsibility in regards to the septic system is questionable. I can't say whether you do or don't, but I suggest that you don't assume that you are not in any way responsible for what might be the outcome of adding two bedrooms to the house. How can this be? Well, let's discuss it.

When a house is built and a septic system is designed, the system is designed in accordance with the number of bedrooms contained in the home. If bedrooms are added to a house, the septic system might not be adequate. A lot of people think that the number of bathrooms in a home affects a septic system. This is not an unreasonable assumption, but it is incorrect. The basis for using bedrooms as a measuring stick in sizing a septic system is the number of people who will use the facilities. It is assumed that this is indicated better by the number of bedrooms than by the number of bathrooms. Therefore, adding bedrooms to a home can trigger a problem with local code officers.

Perhaps you have never run into a situation where a conflict has risen from the addition of bedrooms. I have never been personally involved in this type of incident, but I know contractors who have been. The case that I'm thinking of occurred within the last year or so. Let me tell you about it so that you can better understand how you could be affected.

A couple built a new house. A detached garage, a big one, was also built. The septic system was designed around the house and installed. Then the homeowners decided to have an apartment built over their large garage. They called in a contractor and had the garage attic converted to an apartment. During this process, a problem came up. A code officer discovered that the existing septic system was not designed to handle the additional load created by the apartment. Work was very much underway before this job-stopping problem popped up.

When a stop-work order was issued to the contractor, several things happened. The contractor's crews, who had been scheduled on the conversion job for several more weeks, were at a standstill. Cash flow for the contractor on the job dried up. The homeowners began to fight for their right to create the apartment, and they didn't meet any serious resistance to creating the apartment. They did, however, hit a brick wall on the septic system. The code officer stood firm on a requirement for the septic system to be enlarged. The cost of enlarging the septic system was in the thousands of dollars. This expense was unplanned and caused a lot of trouble.

As you might imagine, a good deal of friction developed between the parties involved. It took weeks and weeks to resolve their problems, but a compromise was reached between the homeowners and the code enforcement office. The contractor was allowed to finish the job and got paid. But this situation could have turned out a lot worse. I suspect that I might now have your attention on how septic systems can become wrapped up in your remodeling business.

The example I've just given you is only one way in which a septic system or well can cause you grief. As we move through this chapter, you are going to see many circumstances surrounding wells and septic systems that can have an adverse affect on you. Some are as simple as digging up a water service by accident. Others are much more complicated. Let's start our exploration with well systems.

Well dangers

Well dangers are very real. As a remodeling contractor, you are not likely to have entire well systems to install. You are, however, fairly likely to have to work with and around these systems. Most of this work is not dangerous to you or your workers, beyond being a financial threat, but there are some physical risks involved. Since personal injury is more important than money, let's start this section with an example of how you or your workers could be seriously injured or even killed.

Old wells

A lot of houses that have municipal water hookups had wells at one time. When the house converted to city water, the well was abandoned. But not all abandoned wells were filled in. Many of them are standing full of water, waiting for a victim. If your customers purchased their home after the conversion from well water was done, they might not have any knowledge of a forgotten well. The old well might have been covered with boards made of wood. As you know, boards rot in time. If you, or one of your people, happen to step on the rotted boards covering an old well, some serious damage can be done. If you think accidents like this don't happen, you're wrong. I came very close to losing my daughter to a well a couple of years ago.

My wife and I rented a house while we were building our new home. The house we rented was situated on an old family farm. Part of this farm included an old well. We didn't know the well even existed. The well had been covered with a wood top. The man who plowed the snow in our driveway hit the cover of the well while pushing up a pile of snow. The plower didn't know the well was there or that it had been hit. When the snow ceased, my wife, my five-year-old daughter (at that time), my daughter's beagle, and I went out to play in the snow.

If you have kids, you might know that a big pile of snow is to a kid what a magnet is to iron. Afton raced to the snow pile and began sliding and playing on it. I was right there with her. Kimberley, my wife, was starting to build a snow sculpture. Daisy, the dog, was playing around the snow pile. After a while, we noticed that Daisy was nowhere to be seen. We called her, but she didn't come. We started looking for her.

As we searched for Daisy, we saw plenty of tracks in the snow around the pile, but there were no tracks going out into the fields. This perplexed us. Then Kimberley heard a soft sound. Following the sound, we found a hole in the snow, at the base of the pile that Afton and I had been playing on. The hole lead into the old well, and Daisy had fallen into the water. We could see her paddling around in the well, but I knew that in the freezing temperature of a Maine winter that the dog couldn't last long.

As soon as I knew what had happened, I had Kimberley take Afton over to the house. I found a length of rope and worked desperately to save Daisy. After a few attempts, I was able to get a loop in the rope around the dog. I feared that pulling her up with the rope might damage her, but I was sure the well would kill her. Anyway, I got Daisy out of the well and we rushed her to a veterinarian. She survived. But I still get the quivers when I think of how it could have been Afton falling into the well.

If you're thinking that this story is just a one-in-a-million example, I can tell you that I fell into a well myself several years ago. The old well was covered with vegetation, and I stepped right into it. Fortunately, I was young enough and strong enough that I caught myself at the lip of the well and was able to climb out. I might not have been so lucky. Don't take abandoned wells for granted. And don't think that abandoned wells are the only ones that can get you.

Under a house

A well is sometimes installed under a house. This practice is not normal, but there have been occasions when houses have had their water wells installed under them. This is one of the last places most people would ever think to look for a well. If you happen to be crawling around under a house and find a well like this the hard way, you could be in serious trouble.

The point I'm trying to make here is that it can be very difficult to guess where a well will be found. Dug wells have large diameters that can easily swallow a full-grown human being. Very old wells were often lined with rocks. Newer wells are lined with concrete cylinders. Neither of these wells are good to fall into. A rock well does offer some possibility for escape, by climbing the rocks, but no well is easy to get out of. Your best defense against a well is to not wind up in one of them by accident. You should always be alert to the possible presence of a well.

Types of wells

There are different types of wells. Three types are the most common. They are drilled wells, dug wells, and driven wells. Drilled wells and dug wells are, by far, the most common types of water wells used in conjunction with residential properties.

Drilled wells

Drilled wells have small diameters. The casing for a well of this type normally has a 6-inch diameter. Some of them have a 4-inch diameter. The well casing is usually made of steel. Drilled wells are typically deep. A depth in excess of 100 feet is common. My drilled well is over 400 feet deep.

Drilled wells are normally more dependable than dug wells. Due to the depth of a drilled well, it is not as likely to dry up in hot months. The cost of installing a drilled well is substantially more than that of a dug well. As a remodeling contractor, you will probably not be involved with the drilling of a well. For this reason, we won't dwell on all of the details involved with installing a well. I would prefer to concentrate on events that are likely to affect you when working with or around a drilled well.

The casing for a drilled well extends above ground level, but the height of this extension varies. In most cases, the well is a foot or more above grade level. This makes the well easy to see under normal circumstances. Still, you might be surprised how often these well casings are hit with backhoes and bulldozers during the construction of room additions. Unless you are operating the piece of equipment that hits a well casing, you might assume you are not liable for any damage done. This might not be the case. As a general contractor, you are very likely to be first in line for attack from a distraught homeowner.

The casing used with a drilled well is small enough that it can be hidden by shrubbery very easily. This makes the well casing more susceptible to damage than it might be if it were a dug well. Unless this type of well is hit with equipment, there is very little risk of damaging the well. One exception could be blasting with explosives. For example, blasting out bedrock to obtain a deeper footing could affect the well. I know of wells that have gone dry after blasting was done in the vicinity. This is a problem that home builders face more so than remodelers, but it is worth remembering.

Dug wells

When I lived in Virginia, dug wells were very common. Unlike Maine, where nearly every house with a well has a drilled well, dug wells were more prolific than drilled wells in Virginia. Most of the houses I built for customers, and all of the houses I built for myself, had dug wells. The water table in the area where I worked was good enough to keep shallow wells supplied with water under all but the driest of conditions. This is not always true, and some dug wells do dry up frequently.

A dug well differs from a drilled well in many ways. The two most noticeable are the depth of the well and the diameter of the well casing. Dug wells are also called shallow wells. This is because they rarely go deeper than 35 feet. The diameter of a dug well can easily span 3 feet. This is considerably larger than the typical 6-inch diameter of a drilled well.

The casing for a dug well might terminate just above ground level, or it might rise above the finished grade for a foot or more. This casing is usually made of preformed concrete. The covers for most modern dug wells are also made of concrete. They are quite heavy and not easily moved. This helps to prevent curious children from falling into the wells. Just as equipment can hit and damage a drilled well, so can they have this effect on a dug well. However, the bulk of a dug well is usually enough to keep equipment operators from hitting them. If the well casing terminates near the ground level, however, it is conceivable that an operator could run into the well cap or the top of the casing without seeing it first.

If you will have equipment working around a house where a well might be at risk, take some safety precautions. Drive a few stakes in the ground and wrap colorful ribbon around them to draw attention to the well. A few dollars spent on stakes and surveyor's tape is a lot cheaper than the cost of repairing damage done to a well.

Water service piping

Water service piping is the pipe that runs from a well or a city water main to a house. This pipe conveys potable water from a water source to the interior plumbing system of a home. A water service pipe is usually located below the local frost line, but there are times when they are closer to the surface. For example, my land has a lot of bedrock near the surface. This fact forced me to install my water service only about 18 inches below ground. In Maine, a water service should be installed at least 4 feet below grade to prevent freezing. I couldn't do this without blasting out rock, so my water service is close to the top of the ground. To keep the pipe from freezing, I use an in-line heat tape. But my point is this. Any contractor in Maine would expect my water line to be at least twice as deep as it is. It would be easy for a contractor to dig up my water service by accident. Since it would be logical to assume that the pipe is buried much deeper than it is, an excavation contractor probably wouldn't think twice about digging to a depth of 2 or 3 feet. In my case, this would be more than deep enough to destroy my water service.

If you are going to be digging footings for an addition, or excavating for any reason, you need to make sure that there are no utilities in the area where you will be digging. This applies to water services, telephone lines, electrical lines, gas pipes, sewers, and so forth. When you are concerned about digging, you can check to see where the well pipe leaves the well and where it enters the home. This doesn't guarantee that the depth will be uniform along the trench where the pipe is buried, but such an inspection is good insurance.

To see how deep a pipe is when it leaves a well, you must remove the well cover. In the case of a drilled well, this will entail removing a few screws, lifting off the well cap, and looking down in the well casing. You will see a fitting, called a *pitless adapter*, attached to the side of the well casing. A pipe will extend from the fitting down into the well. This fitting marks the depth at which the water service enters its trench.

A trip into or under the house should disclose the location where a water service enters. Once the water service is located, you can estimate how deeply it is buried in the ground. Once you have a depth for the starting and ending point of a water service, you can make a reasonable estimate of how deep the pipe is. This information will help you avoid cutting the water service as you dig.

Septic systems

Septic systems pose more problems for remodelers than wells do. We've just seen that the risks associated with wells is minimal for remodelers. Dealing with septic systems can be more dangerous, at least from a financial point of view. The cost of a septic system can range from just a few thousand dollars to well over 10,000 dollars. Damaging a system can be a very expensive lesson to learn.

How are you or your crews likely to damage a septic system? It depends on the conditions surrounding the system that you are working with or around. For example, there are many old septic tanks here in Maine that are made of metal. These metal tanks deteriorate over time. Eventually, they have to be replaced. But when they are replaced, the entire septic system might have to be brought up to current code requirements, and this can open a whole new can of worms. Let me tell you about a personal experience I had along these lines.

Three or four years ago, some of my people drove a big truck over a metal septic tank by accident. The weight of the truck crushed the top of the tank, and the truck was stuck temporarily in the septic tank. The owner of the house was furious. He pointed out to me that the old septic system was far too small to meet current code criteria and that he didn't own enough land around the house to install a larger, to-code system. You talk about sweating bullets, I was drenched in sweat. I could just see my insurance company trying to settle this claim.

Based on the information given to me by the homeowner, it was entirely possible that my people had rendered his house nearly useless. If the code enforcement office condemned the septic tank and the homeowner had no place to install a larger system, the entire house would be uninhabitable. I still shudder to think of what the liability cost for this type of problem would be. And all it took to get me into this mess was having someone park a truck in the driveway. Yes, the driver missed the driveway by a few feet and hit an underground tank that was not visible. But who would have thought that such a big risk could come from such a simple act as parking a truck? As it turned out, the tank was not damaged beyond repair, and I escaped what could have been a very devastating financial disaster. Still, this example shows how quickly and how easily a contractor can wind up in a world of trouble when a septic system is involved.

The only way

Driving a truck over a metal septic tank is not the only way to damage a septic system. Let's say that you've been hired to build a room addition. You contact your excavator and get equipment on the site. As the backhoe begins digging, some perforated pipe turns up. Guess what? Your digger has just damaged a septic field.

A lot of homeowners know where their septic tanks are, but not so many people know where their leach field is. This is because septic tanks have to be pumped out periodically, but there is no routine maintenance involved with a leach field. If a house has a nice lawn, the septic field can sometimes be located by looking for lush grass. While this is a good indicator, it is not always proof positive of where a leach field is or how big it is. Before you start digging around a house that is served by a septic system, you should pinpoint the location of it.

Septic designs are required for the installation of a septic system. This design shows the location of the house, the water well, and the septic system. Contractors are supposed to install septic systems in accordance with the design filed to obtain a permit for the work. I say supposed to because it doesn't always happen that way. However, if you work on the assumption that a septic system is where the official design says it is supposed to be, you reduce your risk of liability. A trip to the local authorities who issue septic permits should allow you access to the septic design for a house. This research might seem like a waste of time, but if it allows you to avoid a major expense in damaging and repairing a septic system, the lost time will become very valuable.

Heavy equipment

Heavy equipment can damage a septic system. Running concrete trucks, bulldozers, and other heavy equipment over a septic field can cause the field to collapse. This would not normally happen with just one or two passes over the field, but depending on the depth of the field, it could. It is also very likely that a piece of heavy equipment placed on top of a septic tank, whether metal or concrete, could damage the system.

The sewer

The sewer running from a house to a septic tank might not be very deep in the ground. It could be just 1 foot below the surface where it leaves a home. Digging around the sewer could break it. This type of damage is much easier and much less expensive to repair than a leach field or septic tank, but it is still a problem you should try to avoid.

Overloading

Overloading a septic system by building additional bedrooms in a house is one of the fastest, most expensive ways to learn why septic systems should not be overlooked by a remodeler. (See Figs. 13-1, 13-2, and 13-3.) If a code officer discovers a violation of this type and demands that the septic system be enlarged, there is going to be plenty of expense and trouble for someone, and that someone might be you.

Research

Research is the best way to avoid trouble with wells and septic systems. If you will be doing any type of work that might interfere with either of these types of systems, confirm as much information as possible about the existence of a well or septic system. Ask the homeowners for information. Look for yourself to see if the home is served by a private well or sewage disposal system. Don't do any work until you are sure that you will not damage an existing system.

Septic Tank Capacity

Single-family dwellings Number of bedrooms	Multiple dwelling units or apartments One bedroom each	Other uses; Maximum fixture units served	Minimum septic tank capacity in gallons
1–3		20	1000
4	2	25	1200
5 or 6	3	33	1500
7 or 8	4	45	2000
	5	55	2250
	6	60	2500
	7	70	2750
	8	80	3000
	9	90	3250
	10	100	3500

13-1 *Septic tank capacities.*

Length of Subsoil Drainage Lines

Number of people served	Slow absorption	Medium absorption	Rapid absorption
1–4	200	150	100
5–9	700	350	200
10–14	1,000	500	340
15–20	1,250	650	475

13-2 *Recommended subsoil drain lengths.*

Soil Absorption Ratings

	Slow absorption	*Medium absorption*	*Rapid absorption*
Seconds required for water to drop 1 in.	5–30	3–5	0–3

13-3 *Soil absorption ratings.*

14

Wall coverings

When we choose to talk about wall coverings, the potential topics cover a broad spectrum. We could start with paint, since it is one of the most used wall coverings. But is it? Is paint a wall covering, or is drywall a wall covering? Depending on the phase of your job, either one could be the wall covering at issue. Once walls are framed and all rough-in work is done, wall coverings are needed. This class of wall coverings will typically include drywall and paneling, though other types could be included. If we assume drywall is used to cover stud walls, as it usually is, we can then focus on paint as a wall covering. But in addition to paint, we could discuss tile and wallpaper. Well, this chapter is going to cover both types of wall coverings and all the major options within each classification.

Remodeling contractors deal with wall coverings in a number of ways. They cut into them, and they repair them. Wall coverings are removed, replaced, cleaned, and altered. All of this work adds up to a need for knowledge. A good remodeler must be able to offer suggestions on what the most appropriate wall coverings for a specific project are. Can you do this? If you've been in the business for a few years, you should have a good, basic understanding of the most common wall coverings. But are you familiar with various types of tub surrounds to offer a customer when a tile wall around a bathtub needs to be replaced? Have you ever suggested that a customer use weathered barn boards as a wall covering when creating a country kitchen? There are a lot of creative angles to wall coverings that many contractors seldom think about.

When was the last time you recommended that a customer use a brick facade on a family room wall? Have you ever offered customers an option for murals in a child's bedroom? Most contractors wait for their customers to say what they want, and then that is what the remodelers base their bids on. This is not wrong, but if you operate in this manner, you are probably losing some jobs that you could win.

Customers tend to like contractors who make creative suggestions. If you impress a customer with your depth of knowledge and your willingness to make their home special, you've got a leg up on the competition. Many contractors are always in a rush. They feel they don't have time to tinker around with the whims of homeowners. These contractors work up an estimate, call or mail it in, and wait. Sometimes they wait for a very long time because more creative contractors are awarded the job.

You don't have to be an interior decorator to offer helpful advice to confused customers. Put yourself in the customer's place. Average people have no idea of all the options available for various types of work. They are not professional remodelers, and most of their information has come from reading magazines or talking to friends. If you are in touch with current remodeling trends, you can sweep these homeowners off their feet. Price will not matter nearly as much to homeowners who feel they have found a competent contractor who has their best interest at heart.

If you walk into a kitchen that a customer wants remodeled and assume that drywall will be used for the walls, you are probably right on target with every other contractor who comes along to bid the work. But what happens if you suggest tile accents, stenciling around the top of the wall, or a herringbone pattern of tongue-and-groove planks. All of a sudden, you are different. You've captured the customer's attention and set yourself apart from the crowd of contractors competing for the work. This is how enterprising contractors get ahead and stay ahead.

You might feel that wall coverings are mundane subjects. Your personal feeling might be that painted drywall is cost-effective and good enough for any house. It's fine to have your own opinion, but don't shove this line of thinking onto your customers. Present them with creative options and allow them to make their own choices. I think you will find yourself winning more bids and working more consistently.

Covering the studs

What type of material are you going to suggest for covering the studs in rough framing? Drywall is the obvious answer, and it is usually the best answer. But there are times when plain old drywall isn't best. Wood paneling has been popular off and on, and it has many good features. Would you suggest the installation of paneling in a family room? How about in a kitchen? Would you use it as wainscotting in a dining room? Does paneling have a place in a bathroom? Paneling can be used in any room, but it is not always an ideal choice.

Once you get past paneling and drywall, the options for covering studs in modern construction shrink. You could use plaster, but this is hardly ever done in modern building. Other options fall into what I consider a special-use category. Brick might be used in a family room, and so might stone. Old barn boards might make a very comfy country kitchen. Wood siding can give a rustic look to an office or study. Any of these materials can be used to cover rough framing, but they should be used in moderation and with special consideration.

Drywall

Drywall is far and away the most popular form of wall covering when it comes to closing in rough framing on the interior of a home. This material is relatively inexpensive, fairly easy to work with, durable under average conditions, and well accepted within the industry. The popularity of drywall is so great that many people never consider alternative options. As a remodeler, you can go with the flow and use drywall on almost all of your jobs. But you've already seen in this chapter how being a little different in your approach can give you a competitive edge.

There are two basic scenarios that most remodelers face. They are either working with existing wall coverings or starting from scratch with bare studs. This can make a difference in a decision of whether or not to use drywall. If you are doing a facelift on a kitchen that already has drywall installed, you might choose to patch and paint the wallboard. This, of course, is affordable, fast, and pretty easy. If drywall is already in place, and it is in good shape, there is little reason to tear it down, unless a customer wants a completely new look. Even then, you might be able to use the drywall as backing and apply a new type of wall covering, such as paneling, over it.

Drywall is easy to repair. If you need to open up a stud bay to allow the installation of a plumbing vent or electrical wires, you can cut into drywall with little fear of not being able to provide an acceptable patch. This can't be said for some other types of walls. All in all, drywall is a fantastic wall covering.

If you rip out a room down to bare studs, or if you are building a new room, customers might want to consider something other than the day-to-day standby of drywall. If you have bare studs to work with, you are unlimited in the types of wall coverings you can offer a customer. When cost is a concern, drywall will usually prove to be the most acceptable type of wall covering. But you must factor in all the expenses associated with it. The drywall has to be purchased. Then it must be installed and finished. Once the drywall is finished, some type of finish wall covering, like paint or wallpaper, must be added. If you total up the cost for each of these phases of work, installing a good grade of prefinished wood paneling might prove to be cheaper. It will certainly be faster. All of this must be considered when planning on what wall covering to use.

When money is not as much of an issue as appearance, some of the more creative wall coverings might be more desirable. These could range from brick to weathered boards, to half logs, to wood siding or planks. Special wall coverings should not be used in just any room or in just any way. But used judiciously, these accent coverings can set a tone for a room. This is especially true when a rustic feeling is being sought, as might be the case in a country kitchen, a family room, or a study.

Problems associated with drywall are many. First, there is the dust from sanding that must be controlled. If a contractor is not careful, the sanding of drywall in a work area can invade other parts of a home, creating a considerable mess. Who cleans up this mess? You guessed it—the contractor. Time is a big drawback to drywall. The boards can be hung quickly enough, but the finishing, priming, and painting process can take weeks. Compared to prefinished paneling, where the job is done as soon as the sheets are installed, drywall is a loser in terms of time.

Another potential drywall problem can arise after a job is done. Seams can show, joints can crack, and the boards themselves can be damaged easily. This is not the case with paneling and some other types of wall coverings. Since no contractor likes callbacks, this reason could be all the proof needed to look for an alternative wall covering.

Drywall requires some type of finish wall covering. If we assume this will be paint, someone will have to maintain the paint over a course of years. The walls will become dirty and the paint will need to be replaced periodically. A cost-conscious homeowner might be willing to pay more up front for a maintenance-free wall covering, such a prefinished paneling. This is something else that you should take into consideration when giving advice to your customers.

Now that we have beaten down drywall, let's pick it back up. The initial cost of installing drywall is usually less expensive than comparable wall coverings. Under normal conditions, drywall will last for years and years. Due to its nature, drywall is easy to repair if it becomes damaged. The decorating opportunities when working with drywall are practically unlimited. The wallboard can be covered with paint, tile, wallpaper, or other creative options. This allows a homeowner to create a custom look in a house. If light walls are wanted, they can be had. When a darker color is desirable, it is no problem to obtain. A pink room that was used as a nursery for a first child can easily be changed to a blue room for a second child. Drywall does offer a host of advantages, and it is the mainstay within the building and remodeling industry.

Paneling

Paneling has been popular off and on for years in residential construction. Many do-it-yourselfers flock to paneling because it is easy to install. You won't find many houses where every interior wall is covered with paneling, but it is not uncommon to discover certain rooms where paneling has been used in homes. Is paneling a good alternative to drywall? It depends on several factors.

If a customer wants wood paneling installed, then wood paneling should be installed. Should you make professional recommendations for paneling? There are times, I believe, when you should. If a customer is asking for a formal dining room or living room where wainscoting will be installed, high-quality wood paneling is a sensible solution. Paneling is also a reasonable alternative in rooms that will receive rough treatment along the walls.

If a customer calls you to build a play room for a child, what are you going to recommend for the wall covering? Concrete might be the most appropriate choice in some ways, but it will not likely be one of your options. Most contractors would recommend either drywall or paneling. I would favor paneling in many ways. When a tricycle runs into drywall, some damage to the wall is likely to occur. The same collision with a paneled wall would probably never be evident. Kids often play rough, and drywall is easy to dent and damage. Paneling is not. One drawback to paneling in a playroom is that it could become damaged to a point where replacement is needed. An example of this could be an enthusiastic painter who decided to paint a pin-the-tale-on-the-donkey game on the paneling. If this were done on drywall, the artistic creation could be painted over. With most types of paneling, the affected paneling would have to be replaced.

People frequently install paneling in basement conversions. Basements tend to be dark to begin with, and installing a dark paneling worsens the situation. Rooms should be light and airy, for the most part. If paneling is used, the color of the paneling should be selected carefully.

I'm sure you've seen the cheap paneling advertised in the weekend paper. So has just about every homeowner considering a remodeling project. This super-cheap paneling is no bargain. I've used it before, in some of my personal rental property, and it is not the type of product that I would install for paying customers. Perhaps I should qualify my statement. The paneling I'm discussing might work very well if it were installed over existing drywall, but when nailed directly to stud walls, the panels warp, twist, and do all sorts of crazy things. If you are going to introduce your customers to paneling, make sure they shop for quality products.

Special wall coverings

When you venture into special wall coverings, you must understand why they are special. Installing weathered barn boards in a master bedroom or a living room is probably not a good idea. But putting them in a country kitchen could win you some awards. An interior brick wall is not common, but it can add warmth to a room, in terms of atmosphere, and it provides a nearly indestructible barrier for children to play around. My parents had a brick wall installed in the family room of one of their houses when I was a child, and I'm still enamored by it. As a contractor, I've used brick in family rooms where a masonry fireplace was centered on a wall. Brick has been used in several of the kitchen jobs I've done. The use of brick gets expensive and it can be too overbearing for a room, so don't get carried away with it.

Exterior siding, such as cedar or pine, can be used to give a room a rustic decor. I've done this in various jobs, and all of the customers have loved their new rooms. Tongue-and-groove boards also work well in this way. The use of wood siding and boards can make a very dramatic statement, and the designs that are possible when working with wood can give a home a custom, signature look.

How many bathrooms have you remodeled that were covered in water-resistant paneling? I've dealt with more of them than I care to remember. During my career, I've torn out a lot of this bathroom board, but I've only installed it once, and I would never do it again. In fact, a few months ago a customer asked me to install some of this hardboard in his bathroom. I agreed to do all of his remodeling work, except for the walls. The customer insisted on using the hardboard, and I stood firm on refusing to install it. The homeowner and one of his friends installed the wall covering themselves, and it didn't turn out very well. I tried to tell him, but he just wouldn't listen. I'm sure there must be occasions when this material is suitable, but I can't think of one.

Tub surrounds are often installed by remodelers. Most of these units are meant to be installed over water-resistant drywall, but a few are made to install directly over stud walls. In my experience, the only tub surrounds that work well when attached directly to wall studs are heavy fiberglass models. Thin fiberglass units, plastic surrounds, and other types of surrounds do best when installed over drywall.

Once you get the stud walls covered, you have to apply a finish coat in many cases. Since most walls are covered with drywall, the options for finish coats are numerous. Even when wood siding or planks are used as interior walls, some type of finish coat is needed. Brick and prefinished paneling don't call for this additional work, but most walls do. So let's talk now about finish wall coverings.

Finish wall coverings

Finish wall coverings come in many types, shapes, and colors. The ways these products are installed are as diverse as the products themselves. Considering the number of potential options, it is easy to understand why customers can become confused when trying to sort through the maze of choices. Good remodelers are aware of this, and they strive to clear the confusion for their customers. To better prepare you for this task, let's talk about specific types of finish wall coverings.

Priming

Priming surfaces prior to painting should be considered essential. A quality primer will allow paint to cover better. Even if a wall is going to be covered with wallpaper, some type of primer should be installed first. If wallpaper is applied to an unprimed wall, removing the wallpaper at a later date will be difficult. The adhesive used with the wallpaper will most likely pull off the paper coating of drywall when the wallpaper is removed. Priming the drywall prior to installing wallpaper will prevent this.

A good primer is every bit as important as a good paint. If you will be painting a wall, prime it first. It is usually a good idea to have the primer tinted to a color that will work well with the finish coats of paint used. Regardless of what you will use as a finish wall covering, buy and install a primer that is recommended for use with the finish product that will be used.

Latex paint

Latex paint is the most common type of paint used in modern construction. This paint doesn't emit offensive odors, it cleans up easily, and it dries quickly. These are all good characteristics. Latex paint is very durable, and it resists mildew. With so much going for it, there is no wonder that latex paint is so popular. However, if you will be painting over existing oil-based paint, latex paint might not be the best choice for the job.

Oil-based paint

Oil-based paint gives off odors that are offensive to many people. Some people have allergic reactions to the vapors. Oil-based paint is slow to dry, and cleaning up this paint is both messy and time-consuming. Many professional painters believe the durability of an oil-based paint makes the negative points of it acceptable, but others disagree.

Acrylic paint

Acrylic paint is in the latex family. This paint can be thinned with water, and it dries even faster than standard latex paint. Another favorable quality of this paint is that it covers well on almost any type of building material.

Alkyd paint

Alkyd paint is normally used in conjunction with oil-based paint. This is a synthetic-resin paint that is thinned with a solvent. Alkyd paint dries more quickly than oil-based paint, but much slower than latex. When you have to cover existing oil-based paint, alkyd paint will cover very well.

Wallpaper

If you get involved with wallpaper, you will soon find that there are a multitude of options available. Matching wallpaper to your specific needs is not always easy. Professionals in retail stores can be a lot of help in this matter, but you won't have these people with you when you begin your estimating process with homeowners. For this reason, you need to gather some background information to talk intelligently about wallpaper.

Vinyl-coated

Vinyl-coated wallpaper can be used in any room where excessive humidity is not a problem. The price for this type of wallpaper varies a great deal. Hanging vinyl wallpaper is not particularly complicated, and this is a popular type of wallpaper.

Wet-look vinyl is often used in areas where moisture is present. Rooms like bathrooms, kitchens, and laundry rooms lend themselves to wet-look vinyl. The cost for this paper is moderate, but lining paper should be factored into the cost. If any wall being covered has imperfections on it, they will likely show through unless a lining paper is used.

Lining paper
Lining paper is used to give a good, smooth surface for finish papers to be applied to. The inexpensive cost of lining paper does not make it a major financial inconvenience. But if it is not used, the finished product, even of a high-quality paper, can turn out poorly. Wheat paste is normally used to apply lining paper.

Paper-backed vinyl
Paper-backed vinyl wallpaper is a great all-purpose wallpaper. It is suitable for use in high-traffic areas and high-humidity areas. Prices on this paper range considerably. All in all, paper-backed vinyl is very hard to beat.

Cloth-backed vinyl
Cloth-backed vinyl can be used in the same rooms as paper-backed vinyl, but there are more drawbacks to the cloth-backed paper. Price is one of them; this paper is expensive. Stiffness can also be a problem with cloth-backed vinyl. I'm not sure why anyone would opt for cloth-backed paper when paper-backed vinyl is readily available.

Foil
Foil wallpaper works well in rooms when constant cleaning is needed, such as bathrooms and kitchens. Lining paper should be used whenever a foil paper is to be installed. You should also be aware that the price for foil paper might be a bit steep for some budgets.

Burlap
Burlap-style wallpaper can be beautiful, but it should not be used in rooms where it will take a beating. If a room will be damp, like in a bathroom, burlap should not be used. Kitchens are another place where a burlap-type paper shouldn't be used. The grease in a kitchen can wreak havoc with a grass-cloth or burlap-type paper.

Accent paper
Accent paper has become very popular. How many kitchens have you seen with pineapples spreading around the tops of walls? Some kitchens have designs stenciled into them, and others use accent pa-

pers to achieve a similar look. Both methods are effective. There are dozens and dozens of accent pieces available. The best way to become familiar with all of these options is to spend some time looking thorough catalogs.

Tile

Tile can be an excellent wall covering. It can also be used very effectively as an accent. When tile is installed as a backsplash in a kitchen, it is easy to clean. It's also attractive, but it tends to be expensive. Tile has been used in bathrooms for years. It is normally installed about half way up the walls and around bathing units. Trends have moved away from tile, except in expensive homes, but people still like it. The reason it doesn't show up as often is cost. Tile and its installation are not cheap.

Ceramic tile comes in various shapes, a multitude of colors, and a variety of designs. There is so much that can be done with it that it could boggle the mind. I incorporate tile into many of my jobs, and I suggest that you consider doing the same thing.

Tub surrounds

Tub surrounds are normally available in plastic and fiberglass. I prefer the fiberglass ones. Many of my bathroom jobs have involved the replacement of faulty tub surrounds and leaking tile. As you probably know, the grouting between tile often allows water to seep past it. It is possible to regrout tile, but my experience shows that most people prefer to have the leaking tile replaced.

My standard procedure for the replacement of a bad tub surround is to strip the walls down to the bare studs. Then I install water-resistant drywall and install a quality, fiberglass tub surround. My favorite type is fairly thin and is applied directly to drywall with an adhesive. I've used this type of surround for probably 15 years without ever having a callback on one.

You can buy cheap tub surrounds. I've seen them retail for less than $50. The type that I use wholesales for between $250 and $300. This is a lot more money, but I feel the expense is worthwhile. Cheap surrounds tend to fall off the walls that they are applied to. I suppose this is due to the adhesive, but I'm not sure. What I am sure of is that the high-quality fiberglass units I install don't fall off.

Some fiberglass surrounds are meant to be installed directly to bare studs. I've used these types of units, and they work fine. I have no complaints against these enclosures. Still, I find the glue-on type to be better accepted among homeowners. I don't know why this is, but it's proven to be true for me.

If you really want to spend a lot of money on a tub surround, you can invest in some of the thick, marblelike surrounds available. These surrounds are very attractive and extremely durable. They are a little harder to work with, and they are a lot more expensive, but there are times when these surrounds are the ideal choice.

Lay it out

When you are talking about wall coverings with your customers, lay it all out for them. Carry samples with you if you want, but one way or the other, be prepared to discuss the abundance of options available. Your performance in this area can have a direct effect on the success of your business. Learn what you need to know so that you can provide customers with enough information to make informed decisions.

15

Floor coverings

Floor coverings are an exciting part of a remodeling job for home-owners. People like the thrill of picking out new flooring and seeing it installed. Contractors enjoy the flooring phase because they know the job is winding down and their final payments will be coming in soon. But for the flooring phase to go smoothly on the job, someone has do to a good bit of preliminary work. Without good planning in the early stages of a job, the flooring phase can get beastly. I say this based on some past personal experiences.

My wife and I built a house for a man many years ago. The gentleman was part owner in a survey and engineering firm that we dealt with. We all knew each other, but even with the friendly background, we kept the construction project on a business level. Most of the job worked out fine, but we ran into some problems when carpeting was installed in the home. The vinyl floors were fine, but the customer was furious about his carpet. Let me tell you what happened.

Kimberley, my wife, handled product selections with customers. This involved all sorts of choices, but in this particular case the choice was carpeting. Kimberley met our customer at one of the carpet showrooms we used at that time. After awhile, the customer settled in on specific brands, models, and colors for all of his finish flooring. The selections were made from standard-size samples. As was our standard procedure, Kimberley filled out a selection form and had the customer sign it. The form detailed all aspects of the flooring, so that there could be no confusion when the time came to buy and install it.

A month or so passed before it was time to order the flooring. As part of our standard procedure, the customer was given an opportunity to change his mind on his flooring choices. We always tried to give customers as much opportunity to customize their homes as we could, and we always confirmed selections before placing orders. In this case, the customer was happy with his initial selections, so the flooring was ordered. The supplier was also one of our installers, so crews went to the job site and began the installation.

I arrived on the job one day to find installers hard at work. The vinyl floor was already installed, and it looked great. The carpeting was perhaps half installed, and I wondered about the color. It looked like a peach or pink color, and this seemed a little out of character with other choices the customer had made. Feeling some concern, I checked the markings on the carpeting and called them into my office. One of our administrative people pulled the customer's file and checked the selection sheet. Sure enough, this was the carpet he had picked out and signed for. I talked to my carpenters for a short while and left.

While on my way to another job site, I received a call from my office. The purpose of the call was to inform me that the customer whose house I had just left was on another line and wanted to talk to me. In fact, he wanted to meet me on the job site. I already had a good idea of what this was all about. Anyway, I doubled back and met with the customer at his new house.

When I arrived on the job site, I was met at my truck by an agitated customer. He didn't seem angry at me, but he was obviously stressed out. To make this long story shorter, I will simply say that he didn't like his new carpet, most of which was already installed. He swore that it was the wrong flooring and that he would have never picked a pink carpet. The color was more peach than pink, but there was no reason to argue this point.

I explained to the customer that I had seen the flooring and had been suspicious myself. Then I told him that I had confirmed, with the selection sheet, that this was in fact the flooring that he had hand picked and signed for. Now the guy started to get mad at me. He wanted different carpeting. I was not at fault and I couldn't afford to just give him new carpeting, so I used my best negotiating skills to calm him. In the long run, we wound up in my office looking over the selection sheet. It took a while, but the customer finally admitted that the carpet being installed was the carpet he had requested.

This job went to completion without any further trouble, but the disappointment surrounding the carpeting tainted the job. Kimberley and I had done all we could in getting a selection sheet signed. We didn't have to go to court, but the signed request would have been a great defense if a court battle had ensued. Unfortunately, the customer was not happy with his flooring selection, and the event took away much of the excitement a new homeowner should be able to enjoy. I felt bad for the customer, but there was not much I could afford to do. This is a case where everything was done right and a job

still soured. You can imagine what might happen if the proper attention to detail is not observed when it comes to flooring.

Replacing floor coverings

Replacing floor coverings is a typical part of many remodeling jobs.
There are few rooms remodeled where the flooring is not replaced.
Some existing floors are left intact and cleaned, but a majority of them
are replaced. Knowing this, you should be up to speed on various
flooring options. It is also necessary for you to know what to expect
in preparation for a flooring replacement. We'll talk about types of
flooring in just a little while. For now, let's concentrate on the other
issues that might become a part of your next flooring job.

Carpet replacements

Carpet replacements are probably the easiest type of flooring replacements. The very nature of carpet lends itself to hiding little flaws in existing subflooring. When a carpet pad is laid, it compensates for most
minor imperfections in the base flooring. By the time carpet is installed,
small ridges, little nail pops, and similar situations are not noticed. This
doesn't mean that you should take new carpeting for granted.

You've already seen an example of how a customer might choose
a particular type or color of carpet and love it in the showroom, only
to hate it once it is installed. Since carpet selections are frequently
made from very small samples, it is easy for a pattern or color to appear different when it is installed. Just the type of lighting being used
when carpeting is picked out can give it a color that is not the same
as it will appear once installed in a home. This is a situation that you
must be aware of and that you should inform your customers of. It
will prove advantageous for you to have customers sign a selection
sheet before you purchase or install any flooring.

As common as it is for carpet colors to seem as if they have
changed from the time they left the showroom to the time they are installed, it is even more common for patterns to give the impression of
magical changes. Try to have your customers make selections from
the largest samples available. The bigger the sample is, the less likely
it is that the customer will be disappointed later.

It is difficult to find anything more than a small sample for customers to choose from. When this is the case, you can suggest that
the customer take the sample home and look at it. Hopefully, your
supplier will have enough samples to allow in-home selection. This

process will, at least, give customers a view of the carpet in the same light that it will be seen in once it is installed.

When your customers pick a particular carpet for their home, record all available information from the sample on a selection sheet. Have your customers compare the information on the sample sheet with that found on the carpet sample. Once they confirm that the information on the selection sheet is accurate, have them sign in acceptance of their choice. This will not prevent the homeowners from getting angry when the carpet is installed, if it is not what they have envisioned, but it will give you solid footing to go to court on.

When you do an estimate that will require the installation of new carpeting, you have to check the existing condition of the subflooring. It will be fine in most cases. However, if you suspect problems with the base flooring, now is the time to express your concerns. Don't wait until you've contracted the job to tell customers that new subflooring will be needed to make a satisfactory installation.

Who is going to assume responsibility for the old carpeting and pad that will be removed? This is normally considered the responsibility of the remodeler. With the increasing cost and difficulty associated with debris removal, you should determine who is going to take charge of the old material before you agree to install new floor coverings.

Seams in carpeting is another issue that you should discuss with your customers before a job is taken. Most carpet is available in a maximum width of 12 feet. There are some brands that can be purchased with widths of 14 feet, but you need to know what the maximum width of your carpet line is before you sit down with potential customers.

Making a seam with carpet is not difficult, and the seam is often hard to spot. But seams sometimes puff up. This gives their location a noticeable hump, and it might be all it takes to turn a nice customer into a nasty one. The more you prepare a customer before work is started, the smoother the job will go.

Vinyl flooring

Vinyl flooring is often used in kitchens and bathrooms. Since these two rooms are often the first to be remodeled in a home, it stands to reason that remodelers deal with a lot of vinyl flooring. It is usually sheet vinyl, but it is sometimes in the form of square tiles. In either case, vinyl is very different from carpet in terms of subfloor preparation. Carpet can be laid over a so-so subfloor with acceptable results. This is not the case with vinyl.

When you look at a job where the vinyl floor will be replaced with a new one, there are many decisions you must make before presenting a price. Will the new vinyl be installed directly over the old vinyl? How hard will the old vinyl be to remove? What condition is the subfloor in? Will underlayment have to be installed? Is the room large enough to cause problems with seams? All of these are valid questions.

It is possible to install new sheet vinyl over existing vinyl. Personally, I don't recommend it, but it can be done. The existing floor must be in good shape and it must be clean. By clean, I mean free of wax, grease, or other elements that will interfere with the holding power of adhesives. If the old floor has cuts, holes, humps, or other defects in it, you should plan on removing it. Vinyl, unlike carpet, is unforgiving. If the base on which vinyl is installed is not flat and in good shape, the faults will show through the new flooring.

Carpet removal is pretty simple. The pad can be a pain to get out, but normally the removal work goes well. This is not always the case with vinyl. Some vinyl floors are taped into place, and they pull out easily. Sheet vinyl that was installed with a high-quality adhesive is much more difficult to get out. Vinyl tiles will usually come out if they are heated with a heat gun, but the old adhesive, from sheet vinyl or vinyl tiles, will normally have to be dealt with. Most remodelers I know don't attempt to remove the old adhesive. They just put down new underlayment. The cost of this material is offset by a savings in labor.

Sheet vinyl that has to be installed with seams presents a liability. The seam might work loose and curl up. Heavy traffic can affect the seam and cause the flooring to peel back. If seams can be avoided, they should be. Even going to extra expense for a higher grade of flooring that comes in a wider width is worthwhile if you can eliminate seams.

New underlayment is always a good idea. The better surface you have to work with, the less likely you are to have troubles down the road. I won't take a vinyl job unless the property owner is willing to authorize the installation of new underlayment. If the existing subfloor is found to be in satisfactory shape, I credit back the costs involved with installing new underlayment. But when underlayment is needed, I already have authorization and a budget for it. I find it is needed more often than not.

Rotted subfloors have been a consistent source of problems for me in bathroom remodeling. This is not to say that every bathroom floor has to be replaced, but a certain percentage of jobs will require all new subflooring and underlayment. I probe the subfloor of a bathroom to see if the subflooring has rotted. Common locations for problems are around the bases of toilets and the edges of bathtubs. There is occasionally a problem under a lavatory, but not very often.

Kitchen subflooring suffers from water damage sometimes. Finding a bad floor in a kitchen is more rare than finding one in a bathroom, but the odds are good that you will run into a rotted subfloor in a kitchen at some time. The dishwasher might leak or the kitchen sink might be at fault. A little probing during an estimate call is good insurance. It also builds confidence in your potential customers. If you are the only contractor to probe likely problem areas for possible water damage, the homeowners will take notice. Your attention to detail should impress them favorably.

Other types

Other types of flooring are not replaced as often as carpet and vinyl. For example, hardwood flooring is almost never replaced. It is often refinished, but rarely replaced. Tile floors endure the test of time, and they are not normally slated for replacement. On the occasions when a long-lasting floor is going to be replaced, attention must be paid to the base flooring conditions. You might very well have to contend with the removal of a mortar base or the installation of new subflooring. Take these expenses into consideration before you offer any price estimates to customers.

Flooring options

Flooring options are abundant. You can offer your customers hundreds of choices in vinyl flooring. The same can be said for carpet. If the customer wants a wood floor, you can suggest a narrow board or a wide plank. There are several types of wood that you can recommend. In terms of tile, there are a host of choices awaiting an excited homeowner. Then there are less conventional flooring options, such as brick. Let's take a few moments to review some of the options you might wish to offer your customers.

Carpet

When you are discussing carpet with your customers, one of the first considerations should be the pad that will be used in conjunction with the carpet. To set a budget for carpeting, you must factor in the cost of both carpeting and padding. Some types of carpeting, like commercial-grade carpeting, have an integral pad, but most carpeting used in homes will require a separate pad. The quality of this padding can have a tremendous effect on the carpet being installed. A great carpet on a cheap pad will not look as good or last as long as a moderate carpet on a great pad. The carpet pad actually prolongs the life of carpeting. It is also responsible for having footprints bounce out of the carpeting. Don't allow your customers to skimp on the padding. If the flooring budget is tight, recommend a high-quality pad and a midrange carpet.

Once you get past the pad issue, you are ready to discuss types of carpeting. There are several types of carpeting to choose from, and each type has its own advantages and disadvantages. (See Figs. 15-1 and 15-2.) Nylon carpet, for example, is an excellent all-around choice. The fibers are extremely tough and durable. Mildew and moths don't present problems for nylon, and this type of carpet is available in many price ranges. The biggest drawback to nylon is its tendency to build up static electricity.

- *Polyester:*
  ~Bright colors
  ~Resists mildew and moisture
  ~Stays clean
- *Olefin:*
  ~Very durable
  ~Resists mildew and moisture
  ~Very stain-resistant
- *Wool:*
  ~Durable
  ~Abrasion-resistant
  ~Reasonably easy to clean
  ~Should be protected against moths
  ~Resists abrasion

- *Acrylic:*
  ~Resists mildew
  ~Resists insects
  ~Remains clean
  ~Resists abrasion
- *Nylon:*
  ~Extremely durable
  ~Resists abrasion
  ~Resists mildew
  ~Resists moths
  ~Remains clean
  ~Tends to create static electricity

15-1 *Carpet features.*

Wool

Wool carpeting is not used much in today's construction and remodeling market. The expense of wool is one reason why it is not installed more often. While wool is durable and resists abrasion, it is susceptible to moths. Cost is probably the biggest shortcoming of wool carpeting.

Polyester

How does polyester stack up in the carpet industry? It ranks high in performance and popularity. The wide array of bright colors available in polyester make it eye-catching. Since it resists moisture and mildew, it is a practical choice. The price tag on polyester falls into a midrange that most homeowners can afford. Anyone considering new carpet should give some thought to a polyester product.

Cost Comparison of Carpet Fibers	
Polyester	Moderate cost
Olefin	Prices vary
Wool	Expensive
Acrylic	Moderate cost
Nylon	Prices vary
Polyester	Moderate cost

15-2 *Carpet cost comparisons.*

Acrylic

If your customer is looking for a carpet that seems to do it all, acrylic might be their choice. This material comes in a vast array of colors. It resists moisture and mildew, and it doesn't crush down easily. Add to this its ability to stand up against abrasions, and you've got a winner. One drawback to acrylic, however, is its likelihood of shedding. The material will sometimes produce little balls of fluff. This tendency to pill up might work against acrylic, but overall, it is a good, moderately priced carpet fiber.

Olefin

If children are going to be active on a carpet, olefin might be the best choice. This material is superresistant to stain. It resists moisture and it is nonabsorbent. Prices for olefin cover a broad spectrum. The cheapest versions might crush under heavy traffic, and this is probably its weakest point.

Vinyl

Vinyl flooring is very popular in bathrooms and kitchens. It is also installed frequently in laundry rooms and entryways. Eat-in breakfast areas are normally floored with vinyl. Other rooms and areas of homes sometimes use vinyl flooring, but the locations just mentioned are, by far, the most popular places for vinyl. When it comes to vinyl flooring, sheet vinyl is the most widely used. Vinyl tiles are available, but they seldom see much use.

When you set out to shop for sheet vinyl, you could be amazed at the wide range in prices. One piece of flooring might be priced at less than $4 per yard, while another is more than $30 per yard. Most builder-grade vinyl runs in the $13–$16 range in my area. Why is there such a spread in prices? There are numerous reasons, one of which is quality.

Cheap vinyl flooring might not be a bargain. The floor can be difficult to install. It can have little to no shine that will remain after a few cleanings. Within reason, you normally get what you pay for with vinyl flooring. I consider the lowest grade acceptable to be one that is approved for use in FHA and VA homes. If a material is FHA/VA approved, I assume it will work in an average home. But if your customer has strong financial resources and an eye for decorating, a sizable upgrade in quality might be beneficial.

Vinyl flooring can be purchased in so many colors and patterns that it can take days for customers to figure out what they want. Just as we discussed earlier about carpeting, large selection samples make getting the right vinyl easier. Many samples for vinyl flooring are very small. This makes it nearly impossible to predict a particular pattern. Ask your supplier to provide you with samples that are large enough to make selection fun and conclusive.

What makes an expensive vinyl better than a cheap vinyl? The difference might be in how thick the flooring is or how well cushioned it is. The finish on the flooring, such as a no-wax finish, will affect price. Some no-wax finishes are better than others. A vinyl floor's ability to resist cuts and scratches can make it more valuable. A lot of shopping has to go into finding the best value in vinyl flooring.

Stick-on tiles are often installed by do-it-yourselfers. I used these tiles one time. The job was a kitchen in one of my old rental properties. This was the first and last time I ever used vinyl tiles. My experience has shown that individual vinyl tiles cause more warranty trouble for contractors than sheet vinyl does. Customers seem to get discouraged when trying to clean the many seams in floor covered with vinyl tiles. Some customers will want these individual tiles, and it is up to you to decide if you are willing to install and stand behind them. The use of individual tiles in a foyer can be justified, but I would shy away from them in most other locations. If you agree to install these tiles, make sure your installer does the job by the book. Insist that all installation guidelines provided by the manufacturer are followed. I believe that many of the problems associated with vinyl tiles are due to the failure to observe the manufacturer's installment recommendations.

Tile

Ceramic and quarry tile make a nice floor. (See Figs. 15-3 and 15-4.) In the old days, the masonry base required to set tile added a lot of weight to a floor. With today's adhesives, the amount of weight associated with a tile floor is pretty much limited to the weight of just the tile. Tile floors can last a very long time, and they are easy to clean. There are some drawbacks, though. Tile floors are generally colder than other types of floor covering. They can also be very slippery when wet, and this is a disadvantage in bathrooms, kitchens, laundry rooms, and foyers, where water is often found on the floor. Tile with a raised surface for increased traction is a safer bet in these cases.

- *Ceramic tile:*
  ~Sizes range from 1-inch squares to 12-inch squares
  ~Most tiles have a thickness of ⁵⁄₁₆ inch
- *Ceramic mosaic tile:*
  ~Sizes range from 1-inch squares to 2-inch squares
  ~Also available in rectangular shapes, generally 1 × 2 inches
  ~Average thickness is ¼ inch
- *Quarry tile:*
  ~Sizes range from 6-inch squares to 8-inch squares
  ~Rectangular tile is available in 4-x-8-inch size
  ~Typical thickness is ½ inch

15-3 *Tile sizes.*

Difficulty Rating for Installing Tile

Ceramic tile:	Fairly easy
Ceramic mosaic tile:	Easy
Quarry tile:	Fairly difficult

15-4 *Difficulty rating for installing tile.*

Cost can be a prohibitive factor in a tile floor. If money is tight, tile is not a good choice. Sheet vinyl is much less expensive to buy and install, and it provides a very functional floor. However, tile opens up the arena of creativity and provides some stunning floors.

One complaint with tile in kitchens is the fact that fragile items dropped on a tile floor are more prone to breakage. This is true. A drinking glass or plate dropped on a tile floor is more likely to break that it would be if it were dropped on sheet vinyl or carpet.

Where should tile floors be installed? Kitchens and bathrooms are natural locations for tile. Laundry rooms are a good place for tile, and so are foyers. Sun rooms also offer a good environment for tile. Homes that are built around a solar basis often use tile as a storage mass. When and where to use tile will be up to your customers. All you have to do is be knowledgeable about the various options and the installment process involved with them.

Wood floors

Wood floors are not installed with the same frequency that they once were. Cost is a big factor in this. But money isn't the only reason people don't install more wood floors. The upkeep of a wood floor can be a bit of a bother. Keeping the floors sealed, waxed, and buffed requires a lot more effort than running a vacuum cleaner over a piece of wall-to-wall carpeting. The hectic schedule that most people face today leaves little time for taking care of a formal wood floor. Yet a number of people want wood floors.

When you get into wood floors, you must learn about the various types available. Hardwood floors are the most common, but a lot of people prefer a softwood floor. Some people want narrow strips, and others want wide planks. A few people want wood squares that are installed like tile. Standard procedure usually involves unfinished wood floors, but prefinished flooring materials are available. The grade of the wood used in the flooring has a lot to do with the finished look. Homeowners seeking a rustic appearance will like rough-grade softwood floors. A customer who wants a formal floor for a dining room will probably select an oak strip floor.

Even after a particular wood floor is decided on, the question of a finished sealer will come up. Picking a type of finish can be as hard, if not harder, than choosing a favorite carpet color. When you are working with your customers to establish a particular finish, you should make sure that the customer sees a sample of the finish. This sample should be applied to the same type of wood that will be used on the flooring. What might look good on an oak floor could look horrible on a birch floor. It is imperative that the finish be compared on a proper type of wood.

Brick

Brick and other types of special floors are not common, but they are used from time to time. For example, a brick floor can add a lot of charm to a country kitchen. On the other hand, installing a brick floor in a powder room would normally be considered strange and unusual. Full-size bricks, when used for flooring, bring the finished floor level to a higher height. This can be overcome by using brick sections that are intended to be used as flooring.

Slate

Slate and flagstone have been used over the years as a finish flooring. A typical location for this type of heavy floor is in a foyer. The cost of installing such a floor is steep, and the floor is typically slippery when wet. Some kitchens use this type of flooring, but overall, slate and flagstone are reserved for use in breezeways and entryways.

A big part

Flooring is a big part of some remodeling jobs, and the budget for flooring can easily reach into the thousands of dollars. With the expense being so great, there is no wonder that consumers want to be careful in their selections. The flooring market is so vast that a contractor has to dedicate significant time to learning it. As with other phases of your business, the more you learn about flooring, the better off you will be.

16

Interior trim

Interior trim doesn't typically play a large role in remodeling jobs. The most difficult part of interior trim when installing it in a remodeling job is matching it to existing trim. This can be a real problem, especially in older homes. Most homeowners recognize the fact that making exact matches between new trim and old trim is not an easy or inexpensive task, but this doesn't mean that they don't want the merger to be as attractive as possible.

What type of trim do you install most often? I would guess it is colonial trim. This is, by far, the most popular type of trim in modern construction. Some jobs are done with clamshell trim, and others are done with rustic boards. The choice of which trim to use is strictly cosmetic. There is no structural value to the material, and one type of trim will hide a crack or seam as well as any other type will. So what's the big deal with trim? Appearance. People like to live in homes that look good, and trim provides much in terms of physical appearance.

Go with the flow

When it comes to trim, it usually pays to go with the flow. If a majority of homes in an area have colonial trim in them, it would not be wise to install clamshell trim in a house. The appraised value of the home would likely suffer. Colonial trim is so well accepted that it is hard to go wrong with it. One exception would be homes with a rustic flair. When a house is capturing a pioneer spirit, plain dimensional lumber works well as a trim. Clamshell trim and vinyl baseboard don't have much place in a competitive remodeling market. These materials are typically used in projects when money is the measuring stick used to make decisions. However, saving money on trim can cost money later on, such as on an appraisal.

Almost all the houses I build and remodel are fitted with colonial trim. This is not just my personal preference. It's a decision I've made based on years of experience. I've seen how people respond to various types of trim, and I've never had anyone complain about colonial trim. During my time in this business, I've met with a lot of real estate appraisers. These meetings and consultations have proven colonial trim to be a safe bet. For these reasons, I stick with it.

I know a contractor who swears by your basic 1-by material as a finish trim. He uses it everywhere he can. I think this type of trim is fine in a rustic home, but I can't see it in a formal setting. You must have your own preference in terms of trim, and this might drive you to lead customers to your favorite. As professionals, we have to remember that we work for our customers. It is our obligation to make them aware of their many choices, but we should not insist that they take all of our advice. You should lay out the options for your customers and allow them to choose for themselves.

Fingerjoint trim

Do you use much fingerjoint trim? Some contractors swear by it, and others swear at it. I don't see anything wrong with using fingerjoint trim when it is going to be painted. If the trim is going to be stained, fingerjoint is not a good choice. But fingerjoint is less expensive than stain-grade trim. And when painted, fingerjoint trim looks the same as clear trim.

Solid trim

Solid trim costs more than fingerjoint trim, but it is the best type of trim to use when stain will be applied to the wood. Some people call solid trim clear trim, and others call it stain-grade trim. I normally refer to it as stain-grade trim. Regardless of what you call it, solid trim doesn't have all the visible joints that exist in fingerjoint trim.

I've seen people use fingerjoint trim and stain it. I can attest to the fact that it doesn't look good. On one occasion, fingerjoint trim was used around interior doors while solid trim was used elsewhere. All of the trim was stained. The result was less than desirable. When fingerjoint trim is stained, it is not a pretty picture.

Matching old trim

Matching old trim with new trim can be quite a challenge. There are many times when this just isn't possible with standard, stock trim. But if your customer is willing to pay, you can have custom trim made. It is also possible to buy replica trim from specialty suppliers, but don't expect the price to be meager. Your customers will have to be committed to making an investment in continuity. If not, you will just have to mix and match the trim.

If you happen to be a dedicated woodworker, you might make your own replica trim. If you do this, you can expect to net a tidy sum for your trouble. The money to be made in matching old trim can be staggering. But you've got to have customers who are willing to pay dearly for their desires. This is not always the case. A lot of people don't object to mixing modern trim with authentic trim, and this is a subject that you will have to work out with your customers.

Meticulous work

Interior trim is meticulous work when it is installed properly. A sharp saw and a sharp eye are key elements to fine trim work. Cutting angles that fit together tightly are essential to a professional trim job. If you can make good cuts, you might say that you are cut out to be a trim carpenter.

Do you use air equipment? Many trim carpenters are now using pneumatic nailers. If you are in this group, you are probably familiar with your tools. However, some trim carpenters don't set their air equipment up right. They don't shoot the nails deep enough. This causes problems for the painters. If you use air gear, make sure it is set to sink the nails in deeply enough. If you're still hammering nails in by hand, don't forget your nail set. If your painters have to go around and set a bunch of nails, you're going to have some irate painters on your hands.

Not much to say

There is really not much to say about interior trim that a professional doesn't already know. The key to interior trim is patience. Surprises rarely pop up when installing trim, and choices of standard trim are not numerous. The simplicity of installing trim doesn't allow for long discussions. So rather than waste your time with long-winded, roundabout talks pertaining to trim, let's move on to the next chapter. We're going to talk about cabinets and counters, and there will be more valuable information to discuss.

17

Cabinets and counters

If you're remodeling a kitchen, you're almost certain to work with cabinets and counters. Bathroom remodeling can also put you into contact with these elements. If you're a seasoned remodeler, you already know how much a set of cabinets can cost. You're probably also aware of the broad spectrum of prices affixed to cabinets. Counters can also be plenty expensive. If you've ever miscut a sink hole in a new countertop, you probably know all too well how much a counter can cost. When you consider that a set of kitchen cabinets can cost less than $2,000 or more than $10,000, it's easy to see why the subject is worthy of your attention.

Kitchen remodeling is certainly one of the most popular forms of remodeling for homeowners. Statistics show that kitchen remodeling is one of the safest home improvements a homeowner can invest in. With such a current interest in kitchen remodeling, there has been a surge in the cabinet industry. Cabinet manufacturers are offering more designs and styles than ever before. There are do-it-yourself videos available to show homeowners how to reface their existing cabinets. Major retailers are coventuring with remodelers to offer replacement doors and drawer fronts to be used in giving old cabinets facelifts. When you sit down with a potential customer for a kitchen job, you might have to explain the pros and cons of refacing, replacement doors, and new cabinets. Are you prepared to do this? Let's find out.

An average homeowner

Assume that I'm an average homeowner. I've asked you over to discuss the options for improving the look of my kitchen. As we sit at the dining room table, I begin asking you questions. I'm expecting some legitimate answers, so let's see how you do.

New doors

I've heard about ways to give my existing cabinets a new look by installing new doors and drawer fronts, what can you tell me about this procedure? How will I make the rest of my cabinet surfaces match the new doors and drawer fronts? Where will the new hardware come from? Will I have a choice in door pulls and hinges? How much money will I save by having my old cabinets updated instead of replaced?

How are you doing with your answers? The replacement of doors and drawer fronts is a common procedure. This work goes quickly. It can be completed in a day or less. As for the rest of the cabinet surfaces, they can be covered with a veneer or an adhesive paper that will match the new doors and drawer fronts. Hardware can come from any number of sources. It is available from standard suppliers of building supplies, as well as specialty suppliers. The amount of money saved by refacing instead of replacing can be quite substantial. An exact amount is difficult to arrive at on a generic basis, but it could easily amount to thousands of dollars. Now let's get back to our make-believe estimate interview.

Can you tell me the pros and cons of a wood veneer over a wood-look adhesive paper? How long will a refacing job last? Explain to me the advantages of replacing my old cabinets. How long will it take to get new cabinets? Would you recommend store-bought cabinets or custom-made cabinets? Let's review these questions and some potential answers.

If money is of a major concern, wood-grain adhesive paper can be used to give a new appearance to old cabinets. This is the cheap way out, and it does come with some potential problems. The paper can be tricky to install. Keeping wrinkles and bubbles out of the paper is not always easy. Since the covering is paper, it can be cut or torn. If this happens, the whole facelift can be ruined. Sometimes a patch can be made, but more often than not, an entire piece of the paper has to be replaced.

Wood veneer is a better option than adhesive paper when putting a false front on kitchen cabinets. The veneer is usually applied with a contact cement. Since the veneer is made of wood, it looks real. The veneer won't tear or rip, and it passes the touch test. In my opinion, wood veneer is the only way to go when refacing cabinets.

A quality refacing job can last years. It might not be as durable as a new set of cabinets, but for the cost, it's a good value. There are some advantages to doing a complete replacement instead of a refacing job. When you're forced to work with existing cabinets, you're limited in your options. Tearing out old cabinets and replacing them with new ones will provide an opportunity for the creative use of all types of cabinets. Turntable cabinets can be put into the system. Cabinets that house recycling bins can be installed. A myriad of possibilities exist when you start from scratch.

Timing can be crucial when dealing with kitchen cabinets. It can take months to have a set of custom cabinets made and delivered. Stock cabinets, on the other hand, might be available for immediate pickup. Most production cabinets can be ordered and delivered in less than three weeks. All of this comes into play when making a buying decision.

With the many alternatives available in production cabinets, there is little reason to pay extra and wait longer for custom cabinets. The quality of production cabinets has reached a level where it can be very difficult to tell a stock cabinet from a custom cabinet. When you weigh out the price and the delivery time of each type of cabinet, production cabinets will win the race every time. There are certainly occasions when custom cabinets are in order. If a person wants a unique cabinet arrangement, custom units will be the only way to go.

Counters

Helping your customers make decisions on counters can be almost as difficult as helping them choose cabinets. If nothing else, the multitude of colors and patterns will keep your customers confused for a good while. Will you recommend a square-edge counter or a round-edge unit? What type of backsplash will you suggest? Are you going to offer to make up a counter on site, or will you have your customer order a top from one of your suppliers? Is a laminate top the only type you plan to offer your customers? Have you considered a tile counter? What about a marble-type counter? Do you think your customer will prefer a slick finish or a pebble finish? Did you know there were this many questions that could come at you so quickly just on the subject of counters? Customers you sit down with might hit you with a lot more questions, and you should be prepared to answer them.

Many people don't give much thought to their counters. They go to a showroom, pick out a color and a pattern, and tell their contractor to order it. It is usually a safe bet that a customer will order a butcher-block design in neutral browns and tans. I know this is the type of laminate top that I get the most demand for.

If you want to take the path of least resistance, you can do as your customer says and order the top. However, if you want to make a good impression, and possibly a little extra money, you can educate your buyer concerning the other counters that are available. Many homeowners never stop to think about any type of top other than what they have been used to. If the people have lived in apartments and tract housing, a basic laminate top is what they will assume is standard procedure. Can you imagine how these customers might respond if you show them pictures of nice tile counters? If you will be using the job as a reference, it is in your best interest to make the work as nice as possible, and this includes making it a little out of the ordinary. I'm not suggesting that you twist a customer's arm to get a flashy counter installed, but it never hurts to apprise people of their options.

Let's assume your customers are dead set on a plain laminate top. Can you sell them on the idea of installing a tile backsplash between the top and the bottom of their wall cabinets? If you can, there will be a few extra bucks in the job for you, and you will have a better grade of work to use as a reference. The customer will get an easy-to-clean wall of tile, and you will be an above-average remodeler with regard to your base grade work.

Do you ever build your own counters? If you don't, you should consider it. At the very least, you should find a subcontractor who can do custom, on-site countertops. If you stay in remodeling long enough, you are sure to have an occasion when a site-built top will be of great interest to a customer. I can give you an example of this from one of my recent jobs.

I was putting together a new kitchen package a few months ago. The job involved a corner sink. With the double-bowl corner sink, a stock laminate counter was not a great idea. The seams for the top would meet under the drains of each sink bowl. Not wanting seams where water infiltration might be likely, it was necessary to look for an alternative. In this particular job, a postform top would have cost me about $300. But since this type of stock top was not desirable, due to the location of seams, I investigated other options. One of these alternatives was a more custom type of top. This counter would be seamed away from the sink, but the price for the top would have been a little more than $600. None of these prices included installation.

After weighing my options on prefab counters, I looked into having the top built on site. Building the counter right in the kitchen would allow me to avoid seams under the sink, and it would speed up the job. Instead of waiting two weeks for an ordered top, I could have one of my subcontractors build the counter in less than a day.

The price I was quoted for labor and material was less than $450. This option gave me a custom-built counter, which could be installed immediately, for about $150 less than a prefab top that didn't include installation. I chose to have the top built on site, and it turned out great. If I had wanted to, I could have easily charged $600 for the counter and a few hundred more for installation. This price would have been in keeping with the cost of a prefab top, and the job would have still been finished quicker. I would have also been about $350 richer. Not being greedy, I didn't inflate the cost of this work. But I could have pocketed the extra cash without really taking advantage of the customer. The homeowner would have gotten a better counter in less time for the same money as a prefab unit. This example alone proves the value of being prepared to do on-site work with counters.

Bathrooms

When you are remodeling bathrooms, you will probably be installing vanity cabinets and tops. This, of course, is no big deal. Almost anyone can install a vanity base and a molded lavatory top. In many cases, space limitations restrict creativity with bathroom cabinets. But when there is adequate room to work with, a vanity can become a work of art.

Most contractors install production cabinets in bathrooms. I've had custom cabinets made for vanity bases from time to time, but a vast majority of my work has been done with stock cabinets. The hardest part about this type of work is helping the customer decide on a particular type or design. When there is enough room to work with, the options for a vanity base are considerable.

If you only have a 30-inch space to work with, you're not going to be able to do much in the way of exotic cabinetry. This type of small space will basically limit you to a base cabinet with one door and no drawers. There are a few cabinets available in this size with drawers, but they are not common. The larger the space you have to work with, the more you have to offer your customers.

If the space available in a bathroom for a vanity is long enough, you can suggest a double-bowl vanity. Customers can choose base cabinets that have doors under the lavatory bowl and drawers on one side or even on both sides. A fairly standard layout is a cabinet with a door under the lavatory bowl and drawers on both sides. This provides his-and-her drawer space.

One design that has been very popular with my customers is a base cabinet with an offset top. The cabinet houses a lavatory, and the top extends for some distance to create a makeup counter. Add some strip lights, a big mirror, and a seating arrangement, and the homeowner has a fantastic place to get ready for work or play. This type of dressing area is very popular in the areas where I've worked.

Vanities can be focal points of bathrooms. The wood, the doors, the shape, and the size of a vanity can all work to create a haven, rather than a simple bathroom. When vanities are used, counters are needed. These can be cultured marble tops with integral lavatory bowls or laminated tops with drop-in or self-rimming lavatory bowls. Self-rimming bowls look better, are easier to clean around, and are not as prone to leaking. Cultured marble tops are usually chosen when a vanity is used. Sometimes a more expensive type of top is picked, and a few people prefer a laminate top. My experience has shown, however, that a cultured marble top, with an integral lavatory bowl, is a big favorite over other options.

Construction features

Customers might want you to point out construction features as they apply to cabinets and counters. (See Fig. 17-1.) This is not very difficult if you know your product line. What are some of the features that you recommend customers look for in a quality cabinet? Views on what makes a good cabinet can vary from person to person, but there are some benchmarks that most contractors agree on.

Most contractors agree that good cabinets are enclosed fully, meaning that they have backs in them. Not all cabinets do. Cabinets without backs are not as sturdy as those that do have backs. How much of the cabinet is made of wood? The more wood that a cabinet contains, the higher it is usually thought of. Were butt joints used in the construction of the cabinet? Dovetail and mortise joints are recognized to be of a higher quality than butt joints. Do the drawers of a cabinet open and close with ease? Drawers should be set into place on smooth glides. If a drawer is jerky to open or close, the quality of the cabinet is probably low. This type of problem could result from a sloppy installation, but it is more often the sign of a cheap cabinet. Are the shelves in the cabinet adjustable? They should be. How many adjustment options are there, and how difficult is it to move shelves around? Good cabinets offer a variety of possible shelf heights, and the movement of shelves should be simple.

I believe that customers should see and try cabinets before they buy them. If you are selling stock cabinets, your customers should be able to go to a showroom and compare various styles and types.

Kitchen Cabinet Features

Type of cabinet	Features
Steel	Noisy
	Might rust
	Poor resale value
Hardwood	Sturdy
	Durable
	Easy to maintain
	Excellent resale value
Hardboard	Sturdy
	Durable
	Easy to maintain
	Good resale value
Particleboard	Sturdy
	Normally durable
	Easy to maintain
	Fair resale value

17-1 *Features of kitchen cabinets.*

When custom cabinets are going to be made, the customer can't see and touch the exact cabinets that will be used until they are made. But a cabinet maker should have samples of the types of cabinets offered for sale. These samples can provide a glimpse of what to expect in custom cabinets being ordered.

The cost of kitchen cabinets can be extremely high. With so much money on the line, customers owe it to themselves to try before they buy. In other words, they should go out and look around at all types of cabinets. Particular attention should be paid to construction features. A cabinet that has terrific eye-appeal might be a piece of junk.

Getting a cabinet with rotating shelves that don't turn smoothly can be disappointing. Wall cabinets with doors that won't stay shut are a nuisance. Drawers that stick and scrape are no good. You should take your customers to showrooms and let them play with sample cabinets. Encourage them to open and close doors, spin turntables, use drawers, and evaluate all the various types of cabinets.

While you are at the showroom with your customers, you should discuss door styles and hardware. Will the doors have raised panels? Do leaded-glass doors fit your customer's budget and design? Will the customer want finger grooves or door and drawer pulls? Answer as many questions as you can in the showroom. There is no better place to work through confusion with cabinets and counters than in a showroom.

Balance

It can be difficult to balance a budget and desire at the same time. When I figure a job that will involve new kitchen cabinets, I plug in an allowance for the cost of the cabinets. For example, my proposal will state that my price is based on a cabinet allowance of $2,800 (at my wholesale cost). The customer can spend more or less, but since I have no way of knowing what taste in cabinets the customer has, I have to use a random figure. When I pick an allowance figure, I base it on my gut feeling. Some people spend less than $1,500 on cabinets. Others spend $7,000, or more. On average, I've found the wholesale cost of cabinets for most of my jobs to range between $2,500 and $3,500.

When you take your customers shopping for cabinets, you are very likely to see them go through a bit of agony. They know they have a budget to work with, but they have trouble deciding what to do. On the one hand, they want to choose something that costs less than their allocated sum. This will save them money on the overall cost of the job. But then they find a higher-priced cabinet style that they like better. It might very well be within their budget, but pushing it. Then there will be the cabinets they really love. These units, of course, are way above the budgeted price. So what is the customer to do? You might be asked to help settle the dilemma.

I recently had a situation just like the one I've described. My wife and I built a new house. During the cabinet stage, we went to the showroom to pick and choose. We knew from the start what brand of cabinet we wanted. After building 60 homes a year and running a very active remodeling business for over a decade, we had no doubt about the cabinet manufacturer that we trusted most. But we were faced with the money crunch. With as much experience as we both have in the construction and remodeling field, Kimberley and I still got caught in the pricing web.

We had set a budget of $2,500 for our kitchen cabinets. For the first time in any of the houses we have built for personal use, we wanted white cabinets. When we visited the showroom, we were not surprised to see a broad selection of styles and options. We're used to this from being in the business. But we were like many other consumers who are trying to decide on which cabinets to choose—confused!

All of the cabinet styles we were looking at were of a good quality. The least expensive design was all white. The cabinets had flat doors and finger grooves. This particular set of cabinets would have cost us about $1,800. We contemplated the opportunity to save $700 on our allowance. I felt, however, that the cabinets were too clinical looking. They gave me the impression of being in a medical facility. We moved on to the next pricing level.

The second set of cabinets we examined would cost about $2,300. This was still less than our budgeted amount, and the cabinets looked more residential than the first group did. They still didn't feel quite right. There were livable, and we were both willing to accept them, but neither of us were thrilled with them. This led us to a third level.

When we reached a higher price range, about $3,300, we got to cabinets that were white with oak trim. The oak strips around the finger grooves were a nice touch, and they wouldn't show dirty fingerprints the way a stark white cabinet would. Kimberley and I both really liked the oak accents. After considerable discussion, we decided to go with the oak. All of a sudden, we were $800 over budget, but how many houses do most people build for themselves? We've lived with the cabinets now for about four months, and we still love them.

I've told you this story to put into perspective what your customers might go through at a showroom. With all the years of experience I have in remodeling and construction, I still struggled with a cabinet selection. If someone like myself can have this type of problem, you can image how an average homeowner might feel? As a professional, you should be available to assist your customers in making their decisions. The people selling cabinets are going to stress sales features. It's up to you to show your customers all angles of a cabinet selection. If you take the time to explain construction features, cost factors (Fig. 17-2), market appeal, and other elements of cabinets, your customers will make decisions based on facts, not just sales hype.

Type of cabinet	Price range
Kitchen Cabinet Price Ranges	
Steel	Typically inexpensive, but high-priced units exist
Hardwood	Typically moderately priced, but can be expensive
Hardboard	Typically moderately priced
Particleboard	Typically low in price, but can reach into moderate range

17-2 *Price ranges of kitchen cabinets.*

Lowball prices

How many times have you seen lowball prices on cabinets in sales flyers? Almost any building supply center that caters to homeowners will carry some type of low-priced cabinets that can be advertised to pull people in. Many times the prices are not the bargain that they seem to be. It is not unusual for the rock-bottom prices of cabinets to exclude the finishing of the cabinets. I've had customers come to me with flyers and express a desire for the low-priced cabinets. It's true that unfinished cabinets can sell for half of what a standard production cabinet that has a permanent finish does, but this doesn't make the cheap cabinets a good deal. Even if the quality of the cabinets is not lacking, the cost and trouble of finishing them can outweigh any price savings.

I have a policy that stipulates the use of prefinished cabinets. My company will not assume any responsibility for finishing unfinished cabinets. We will install them if a customer insists, but we will not apply the finish. Finishing cabinets to a uniform look is very difficult and time-consuming. It is not an area of work that I perceive as being profitable for most remodelers. Unless you have resources beyond those of most contractors, you will probably be better off avoiding unfinished cabinets.

Installation problems

Any time you're working with old houses, you're likely to have some installation problems with cabinets and counters. Floors aren't level and walls aren't plumb. These conditions can make installing cabinets and counters very difficult indeed. The problems can be overcome if you catch them early, but when you wait until the cabinets are going in to discover the trouble, you've got a more serious problem.

Anyone who has been a remodeler for long knows that most houses are not perfect. In fact, they are usually far from it. If conditions are not right when cabinets are installed, problems will pop up. Doors might not stay shut. Drawers and slide-out accessories might not work properly. Gaps might exist along the bottoms of base cabinets. The space between a backsplash and a wall can be large enough to drop a pencil through. Face joints along cabinets might not fit up tightly. All of this can come together into a splitting headache for any remodeler who hasn't planned for the problems.

When you do an estimate for replacement cabinets, take a good level with you. Check the existing walls and floor. Even if you are going to gut the room out, check the existing conditions. Furring out walls and leveling floors takes time. If you don't budget this time into your job cost, you're going to lose money. When your level shows that problems with existing construction exist, you should show the trouble to your potential customers. They might not like finding out that additional work is going to be needed to bring existing conditions up to a satisfactory level, but they should appreciate finding out about the added expense before the job is underway.

Setting and hanging cabinets is not difficult work. It's not even very technical. But when a room is not square, a floor is not level, or walls are out of plumb, the job can become tedious, to say the least. Existing walls can be furred out to make them suitable for cabinets. A floor that isn't level can be corrected with underlayment and, possibly, some filler compound. None of this work is a big deal if it is done during the rough-framing stage of a job. It can, however, be extremely difficult once the job is nearly finished and it's time to set cabinets.

Very few homeowners are going to appreciate having a wide piece of trim installed along the top of their backsplash to hide a huge gap. A small bead of caulking (Fig. 17-3) will be the most they are expecting. If you have to put trim along the backsplash, someone messed up in their planning. It's standard procedure to shim up base cabinets, but the end result should not leave a noticeable gap along the floor. Yet I've seen kitchen after kitchen where the base cabinets are jacked up to a point where shoe mold is needed to hide the imperfections. This might or might not be acceptable to a homeowner, but having such a gap shouldn't be necessary. If the floor is worked with prior to installing finish floor covering, there shouldn't be any need for decorative trim to hide gaps.

Characteristics of Caulks

Type of caulk	Relative cost	Life years
Oil	Low	1–3
Vinyl latex	Low	3–5
Acrylic latex	Low	5–10
Silicon acrylic latex	Medium	10–20
Butyl rubber	Medium	5–10
Polysulfide	Medium	20+
Polyurethane	High	20+
Silicone	High	20+
Urethane foam	High	10–20

17-3 *Characteristics of various types of caulk.*

The key to a smooth cabinet installation is planning. If you prepare a kitchen properly, installing cabinets will be simple and fast. Should you neglect to correct framing problems early on, finishing a job to the satisfaction of a customer can be all but impossible. Spend some extra time up front to avoid conflicts near the end of the job.

Most of our discussion has revolved around kitchen cabinets. This is because they are more numerous than bathroom cabinets. However, the same rules apply for vanities. You need to check closely to see that a new cabinet can be installed properly. You must also allow for the vanity top. This is something a lot of contractors forget to do. They think in terms of a 36-inch cabinet and fail to remember that the top will be 37 inches in width. This extra inch can be enough to cause you to pull some hair out. When you are measuring for cabinets, don't forget to allow for the countertops that will go on them.

Damage

A lot of damage can occur near the end of a job, and some of it is likely to be with finished floors and cabinet installations. Using a screw that is too long can result in your having to buy a new cabinet out of your intended profits. If the screw punches through and ruins a cabinet, you are going to be responsible for the damage. Sliding base cabinets into place on a finished floor can cause other damage. If you cut, scrape, or tear a new floor, you will lose some more of your profit. Dropping screws and stepping on them is one way that many contractors inadvertently damage vinyl flooring. Some customers might accept a patch, but others will expect a complete floor replacement. This gets expensive, so you should make sure that you and your crews are careful not to harm new flooring.

Walls often suffer some damage during a cabinet and counter installation. To some extent, this is to be expected. Plan on having your painter do some touchup work after an installation is complete. Ideally, this work should be done as soon as possible. The visual picture a homeowner gets when a new wall is scuffed or gouged is not conducive to referral business.

To create a complete list of potential problems to be encountered during a cabinet installation would take more space than we have. For example, a slip in cutting a sink hole into a cabinet can quickly mean lost money and a delay of weeks. A long screw coming up through a new counter is disastrous. Having a worker lean too hard against an open cabinet door can result in damage that is serious enough to warrant the replacement of a cabinet. Almost all of the risks associated with damaging cabinets can be eliminated with good work habits and strong concentration. Take your time and do the job right the first time. You're getting paid for the initial installation, but if your get careless, you might be paying for repairs and replacements.

We are almost at the end of this book. Our discussions have covered all of the major phases of remodeling. There is, however, one more topic for us to delve into. A lot of people are interested in fireplaces and wood stoves. Either of these could become a part of your next remodeling job. The next chapter will take you through this subject, so let's turn the page and see what's waiting for us.

18

Fireplaces, wood stoves, and chimneys

Fireplaces, wood stoves, and chimneys can be part of a remodeling job. Some people want a wood stove installed to use as a backup heat source. Other people want them to use as an alternative heat source. Fireplaces are desirable in the eyes of many people. With either a fireplace or a wood stove, a chimney of some type is required. The chimney made be made of metal pipe or masonry materials. Fireplaces can be prefab metal units that don't require a lot of alteration in existing construction, or they can be masonry monsters that mandate a footing and substantial changes to existing construction conditions. Some remodelers are not familiar with what is involved in the installation of a fireplace or wood stove. For this reason, we are going to go over the basics. Before we do, however, I want to stress that you should consult with local authorities with regard to current, local code and safety requirements before installing any type of fireplace or stove.

Chimneys

Chimneys have been made with little more than sticks and mud, but this type of construction is no longer acceptable. Today's code requirements for chimneys and flues are much more restrictive, and with good reason. Unlined brick chimneys often lead to unwanted chimney fires. Mud and sticks are not a prime choice in terms of chimney materials. But even after throwing out some of the more primitive methods for building a chimney, we are still left with options. Do you know what they are?

Masonry

Masonry chimneys are looked on as being ideal. They are expensive, and they need to be cleaned periodically, but they are generally considered to be the best type of chimney available. I don't disagree with this view completely, but neither do I feel that a masonry chimney is always best.

When a masonry chimney is built, it must have a solid platform to rest on. This typically entails the use of a footing. If the chimney is to be installed on the outside of a home, substantial work must be done to cut it into the siding. Exterior masonry chimneys are usually covered in brick for appearance purposes, and this runs their cost up. If I were installing a wood stove, I probably would not opt for a masonry chimney. However, if a masonry fireplace is being built, it will be served by a masonry chimney. So how involved is it for a remodeler to undertake the installation of a masonry chimney for an existing house?

The first choice someone has to make is whether the chimney will be installed within the home or on an exterior wall. Interior chimneys can be enclosed with standard building materials, and this eliminates the need for a brick exterior, with the exception of where the chimney exits a roof. When the brick is avoided, there is a substantial savings in cost.

Before a chimney can be installed inside a home, a proper space for it must be found. Local codes will set requirements for clear space around the chimney. When planning an interior chimney location, you must take into account the clearance requirements, the size of the chimney, and the concealment framing. The amount of room needed for all this can be quite a bit. So much, in fact, that an interior chimney of this type might not be practical.

If a chimney is to be installed along an exterior wall, outside of a home, a footing and concrete pad will be needed for support. Existing siding on the home will have to be cut so that the chimney can be built along the sheathing of the home. Then flashing will have to be installed along the length of the chimney. All of this runs the expense of such a job up. Is your customer willing to pay thousands of dollars for a chimney? It could easily cost that much to build a masonry chimney. Is there an alternative? For wood stoves and prefab fireplaces, there is.

Metal chimneys

Metal chimneys are far from cheap, but they are much less expensive than their masonry cousins. Double- and triple-wall metal chimneys can be installed with a minimum amount of clearance. This allows them to be installed in smaller spaces than a masonry unit could be. Almost anyone can install a metal chimney, so the high cost of a mason is not necessary. An average remodeler can easily install a metal chimney, from start to finish, in less than a day. This is much faster than the time it would take to have a masonry chimney built, and there are other advantages to metal chimneys.

Unless a customer wants a brick chimney for status or appearance, there is little reason to use a masonry chimney for anything other than a masonry fireplace. Metal chimneys can be installed inside or outside of homes. When installed outside, the chimney pipe can be enclosed with framing and siding. Inside, the pipe can be hidden with framing and drywall. Framing and siding can be installed around the chimney where it exits a roof.

The relatively low cost of a metal chimney makes it not only a viable option, but also an affordable one. Since metal chimneys have a very smooth finish on the inside, they are not as prone to catch and hold creosote. This is not to say that they shouldn't be cleaned, but they might be less dangerous than a masonry chimney that has rough surfaces along its channel.

Few remodelers are accomplished masons. If you have a customer who wants a masonry chimney, you should have an experienced mason visit the job site with you before making any commitments. The mason will be able to point out alterations that will be needed on the existing construction. This helps to protect you and makes your estimate more accurate.

When a metal chimney is suitable, you might have your own crews take care of the installation. Suppliers of metal chimneys usually stock a variety of kits and accessories to make installations safer and easier. For example, you can get a through-the-wall kit or a through-the-ceiling kit. Each kit will contain special fittings that are designed to provide proper clearance and protection when a chimney pipe penetrates a wall or ceiling.

Let's say, for example, that you have a customer who wants a wood stove installed in a basement where you are doing a conversion job. The house has a basement and one level of living space. There is a standard gable attic over the living space. Your customer wants the chimney to run up through the house and has agreed to forfeit a small section of a room to house the chimney. What will you need to make this installation?

The first thing you will need are three collars that will be used where the chimney comes through the floor, ceiling, and roof. The collar will mount between joists, although you might have to cut out and head off enough space to accommodate it. The first collar will be installed in the basement. The exposed side of the collar will accept standard stove pipe, and the upper side of the collar will accept the metal chimney pipe. This provides support for the chimney and complies with clearance requirements.

A section of chimney pipe is attached to the first collar and subsequent sections are installed, one on top of the other, until the ceiling area is reached. At this point, another collar is needed to make the penetration through the ceiling and into the attic. Chimney pipe is installed on both sides of the collar and is extended up through the attic. A hole is cut in the roof, and a third collar guides the chimney pipe through the roof. Once the pipe is out of the house, it is extended to meet local code requirements. A spark arrestor will normally be installed, and so will a chimney cap. Other supports and accessories might be needed, depending on individual conditions.

Once the chimney is installed and inspected, it can be concealed in a framed chase. Some clearance from combustible materials will be required by local regulations, but the distance will be minimal. This type of installation is fast, easy, safe, and affordable. It is hard to beat.

If the customer had wanted the chimney to extend up the exterior of the home, a through-the-wall kit could have been used. A special collar is used where the chimney penetrates the exterior wall, and then a wall bracket provides support for the vertical chimney on the outside wall. The pipe is run up the side of the house, using special brackets to hold it in place. When the piping is complete, a wood frame can be built around the chimney, leaving required clearance, and the wood frame can be covered with siding. Either of these types of installation are much more simple than what would be required for a masonry chimney.

Fireplaces

There are three basic types of fireplaces that you might be asked to install. The most common, and most expensive, is a full masonry fireplace. A second type of fireplace is a prefab unit that is designed to be built into a wall. The third type of fireplace is a freestanding unit. There are pros and cons to each of these types of fireplaces, so let's discuss them.

Masonry fireplaces

Masonry fireplaces are typically considered to be the most desirable. They can be made to fit almost any location nicely, and they are extremely durable. The biggest drawbacks to masonry fireplaces are their cost to install and the work involved with the installation. Adding a masonry fireplace to an existing house is no small job. It is a major undertaking that will consume many days and a lot of dollars.

One consideration many homeowners look at when assessing fireplaces is the effect they will have on the appraised value of their homes. From my discussions with real estate appraisers, masonry fireplaces do very well when it comes time for an appraisal. While it is unlikely that excess equity will result from adding a masonry fireplace, it is likely that most of the cost will be returned in appraised value. Considering the fact that a masonry fireplace is likely to cost a minimum of $4,000, this is comforting to know.

Built-in fireplaces

Built-in fireplaces cost a fraction of what a masonry fireplace does. Prefab, metal fireplaces can be installed in any room without excessive alteration. Installation is simple. The unit is set in place, metal chimney pipe is run, and a wall is framed up around the fireplace and chimney. These working fireplaces can add a touch of romance to a master bedroom or warmth to a family room.

What is the major drawback to a metal fireplace? Well, it isn't cost because they are cheap in terms of fireplaces. I've had both masonry and metal fireplaces in homes where I have lived. Without question, I have preferred masonry fireplaces. My personal experience as a user of a metal fireplace is that the firebox is too small. The space is typically short and narrow, which restricts log length and burning time between trips to the wood pile. Other than this one complaint, I don't know of any other serious drawback.

Freestanding fireplaces

Freestanding fireplaces were very popular for awhile, but the infatuation with them seems to have waned. These are units that are intended to set out in the floor of a room. A chimney pipe extends off the top of the unit and is usually left out in open view. These fireplaces are inexpensive, in relative terms, and they are easy to install. Some are very attractive and quite functional. The freestanding aspect makes these fireplaces more like a wood stove than a fireplace, in terms of heating capabilities.

One potentially dangerous drawback to a freestanding unit is the risk of someone getting burned. This is especially true when small children will be found in the vicinity. The relatively low cost of freestanding and prefab fireplaces makes up for the fact that neither of these units do great in terms of appraised value.

Wood stoves

Wood stoves don't require as much work to install as most fireplaces do. A chimney is built and the wood stove is set in place. A stove pipe connects the stove to the chimney collar, and the job is done. There are, of course, a lot of wood stoves to choose from on the market. Making a decision on which stove to buy might very well be the toughest part of the job. Fortunately, your customers won't expect you to hold their hand while they shop for a stove. As long as you are aware of local code requirements and the methods for installing a safe, acceptable chimney, you are in the clear on wood stoves.

If your customer is planning to have you install a stove, you might suggest a brick hearth and perhaps even a brick heat shield for the wall behind or on either side of the stove. When a suitable heat shield is used, a stove can be safely set closer to a wall. This conserves floor space for your customer. The heat shield may be made of metal, brick, tile, or some other approved material.

Other considerations

Other considerations might come up when talking with customers about wood stoves and fireplaces. For example, your customer might want gas piping run for a gas log. In most jurisdictions, a licensed gas fitter will be required for such an installation. Many licensed plumbers are also licensed gas fitters. If the customer is seeking a sensible source of heat, your conversation might change to gas- or oil-fired wall heaters. Some gas-fired heaters are rated to work safely without any venting to outside air. Most wall units do, however, require a direct-vent system, which is easy to install.

It is difficult to stay up to speed on all the many options available to homeowners when it comes to remodeling. If you sat in your office all day, every day, reviewing trade publications, brochures, and other available data, you might be able to absorb most of what's hot in the market. But few remodelers have time to sit around ferreting out new products and their specifications. You should strive to stay informed, but don't be afraid to ask a customer to allow you to research a subject. If you are asked a question that you are unable to answer with authority, don't bluff the homeowner. Request some time to look into the matter and then present your findings at a later date. It is better to say nothing than to say something that is not correct.

We have reached the end of this book and the beginning of your new outlook on remodeling jobs. I suspect that some of the information and stories that you have read here have changed your perspective on various aspects of your work. As my closing advice, I would like to say that you should never stop improving your depth of knowledge. People who believe they know all there is to know about remodeling are fooling themselves. Every day is a learning experience, and we can all benefit if we pay attention to what is going on around us.

A

Working safely

General Safe Working Habits

1. Wear safety equipment.

2. Observe all safety rules at the particular location.

3. Be aware of any potential dangers in the specific situation.

4. Keep tools in good condition.

A-1 *General safe working habits.*

Safe Dressing Habits

1. Do not wear clothing that can be ignited easily.

2. Do not wear loose clothing, wide sleeves, ties or jewelry (bracelets, necklaces) that can become caught in a tool or otherwise interfere with work. This caution is especially important when working with electrical machinery.

3. Wear gloves to handle hot or cold pipes and fittings.

4. Wear heavy-duty boots. Avoid wearing sneakers on the job. Nails can easily penetrate sneakers and cause a serious injury (especially if the nail is rusty).

5. Always tighten shoelaces. Loose shoelaces can easily cause you to fall, possibly leading to injury to yourself or other workers.

6. Wear a hard hat on major construction sites to protect the head from falling objects.

A-2 *Safe dressing habits.*

Safe Operation of Grinders

1. Read the operating instructions before starting to use the grinder.

2. Do not wear any loose clothing or jewelry.

3. Wear safety glasses or goggles.

4. Do not wear gloves while using the machine.

5. Shut the machine off promptly when you are finished using it.

A-3 *Safe operation of grinders.*

Safe Use of Hand Tools

1. Use the right tool for the job.

2. Read any instructions that come with the tool unless you are thoroughly familiar with its use.

3. Wipe and clean all tools after each use. If any other cleaning is necessary, do it periodically.

4. Keep tools in good condition. Chisels should be kept sharp and any mushroomed heads kept ground smooth; saw blades should be kept sharp; pipe wrenches should be kept free of debris and the teeth kept clean; etc.

5. Do not carry small tools in your pocket, especially when working on a ladder or scaffolding. If you should fall, the tools might penetrate your body and cause serious injury.

A-4 *Safe use of hand tools.*

Safe Use of Electric Tools

1. Always use a three-prong plug with an electric tool.

2. Read all instructions concerning the use of the tool (unless you are thoroughly familiar with its use).

3. Make sure that all electrical equipment is properly grounded. Ground fault circuit interrupters (GFCI) are required by OSHA regulations in many situations.

4. Use proper-sized extension cords. (Undersized wires can burn out a motor, cause damage to the equipment, and present a hazardous situation.

5. Never run an extension cord through water or through any area where it can be cut, kinked, or run over by machinery.

6. Always hook up an extension cord to the equipment and then plug it into the main electrical outlet—not vice versa.

7. Coil up and store extension cords in a dry area.

A-5 *Safe use of electric tools.*

Rules for Working Safely in Ditches or Trenches

1. Be careful of underground utilities when digging.

2. Do not allow people to stand on the top edge of a ditch while workers are in the ditch.

3. Shore all trenches deeper than 4 feet.

4. When digging a trench, be sure to throw the dirt away from the ditch walls (2 feet or more).

5. Be careful to see that no water gets into the trench. Be especially careful in areas with a high water table. Water in a trench can easily undermine the trench walls and lead to a cave-in.

6. Never work in a trench alone.

7. Always have someone nearby—someone who can help you and locate additional help.

8. Always keep a ladder nearby so you can exit the trench quickly if need be.

9. Be watchful at all times. Be aware of any potentially dangerous situations. Remember, even heavy truck traffic nearby can cause a cave-in.

A-6 *Working safely in ditches.*

Safety on Rolling Scaffolds

1. Do not lay tools or other materials on the floor of the scaffold. They can easily move and you could trip over them, or they might fall, hitting someone on the ground.

2. Do not move a scaffold while you are on it.

3. Always lock the wheels when the scaffold is positioned and you are using it.

4. Always keep the scaffold level to maintain a steady platform on which to work.

5. Take no shortcuts. Be watchful at all times and be prepared for any emergencies.

A-7 *Safety on rolling scaffolds.*

Working Safely on a Ladder

1. Use a solid and level footing to set up the ladder.

2. Use a ladder in good condition; do not use one that needs repair.

3. Be sure step ladders are opened fully and locked.

4. When using an extension ladder, place it at least ¼ of its length away from the base of the building.

5. Tie an extension ladder to the building or other support to prevent it from falling or blowing down in high winds.

6. Extend a ladder at least 3 feet over the roof line.

7. Keep both hands free when climbing a ladder.

8. Do not carry tools in your pocket when climbing a ladder. (If you fall, the tools could cut into you and cause serious injury.)

9. Use the ladder the way it should be used. For example, do not allow two people on a ladder designed for use by one person.

10. Keep the ladder and all its steps clean—free of grease, oil, mud, etc.—in order to avoid a fall and possible injury.

A-8 *Safety on a ladder.*

To Prevent Fires

1. Always keep fire extinguishers handy, and be sure that the extinguisher is full and that you know how to use it quickly.

2. Be sure to disconnect and bleed all hoses and regulators used in welding, brazing, soldering, etc.

3. Store cylinders of acetylene, propane, oxygen, and similar substances in an upright position in a well-vented area.

4. Operate all air acetylene, welding, soldering, and related equipment according to the manufacturer's directions.

5. Do not use propane torches or other similar equipment near material that can easily catch fire.

6. Be careful at all times. Be prepared for the worst, and be ready to act.

A-9 *Preventing fires.*

B

Work outlines and budget estimates

Types of Work That Might be Needed to Build an Addition

Survey

Plans

Specifications

Permits

Site preparation

Footings

Foundation

Pest control treatment

Backfill labor, if applicable

Demolition

Repairs to existing wall

Framing

Siding

Roofing

Exterior trim

Exterior hardware

Windows

Doors

Plumbing

Heating/ac

Electrical

Insulation

Drywall

Paint

Interior doors

Interior hardware

Interior trim

Finish floor covering

Wall cabinets

Base cabinets

Countertops

Window treatments

Landscaping

Trash container

Dump fees

Cleanup

Personal touches

Gutters

Decks

B-1 *Types of work needed with additions.*

Work to be Done when Building an Addition (before Physical Work Begins)

Choose style of addition to be built.

Review requirements of space; closets, additional baths, windows, door sizes, etc . . .

Draw a rough draft of addition plans.

Make a list of required materials for the job.

Price materials.

Make a list of subcontractors or general contractors for selection.

Contact contractors for price quotes.

Evaluate your budget and the affordability of the addition.

Make financing arrangements.

Make a final decision on the plans for the addition.

Obtain blueprints.

Apply for the necessary permits.

Choose your contractors and check their references.

Meet with your attorney to draft contracts and other documents.

Schedule work.

Schedule material deliveries.

Schedule contractors.

B-2 *Preliminary work involved with additions.*

Work to be Done
when Building an Addition
(when Physical Work Begins)

Start work.

Inspect work.

Obtain copies of all code enforcement inspections.

Make payments as scheduled in the contracts and obtain signed lien waivers from contractors and suppliers.

Inspect completed job.

Make punch-lists, as necessary.

Make absolute final inspection and approval.

Make final payments, except for retainages.

Make retainage payments.

B-3 *Work outline for additions.*

Budget Estimates for Building a Room Addition

Item/Phase	Labor	Material	Total
Survey			
Plans			
Specifications			
Permits			
Site preparation			
Dig footings			
Concrete for footings			
Pour footings			
Foundation wall material			
Foundation wall labor			
Pest control treatment			
Foundation backfill labor			
Demolition			
Repairs to existing wall			
Framing lumber			
Roof trusses			
Attic vents			
Sheathing			
Framing labor			
Siding			
Siding labor			
Shingles			
Subtotal			

B-4 *Budget estimates for additions.*

Item/Phase	Labor	Material	Total
Roof labor			
Exterior trim material			
Exterior hardware			
Windows			
Doors			
Nails & misc. material			
Shelving			
Pull-down attic stairs			
Misc. carpentry labor			
Rough plumbing material			
Rough plumbing labor			
Plumbing fixtures			
Final plumbing labor			
Rough heating/ac material			
Rough heating/ac labor			
Heating/ac equipment			
Final heating/ac labor			
Rough electrical material			
Rough electrical labor			
Light fixtures			
Final electrical labor			
Insulation			
Insulation labor			
Drywall			
Drywall labor			
Paint			
Subtotal			

B-4 *Continued.*

Item/Phase	Labor	Material	Total
Paint labor			
Interior doors			
Interior hardware			
Interior trim			
Interior trim labor			
Underlayment			
Finish floor covering			
Wall cabinets			
Base cabinets			
Countertops			
Window treatments			
Landscaping			
Trash container deposit			
Trash container delivery			
Dump fees			
Cleanup			
Trash container removal			
Personal touches			
Financing expenses			
Miscellaneous expenses			
Options:			
Concrete for slab			
Wire mesh			
Gravel			
Plastic ground cover			
Pour slab			
Subtotal			

B-4 *Continued.*

Item/Phase	Labor	Material	Total
Finish slab			
Gutters			
Decks			
Unexpected expenses			
Margin of error			
Total projected expenses			

B-4 *Continued.*

Work for Kitchen Remodeling (before Physical Work Begins)

Review requirements of space; additional windows or appliances, eat-in area, built-in seating or storage, lighting, etc.

Draw a rough draft of kitchen plans.

Make a list of required materials for the job.

Price materials.

Make a list of subcontractors or general contractors for selection.

Contact contractors for price quotes.

Evaluate your budget and the affordability of the kitchen project.

Make financing arrangements.

Make a final decision on the plans for the kitchen.

Obtain blueprints, if necessary.

Apply for the necessary permits.

Choose your contractors and check their references.

Meet with your attorney to draft contracts and other documents.

Schedule work.

Schedule material deliveries.

Schedule contractors.

B-5 *Preliminary work involved with kitchen remodeling.*

Work That Might Need to be Done for Kitchen Remodeling

Plans	Subfloor	Hardware
Specifications	Insulation	Wall cabinets
Permits	Drywall	Base cabinets
Trash container	Trim	Countertops
Demolition	Windows	Appliances
Dump fees	Doors	Kitchen accessories
Plumbing	Paint/wallpaper	Cleanup
Electrical	Underlayment	Window treatments
Heating/ac	Finish floor covering	Personal touches

B-6 *Types of work involved with kitchen remodeling.*

Work to be Done for Kitchen Remodeling (when Physical Work Begins)

Start work.

Inspect work.

Obtain copies of all code enforcement inspections.

Make payments as scheduled in the contracts and obtain signed lien waivers from contractors and suppliers.

Inspect completed job.

Make punch-list, if necessary.

Make absolute final inspection and approval.

Make final payments, except for retainages.

Make retainage payments.

B-7 *Work outline for kitchen remodeling.*

Budget Projections for Kitchen Remodeling

Item/Phase	Labor	Material	Total
Plans			
Specifications			
Permits			
Trash container deposit			
Trash container delivery			
Demolition			
Dump fees			
Rough Plumbing			
Rough Electrical			
Rough heating/ac			
Subfloor			
Insulation			
Drywall			
Baseboard trim			
Window trim			
Door trim			
Paint/wallpaper			
Underlayment			
Finish floor covering			
Hardware			
Wall cabinets			
Base cabinets			
Countertops			
Subtotal			

B-8 *Budget estimates for kitchen remodeling.*

Item/Phase	Labor	Material	Total
Plumbing fixtures			
Trim plumbing material			
Final plumbing			
Light fixtures			
Trim electrical material			
Final electrical			
Trim heating/ac material			
Final heating/ac			
Appliances			
Kitchen accessories			
Cleanup			
Trash container removal			
Window treatments			
Personal touches			
Financing expenses			
Miscellaneous expenses			
Unexpected expenses			
Margin of error			
Total projected expenses			

B-8 *Continued.*

Work That Might Need to be
Done for Garage Construction

Survey	Trim	Hardware
Plans	Windows	Landscaping
Specifications	Small door	Cleanup
Permits	Garage doors	Personal touches
Site preparation	Garage door openers	*Options:*
Footings	Electrical	Heating/ac
Pest control	Insulation	Plumbing
Slab floor	Drywall	Interior trim
Framing	Paint	Floor sealant
Siding	Trash container	Apron
Roofing	Dump fees	Driveway repair or extension

B-9 *Types of work needed with garages.*

Work to be Done for Garage Construction (before Physical Work Begins)

Choose style of garage to be built.

Draw a rough draft of garage plans or obtain predrawn plans.

Make, or obtain, a list of required materials for the job.

Price materials.

Make a list of subcontractors or general contractors for selection.

Contact contractors for price quotes.

Evaluate budget and the affordability of the garage.

Make financing arrangements.

Make a final decision on the plans for the garage.

Obtain blueprints.

Apply for the necessary permits.

Choose your contractors and check their references.

Meet with your attorney to draft contracts and other documents.

Schedule work.

Schedule material deliveries.

Schedule contractors.

B-10 *Preliminary work involved with garages.*

Work to be Done for Garage Construction (when Physical Work Begins)

Start work.

Inspect work.

Obtain copies of all code enforcement inspections.

Make payments as scheduled in the contracts and obtain signed lien waivers from contractors and suppliers.

Inspect completed job.

Make punch-list, if necessary.

Make absolute final inspection and approval.

Make final payments, except for retainages.

Make retainage payments.

B-11 *Work outline for garages.*

Budget Projections for the Construction of a Garage

Item/Phase	Labor	Material	Total
Survey			
Plans			
Specifications			
Permits			
Site preparation			
Dig footings			
Concrete for footings			
Pour footings			
Concrete for slab			
Wire mesh			
Gravel			
Plastic ground cover			
Pest control			
Pour slab			
Pour apron			
Finish slab			
Framing lumber			
Roof trusses			
Attic vents			
Sheathing			
Framing labor			
Siding			
Subtotal			

B-12 *Budget estimates for garages.*

Item/Phase	Labor	Material	Total
Siding labor			
Shingles			
Roof labor			
Trim material			
Windows			
Small door			
Garage doors			
Garage door openers			
Overhead door labor			
Nails & misc. material			
Pegboard			
Shelving			
Pull-down attic stairs			
Misc. carpentry labor			
Rough electrical material			
Rough electrical labor			
Light fixtures			
Final electrical labor			
Insulation			
Insulation labor			
Drywall			
Drywall labor			
Paint			
Paint labor			
Trash container deposit			
Trash container delivery			
Subtotal			

B-12 *Continued.*

Item/Phase	Labor	Material	Total
Dump fees			
Hardware			
Landscaping			
Cleanup			
Trash container removal			
Personal touches			
Financing expenses			
Miscellaneous expenses			
Options:			
Heating/ac			
Plumbing			
Interior trim			
Floor sealant			
Driveway repair or extension			
Unexpected expenses			
Margin of error			
Total projected expenses			

B-12 *Continued.*

Types of Work That Might Need to be Done for an Attic Conversion

Plans	Paint
Specifications	Interior doors & hardware
Permits	Interior trim
Demolition	Underlayment
Repairs to existing ceiling	Finish floor covering
Framing	Wall cabinets
Stairs	Base cabinets
Dormer work, if required	Countertops
Plumbing	Window treatments
Heating/ac	Trash container
Electrical	Dump fees
Insulation	Cleanup
Drywall	Personal touches

B-13 *Types of work needed with attic conversions.*

Work for an Attic Conversion
(before Physical Work Begins)

Review requirements of space; stairs, built-in storage, closets, windows, new attic space ventilation, etc.

Draw a rough draft of conversion plans.

Make a list of required materials for the job.

Price materials.

Make a list of subcontractors or general contractors for selection.

Contact contractors for price quotes.

Evaluate your budget and the affordability of the conversion.

Make financing arrangements.

Make a final decision on the plans for the conversion.

Obtain blueprints, if necessary.

Apply for the necessary permits.

Choose your contractors and check their references.

Meet with your attorney to draft contracts and other documents.

Schedule work.

Schedule material deliveries.

Schedule contractors.

B-14 *Preliminary work involved with attic conversions.*

Work to be Done
for an Attic Conversion
(when Physical Work Begins)

Start work.

Inspect work.

Obtain copies of all code enforcement inspections.

Make payments as scheduled in the contracts and obtain signed lien waivers from contractors and suppliers.

Inspect completed job.

Make punch-list, if necessary.

Make absolute final inspection and approval.

Make final payments, except for retainages.

Make retainage payments.

B-15 *Work outline for attic conversions.*

Budget Projects for an Attic Conversion

Item/Phase	Labor	Material	Total
Plans			
Specifications			
Permits			
Demolition			
Repairs to existing ceiling			
Framing lumber			
Framing labor			
Dormer material			
Dormer labor			
Nails & misc. material			
Misc. carpentry labor			
Rough plumbing material			
Rough plumbing labor			
Plumbing fixtures			
Final plumbing labor			
Rough heating/ac material			
Rough heating/ac labor			
Heating/ac equipment			
Final heating/ac labor			
Rough electrical material			
Rough electrical labor			
Light fixtures			
Final electrical labor			
Subtotal			

B-16 *Budget outline for attic conversions.*

Item/Phase	Labor	Material	Total
Insulation			
Insulation labor			
Drywall			
Drywall labor			
Paint			
Paint labor			
Interior doors & hardware			
Interior trim			
Interior trim labor			
Underlayment			
Finish floor covering			
Wall cabinets			
Base cabinets			
Countertops			
Window treatments			
Trash container deposit			
Trash container delivery			
Dump fees			
Cleanup			
Trash container removal			
Personal touches			
Financing expenses			
Miscellaneous expenses			
Unexpected expenses			
Margin of error			
Total projected expenses			

B-16 *Continued.*

Work for Bathroom Remodeling
(before Physical Work Begins)

Obtain various product information.

Review requirements of space; linen closet, door sizes, windows, additional electrical outlets (GFI), fans, etc.

Draw a rough draft of bathroom plans.

Make a list of required materials for the job.

Price materials.

Make a list of subcontractors or general contractors for selection.

Contact contractors for price quotes.

Evaluate budget and the affordability of the bathroom remodeling.

Make financing arrangements.

Make a final decision on the plans for the bathroom.

Obtain blueprints, if necessary.

Apply for the necessary permits.

Choose your contractors and check their references.

Meet with your attorney to draft contracts and other documents.

Schedule work.

Schedule material deliveries.

Schedule contractors.

B-17 *Preliminary work outline for bathroom remodeling.*

Possible Work for Bathroom Remodeling

Plans	Subfloor	Finish floor covering
Specifications	Insulation	Hardware
Permits	Drywall	Wall cabinets
Trash container	Ceramic tile	Base cabinets
Demolition	Linen closet	Countertops
Dump fees	Trim	Shower enclosure
Plumbing	Windows	Bath accessories
Fixture installation	Doors	Cleanup
Electrical	Paint/wallpaper	Window treatments
Heating/ac	Underlayment	Personal touches

B-18 *Types of work involved with bathroom remodeling.*

Work for Bathroom Remodeling
(when Physical Work Begins)

Start work.

Inspect work.

Obtain copies of all code enforcement inspections.

Make payments as scheduled in the contracts and obtain signed lien waivers from contractors and suppliers.

Inspect completed job.

Make punch-list, if necessary.

Make absolute final inspection and approval.

Make final payments, except for retainages.

Make retainage payments.

B-19 *Work outline for bathroom remodeling.*

C

Business forms

Cash Receipts

Date	Account description	Amount paid	Date received

C-1 *Cash receipts form.*

Job Cost Log

Item	Quantity	Size

C-2 *Job cost log.*

Accounts Payable

Vendor	Job	Amount due	Date due	Date paid

C-3 *Accounts payable log.*

Petty-Cash Record

Month _____

Year _____

Vendor	Amount	Item	Date	Job

C-4 *Petty-cash log.*

Accounts Receivable

Date	Account description	Amount due	Date due	Date received
	Total due			

C-5 *Accounts receivable log.*

Phone Log

Date	Company name	Contact person	Remarks

C-6 *Phone log.*

Punch List
Bathroom Remodeling Project

Item/phase	O.K.	Repair	Replace	Finish work
Demolition				
Rough plumbing				
Rough electrical				
Rough heating/ac				
Subfloor				
Insulation				
Drywall				
Ceramic tile				
Linen closet				
Baseboard trim				
Window trim				
Door trim				
Paint/wallpaper				
Underlayment				
Finish floor covering				
Linen closet shelves				
Linen closet door				
Closet door hardware				
Main door hardware				
Wall cabinets				
Base cabinets				
Countertops				
Plumbing fixtures				
Subtotal				

C-7 *Bathroom punch list.*

Item/phase	O.K.	Repair	Replace	Finish work
Trim plumbing material				
Final plumbing				
Shower enclosure				
Light fixtures				
Trim electrical material				
Final electrical				
Trim heating/ac material				
Final heating/ac				
Bathroom accessories				
Clean up				

Notes

C-7 *Continued.*

Punch List

Phase	Okay	Needs work

C-8 *Punch list log.*

Inspection Log

Phase	Ordered	Approved
Rough plumbing		
Finish plumbing		
Rough electrical		
Finish electrical		
Rough heating		
Finish heating		
Framing		
Insulation		
Final		

C-9 *Field inspection log.*

Material Specifications

Phase	Item	Brand	Model	Color	Size
Plumbing	Lavatory	WXYA	497	White	19" × 17"
Plumbing	Toilet	ABC12	21	White	12" rough
Plumbing	Shower	KYTCY	41	White	36" × 36"
Electrical	Ceiling fan	SPARK	2345	Gold	30"
Electrical	Light kit	JFOR2	380	White	Standard
Flooring	Carpet	MISTY	32	Grey	14 yards

C-10 *Sample material specifications such as those that should be used when entering into a remodeling or subcontract contract.*

Contractor Rating Sheet

Category	Contractor 1	Contractor 2	Contractor 3
Contractor name			
Returns calls			
Licensed			
Insured			
Bonded			
References			
Price			
Experience			
Years in business			
Work quality			
Availability			
Deposit required			
Detailed quote			
Personality			
Punctual			
Gut reaction			

Notes

_____

_____

_____

_____

_____

C-11 *Contractor rating sheet.*

Subcontractor Questionnaire

Company name _____

Physical company address _____

Company mailing address _____

Company phone number _____

After-hours phone number _____

Company president/owner _____

President/owner address _____

President/owner phone number _____

How long has company been in business _____

Name of insurance company _____

Insurance company phone number _____

Does company have liability insurance _____

Amount of liability insurance coverage _____

Does company have Workman's Comp. insurance _____

Type of work company is licensed to do _____

List business or other license numbers _____

Where are licenses held _____

If applicable, are all workers licensed _____

Are there any lawsuits pending against the company _____

Has the company ever been sued _____

Does the company use subcontractors _____

Is the company bonded _____

Who is the company bonded with _____

Has the company had complaints filed against it _____

Are there any judgments against the company _____

C-12 *Subcontractor questionnaire.*

Material Take-Off

Item	Size	Quantity

C-13 *Take-off form.*

Material Order Log for Follow-Up

Supplier: _____

Date order was placed: _____

Time order was placed: _____

Name of person taking order: _____

Promised delivery date: _____

Order number: _____

Quoted price: _____

Date of follow-up call: _____

Manager's name: _____

Time of call to manager: _____

Manager confirmed delivery date: _____

Manager confirmed price: _____

Notes and Comments

_____

_____

_____

_____

_____

_____

_____

_____

C-14 *Material order follow-up log.*

Paint Record

Type of paint	Supplier	Color	Paint number

C-15 *Paint record log.*

Bid Request

Customer name: _____

Customer address: _____

Customer city/state/zip: _____

Customer phone number: _____

Job location: _____

Plans & specifications dated: _____

Bid requested from: _____

Type of work: _____

Description of material to be quoted: _____

All quotes to be based on attached plans and specifications. No substitutions allowed without written consent of customer.

Please provide quoted prices for the following: _____

_____

All labor, materials, permits, and related fees to complete plumbing as per attached plans and specifications.

All bids must be submitted by: _____

C-16 *Bid request.*

Job Schedule

Phase	Start date	Completion date

C-17 *Job schedule form.*

Job Budget

Phase	Cost
Plans	
Permits	
Demolition	
Framing	
Stairs	
Dormers	
Plumbing	
Heating	
Electrical	
Insulation	
Drywall	
Paint	
Doors	
Hardware	
Underlayment	
Floor coverings	
Cabinets	
Countertops	
Cleanup	
Other	
Total cost	

C-18 *Job budget form.*

Cost Projection

Item/phase	Labor	Material	Total
Plans			
Specifications			
Permits			
Trash container deposit			
Trash container delivery			
Demolition			
Dump fees			
Rough plumbing			
Rough electrical			
Rough heating/ac			
Subfloor			
Insulation			
Drywall			
Ceramic tile			
Linen closet			
Baseboard trim			
Window trim			
Door trim			
Paint/wallpaper			
Underlayment			
Finish floor covering			
Linen closet shelves			
Closet door & hardware			

C-19 *Cost projection form.*

Item/phase	Labor	Material	Total
Main door hardware			
Wall cabinets			
Base cabinets			
Countertops			
Plumbing fixtures			
Trim plumbing material			
Final plumbing			
Shower enclosure			
Light fixtures			
Trim electrical material			
Final electrical			
Trim heating/ac material			
Final heating/ac			
Bathroom accessories			
Clean-up			
Trash container removal			
Window treatments			
Personal touches			
Financing expenses			
Miscellaneous expenses			
Unexpected expenses			
Margin of error			
Total estimated expense			

C-19 *Continued.*

Materials Log

Supplier's name	
Contact person	
Order number	
Date of order	
Delivery date	
Cost of order	

C-20 *Materials order log.*

Subcontractor Schedule

Type of service	Vendor name	Phone number	Date scheduled
Site work			
Footings			
Concrete			
Foundation			
Waterproofing			
Masonry			
Framing			
Roofing			
Siding			
Exterior trim			
Gutters			
Pest control			
Plumbing/R-I			
HVAC/R-I			
Electrical/R-I			
Insulation			
Drywall			
Painter			
Wallpaper			
Tile			
Cabinets			
Countertops			
Interior trim			

C-21 *Subcontractor schedule.*

Type of service	Vendor name	Phone number	Date scheduled
Floor covering			
Plumbing/final			
HVAC/final			
Electrical/final			
Cleaning			
Paving			
Landscaping			

Notes/Changes

C-21 *Continued.*

Commencement and Completion Schedule

The work described above shall be started within 3 days of verbal notice from the customer, the projected start date is _____. The subcontractor shall complete the above work in a professional and expedient manner by no later than twenty (20) days from the start date. Time is of the essence of this subcontract. No extension of time will be valid without the general contractor's written consent. If subcontractor does not complete the work in the time allowed and if the lack of completion is not caused by the general contractor, the subcontractor will be charged one-hundred dollars ($100.00) for every day work is not finished after the completion date. This charge will be deducted from any payments due to the subcontractor for work performed.

C-22 *Commencement and completion schedule clause, like the type that should be in a subcontract agreement.*

Subcontractor Liability for Damages

Subcontractor shall be responsible for any damage caused to existing conditions. This shall include new work performed on the project by other contractors. If the subcontractor damages existing conditions or work performed by other contractors, said subcontractor shall be responsible for the repair of said damages. These repairs may be made by the subcontractor responsible for the damages or another contractor, at the discretion of the general contractor.

If a different contractor repairs the damage, the subcontractor causing the damage may be back-charged for the cost of the repairs. These charges may be deducted from any monies owed to the damaging subcontractor, by the general contractor. The choice for a contractor to repair the damages shall be at the sole discretion of the general contractor.

If no money is owed to the damaging subcontractor, said contractor shall pay the invoiced amount, from the general contractor, within seven business days. If prompt payment is not made, the general contractor may exercise all legal means to collect the requested monies.

The damaging subcontractor shall have no rights to lien the property where work is done for money retained to cover the repair of damages caused by the subcontractor. The general contractor may have the repairs made to his satisfaction.

The damaging subcontractor shall have the opportunity to quote a price for the repairs. The general contractor is under no obligation to engage the damaging subcontractor to make the repairs.

C-23 *Liability for damages schedule clause, like the type that should be in a subcontract agreement.*

Progress Payments

The contractor shall pay the subcontractor once an acceptable insurance certificate has been filled by the subcontractor with the contractor and the contractor approves the finished work. Payment schedule will be as follows:

_____

_____

All payments are subject to a site inspection and approval of work by the contractor.

Before final payment, the subcontractor, if required, shall submit satisfactory evidence to the contractor, that all expenses related to this work have been paid and no lien risk exists on the subject property.

C-24 *Progress payment clause, like the type that should be in a subcontract agreement.*

Working Conditions

Working hours will be 8:00 AM through 4:30 PM, Monday through Friday. Subcontractor may work additional hours if desired.

Subcontractor is required to clean his work debris from the job site on a daily basis and leave the site in a clean and neat condition. Subcontractor shall be responsible for the removal and disposal of all related debris from his job site.

C-25 *Working conditions clause, like the type that should be in a subcontract agreement.*

Contract Assignment

Subcontractor shall not assign this contract or further subcontract the whole of this subcontract without the written consent of the contractor.

C-26 *Contract assignment clause, like the type that should be in a subcontract agreement.*

Laws, Permits, Fees, and Notices

Subcontractor shall be responsible for all required laws, permits, fees, or notices, required to perform the work stated herein.

C-27 *Responsibility clause, like the type that should be in a subcontract agreement.*

Work of Others

Subcontractor shall be responsible for any damage caused to existing conditions or other trade's work. This damage will be repaired and the subcontractor charged for the expense and supervision of this work. The amount charged will be deducted from any payments due to the subcontractor, if any exist.

C-28 *Work of others clause, like the type that should be in a subcontract agreement.*

Warranty

Subcontractor warrants to the contractor all work and materials for one year from the day work is completed.

Indemnification

To the fullest extent allowed by law, the subcontractor shall indemnify and hold harmless the owner, the contractor and all of their agents and employees from and against all claims, damages, losses and expenses.

This Agreement entered into on _____ shall constitute the whole agreement between contractor and subcontractor.

_____   _____

Contractor   Subcontractor

C-29 *Warranty clause, like the type that should be in a subcontract agreement.*

Subcontract Agreement

This agreement, made this _____th day of _____, 19____, shall set forth the whole agreement, in its entirety, between Contractor and Subcontractor.

Contractor: _____, referred to herein as Contractor.

Job location: _____

Subcontractor: _____, referred to herein as Subcontractor.

The Contractor and Subcontractor agree to the following:

Scope of Work

Subcontractor shall perform all work as described below and provide all material to complete the work described below:

Subcontractor shall supply all labor and material to complete the work according to the attached plans and specifications. These attached plans and specifications have been initialed and signed by all parties. The work shall include, but is not limited to, the following:

_____

_____

_____

_____

_____

_____

_____

_____

_____

Commencement and Completion Schedule

The work described above shall be started within three days of verbal notice from Contractor, the projected start date is _____. The

C-30 *Subcontract agreement.*

Subcontractor shall complete the above work in a professional and expedient manner by no later than twenty days from the start date. Time is of the essence in this contract. No extension of time will be valid without the Contractor's written consent. If Subcontractor does not complete the work in the time allowed, and if the lack of completion is not caused by the Contractor, the Subcontractor will be charged fifty dollars ($50.00) per day, for every day work extends beyond the completion date. This charge will be deducted from any payments due to the Subcontractor for work performed.

Contract Sum

The Contractor shall pay the Subcontractor for the performance of completed work subject to additions and deductions as authorized by this agreement or attached addendum. The Contract Sum is
_____($_____).

Progress Payments

The Contractor shall pay the Subcontractor installments as detailed below, once an acceptable insurance certificate has been filed by the Subcontractor with the Contractor: Contractor shall pay the Subcontractor as described:

_____

_____

_____

All payments are subject to a site inspection and approval of work by the Contractor. Before final payment, the Subcontractor, shall submit satisfactory evidence to the Contractor that no lien risk exists on the subject property.

Working Conditions

Working hours will be 8:00 AM through 4:30 PM, Monday through Friday. Subcontractor is required to clean his work debris from the job site on a daily basis and leave the site in a clean and neat condition. Subcontractor shall be responsible for removal & disposal of all debris related to his job description.

Contract Assignment

Subcontractor shall not assign this contract or further subcontract the whole of this subcontract, without the written consent of the Contractor.

C-30 *Continued.*

Laws, Permits, Fees, and Notices

Subcontractor shall be responsible for all required laws, permits, fees, or notices, required to perform the work stated herein.

Work of Others

Subcontractor shall be responsible for any damage caused to existing conditions or other contractor's work. This damage will be repaired, and the Subcontractor charged for the expense and supervision of this work. The Subcontractor shall have the opportunity to quote a price for said repairs, but the Contractor is under no obligation to engage the Subcontractor to make said repairs. If a different subcontractor repairs the damage, the Subcontractor may be back-charged for the cost of the repairs. Any repair costs will be deducted from any payments due to the Subcontractor. If no payments are due the Subcontractor, the Subcontractor shall pay the invoiced amount within ten days.

Warranty

Subcontractor warrants to the Contractor, all work and materials for one year from the final day of work performed.

Indemnification

To the fullest extent allowed by law, the Subcontractor shall indemnify and hold harmless the Owner, the Contractor, and all of their agents and employees from and against all claims, damages, losses and expenses.

This agreement, entered into on _____, 19____, shall constitute the whole agreement between Contractor and Subcontractor.

_____   _____
Contractor   Date   Subcontractor   Date

C-30 *Continued.*

Remodeling Contract

This agreement, made this _____ day of _____,
19____, shall set forth the whole agreement, in its entirety, between
Contractor and Customer.

Contractor: Your Name, referred to herein as Contractor.

Customer: _____, referred
to herein as Customer.

Job name: _____

Job location: _____

The Customer and Contractor agree to the following:

Scope of Work

Contractor shall perform all work as described below and provide all
material to complete the work described below: All work is to be
completed by Contractor in accordance with the attached plans and
specifications. All material is to be supplied by Contractor in accordance
with attached plans and specifications. Said attached plans and
specifications have been acknowledged and signed by Contractor and
Customer.

A brief outline of the work is as follows, and all work referenced in the
attached plans and specifications will be completed to the Customer's
reasonable satisfaction. The following is only a basic outline of the
overall work to be performed:

_____

_____

_____

_____

_____

Commencement and Completion Schedule

The work described above shall be started within three days of verbal
notice from Customer; the projected start date is _____. The
Contractor shall complete the above work in a professional and

C-31 *Remodeling contract.*

expedient manner, by no later than twenty days from the start date. Time is of the essence regarding this contract. No extension of time will be valid, without the Customer's written consent. If Contractor does not complete the work in the time allowed, and if the lack of completion is not caused by the Customer, the Contractor will be charged one-hundred dollars ($100) per day, for every day work is not finished beyond the completion date. This charge will be deducted from any payments due to the Contractor for work performed.

Contract Sum

The Customer shall pay the Contractor for the performance of completed work, subject to additions and deductions, as authorized by this agreement or attached addendum. The contract sum is

_____, ($_____).

Progress Payments

The Customer shall pay the Contractor installments as detailed below, once an acceptable insurance certificate has been filed by the Contractor, with the Customer:

Customer will pay Contractor a deposit of _____
_____, ($_____), when work is started.
Customer will pay _____,
($_____), when all rough-in work is complete.
Customer will pay _____,
($_____) when work is _____ percent complete.
Customer will pay _____,
($_____) when all work is complete and accepted.

All payments are subject to a site inspection and approval of work by the Customer. Before final payment, the Contractor, if required, shall submit satisfactory evidence to the Customer, that all expenses related to this work have been paid and no lien risk exists on the subject property.

Working Conditions

Working hours will be 8:00 AM through 4:30 PM, Monday through Friday. Contractor is required to clean work debris from the job site on a daily basis and to leave the site in a clean and neat condition. Contractor shall be responsible for removal and disposal of all debris related to their job description.

Contract Assignment

Contractor shall not assign this contract or further subcontract the whole of this subcontract without the written consent of the Customer.

C-31 *Continued.*

Laws, Permits, Fees, and Notices

Contractor is responsible for all required laws, permits, fees, or notices required to perform the work stated herein.

Work of Others

Contractor shall be responsible for any damage caused to existing conditions. This shall include work performed on the project by other contractors. If the Contractor damages existing conditions or work performed by other contractors, said Contractor shall be responsible for the repair of said damages. These repairs may be made by the Contractor responsible for the damages or another contractor, at the sole discretion of Customer.

The damaging Contractor shall have the opportunity to quote a price for the repairs. The Customer is under no obligation to engage the damaging Contractor to make the repairs. If a different contractor repairs the damage, the Contractor causing the damage may be back-charged for the cost of the repairs. These charges may be deducted from any monies owed to the damaging Contractor.

If no money is owed to the damaging Contractor, said Contractor shall pay the invoiced amount within seven business days. If prompt payment is not made, the Customer may exercise all legal means to collect the requested monies. The damaging Contractor shall have no rights to lien the Customer's property for money retained to cover the repair of damages caused by the Contractor. The Customer may have the repairs made to his satisfaction.

Warranty

Contractor warrants to the Customer all work and materials, for one year from the final day of work performed.

Indemnification

To the fullest extent allowed by law, the Contractor shall indemnify and hold harmless the Customer and all of their agents and employees from and against all claims, damages, losses and expenses.

This Agreement entered into on _____, 19_____ shall constitute the whole agreement between Customer and Contractor.

Customer	Date	Contractor	Date

Customer	Date

C-31 *Continued.*

Proposal

Date: _____

Customer name: _____
Address: _____
Phone number: _____
Job location: _____

Description of Work

(Your Company Name) will supply, and or coordinate, all labor and material for the above referenced job as follows:

_____

_____

_____

Payment Schedule

Price: _____ ($_____),

Payments to be made as follows:

_____

_____

_____

All payments shall be made in full, upon presentation of each completed invoice. If payment is not made according to the terms above, (Your Company Name) will have the following rights and remedies. (Your Company Name) may charge a monthly service charge of one-and-one-half percent (1.5%), eighteen percent (18%) per year, from the first day default is made. (Your Company Name) may lien the property where the work has been done. (Your Company Name) may use all legal methods in the collection of monies owed to it. (Your Company Name) may seek compensation, at the rate of $30 per hour, for attempts made to collect unpaid monies.

(Your Company Name) may seek payment for legal fees and other costs of collection, to the full extent the law allows.

C-32 *Proposal.*

If the job is not ready for the service or materials requested, as scheduled, and the delay is not due to (Your Company Name's) actions, (Your Company Name) may charge the customer for lost time. This charge will be at a rate of $30 per hour, per man, including travel time.

If you have any questions or don't understand this proposal, seek professional advice. Upon acceptance, this proposal becomes a binding contract between both parties.

Respectfully submitted,

Your name and title
Owner

Acceptance

We the undersigned do hereby agree to, and accept, all the terms and conditions of this proposal. We fully understand the terms and conditions, and hereby consent to enter into this contract.

Your Company Name   Customer

By _____   _____

Title _____   Date _____

Date _____

Proposal Expires in 30 Days, If Not Accepted by All Parties.

C-32 *Continued.*

Change Order

This change order is an integral part of the contract dated _____,
between the Customer, _____ , and the
Contractor, _____, for the work to be
performed. The job location is _____.
The following changes are the only changes to be made. These changes
shall now become a part of the original contract and may not be altered
again without written authorization from all parties.

Changes to be as follow:

_____

_____

_____

_____

_____

These changes will increase/decrease the original contract amount.
Payment for theses changes will be made as follows: _____.
The amount of change in the contract price will be _____
_____ ($). The new total contract price shall be
_____ ($).

The undersigned parties hereby agree that these are the only changes to
be made to the original contract. No verbal agreements will be valid. No
further alterations will be allowed without additional written
authorization, signed by all parties. This change order constitutes the
entire agreement between the parties to alter the original contract.

_____   _____
Customer   Contractor

_____   _____
Date   Date

_____
Customer

_____
Date

C-33 *Change order.*

Quote

This agreement, made this _____ day of _____,
19___, shall set forth the whole agreement, in its entirety, by and
between YOUR COMPANY NAME, herein called Contractor and
_____, herein called Owners.

Job name: _____

Job location: _____

    The Contractor and Owners agree to the following:

Contractor shall perform all work as described below and provide all
material to complete the work described below. Contractor shall supply
all labor and material to complete the work according to the attached
plans and specifications. The work shall include the following:

_____

_____

_____

_____

Schedule

The work described above shall begin within three days of notice from
Owner, with an estimated start date of _____. The Contractor
shall complete the above work in a professional and expedient manner
within _____ days from the start date.

Payment Schedule

Payments shall be made as follows:

_____

_____

This agreement, entered into on _____, shall constitute the
whole agreement between Contractor and Owner.

_____   _____

Contractor   Date   Owner   Date

_____

Owner   Date

C-34 *Quote.*

Subcontractor Contract Addendum

This addendum is an integral part of the contract dated _____,
between the Contractor, _____,
and the Customer(s), _____,
for the work being done on real estate commonly known as _____
_____. The undersigned parties hereby
agree to the following:

_____

_____

_____

_____

_____

_____

_____

_____

The above constitutes the only additions to the above-mentioned
contract, no verbal agreements or other changes shall be valid unless
made in writing and signed by all parties.

_____   _____

Contractors   Date   Customer   Date

                                       _____

                                       Customer   Date

C-35 *Contract addendum.*

Request for Substitutions

Customer name: _____

Customer address: _____

Customer city/state/zip: _____

Customer phone number: _____

Job location: _____

Plans & specifications dated: _____

Bid requested from: _____

Type of work: _____

The following items are being substituted for the items specified in the attached plans and specifications:

_____

_____

_____

_____

_____

Please indicate your acceptance of these substitutions by signing below.

_____   _____

Contractor   Date   Customer   Date

                                          _____

                                        Customer   Date

C-36 *Request for substitutions.*

Certificate of Subcontractor Completion Acceptance

Contractor: _____

Subcontractor: _____

Job name: _____

Job location: _____

Job description: _____

_____

_____

Date of completion: _____

Date of final inspection by contractor: _____

Date of code compliance inspection & approval: _____

Defects found in material or workmanship: _____

_____

_____

Acknowledgment

Contractor acknowledges the completion of all contracted work and accepts all workmanship and materials as being satisfactory. Upon signing this certificate, the Contractor releases the Subcontractor from any responsibility for additional work, except warranty work. Warranty work will be performed for a period of one year from the date of completion. Warranty work will include the repair of any material or workmanship defects occurring between now and the end of the warranty period. All existing workmanship and materials are acceptable to the Contractor and payment will be made, in full, according to the payment schedule in the contract, between the two parties.

_____   _____
Contractor   Date   Subcontractor   Date

C-37 *Subcontractor completion acceptance.*

ABC Remodeling Contractors, Inc.
P. O. Box 555
Wilson, Maine 55555
107-555-5555

I understand that as an Independent Contractor, I am solely responsible for my health, actions, taxes, insurance, transportation and any other responsibilities that may be involved with the work I will be doing as an Independent Contractor.

I will not hold anyone else responsible for any claims or liabilities that may arise from this work or from any cause related to this work. I waive any rights I have or may have to hold anyone liable for any reason as a result of this work.

Independent Contractor _____

Date _____

Witness _____

Date _____

C-38 *Independent contractor agreement.*

Code Violation Notification

Contractor: _____

Contractor's address: _____

City/state/zip: _____

Phone number: _____

Job location: _____

Date: _____

Type of work: _____

Subcontractor: _____

Address: _____

Official Notification of Code Violations

On March _____, 19____, I was notified by the local code enforcement officer of code violations in the work performed by your company. The violations must be corrected within two business days, as per our contract dated March _____, 19____. Please contact the codes officer for a detailed explanation of the violations and required corrections. If the violations are not corrected within the allotted time, you may be penalized, as per our contract, for your actions in delaying the completion of this project. Thank you for your prompt attention to this matter.

_____

General Contractor   Date

C-39 *Code violation notification.*

Form Letter for Soliciting Bids from Subcontractors

Dear Sir:

I am soliciting bids for the work listed below, and I would like to offer you the opportunity to participate in the bidding. If you are interested in giving quoted prices for the <u>Labor/Material</u> for this job, please let me hear from you at the above address. The job will be started _____. Financing has been arranged and the job will be started on schedule. Your quote, if you choose to enter one, must be received no later than

_____.

The proposed work is as follows:

_____

_____

_____

_____

Thank you for your time and consideration in this request.

Sincerely,

Your name and title

C-40 *Bid letter.*

Form Letter for Soliciting Material Quotes

Dear Sir:

I am soliciting bids for the work listed below, and I would like to offer you the opportunity to participate in the bidding. If you are interested in giving quoted prices on <u>material</u> for this job, please let me hear from you, at the above address.

The job will be started in <u>four weeks</u>. Financing has been arranged and the job will be started on schedule. Your quote, if you choose to enter one, must be received no later than _____.

The proposed work is as follows:

_____

_____

_____

Plans and specifications for the work are available upon request.

Thank you for your time and consideration in this request.

Sincerely,

Your name and title

C-41 *Material quote solicitation.*

Long-Form Lien Waiver

Customer name: _____

Customer address: _____

Customer city/state/zip: _____

Customer phone number: _____

Job location: _____

Date: _____

Type of work: _____

The vendor acknowledges receipt of all payments stated below. These payments are in compliance with the written contract between the vendor and the customer. The vendor hereby states that payment for all work done to this date has been paid in full.

The vendor releases and relinquishes any and all rights available to said vendor to place a mechanic or materialman lien against the subject property for the described work. Both parties agree that all work performed to date has been paid for, in full and in compliance with their written contract.

The undersigned vendor releases the customer and the customer's property from any liability for non-payment of material or services extended through this date. The undersigned contractor has read this entire agreement and understands the agreement.

Vendor	*Services*	*Date paid*	*Amount paid*
Plumber	(Rough-in)		
Plumber	(Final)		
Electrician	(Rough-in)		
Electrician	(Final)		
Supplier	(Framing lumber)		

NOTE: This list should include all contractors and suppliers. All vendors are listed on the same lien waiver, and sign above their trade name for each service rendered, at the time of payment.

C-42 *Long-form lien waiver.*

Short-Form Lien Waiver

Customer name: _____

Customer address: _____

Customer city/state/zip: _____

Customer phone number: _____

Job location: _____

Date: _____

Type of work: _____

Contractor: _____

Contractor address: _____

Subcontractor: _____

Subcontractor address: _____

Description of work completed to date: _____

_____

Payments received to date: _____

Payment received on this date: _____

Total amount paid, including this payment: _____

The contractor/subcontractor signing below acknowledges receipt of all payments stated above. These payments are in compliance with the written contract between the parties above. The contractor/subcontractor signing below hereby states payment for all work done to this date has been paid in full.

The contractor/subcontractor signing below releases and relinquishes any and all rights available to place a mechanic or materialman lien against the subject property for the above described work. All parties agree that all work performed to date has been paid for in full and in compliance with their written contract.

The undersigned contractor/subcontractor releases the general contractor/customer from any liability for non-payment of material or services extended through this date. The undersigned contractor/subcontractor has read this entire agreement and understands the agreement.

_____
Contractor/Subcontractor   Date

C-43 *Short-form lien waiver.*

D

Measurements

Multipliers That are Useful to the Trade

To change	To	Multiply by
Inches	Feet	0.0833
Inches	Millimeters	25.4
Feet	Inches	12
Feet	Yards	0.3333
Yards	Feet	3
Square inches	Square feet	0.00694
Square feet	Square inches	144
Square feet	Square yards	0.11111
Square yards	Square feet	9
Cubic inches	Cubic feet	0.00058
Cubic feet	Cubic inches	1728
Cubic feet	Cubic yards	0.03703
Cubic yards	Cubic feet	27
Cubic inches	Gallons	0.00433
Cubic feet	Gallons	7.48
Gallons	Cubic inches	231
Gallons	Cubic feet	0.1337
Gallons	Pounds of water	8.33
Pounds of water	Gallons	0.12004
Ounces	Pounds	0.0625
Pounds	Ounces	16

D-1 *Trade multipliers.*

To change	To	Multiply by
Inches of water	Pounds per square inch	0.0361
Inches of water	Inches of mercury	0.0735
Inches of water	Ounces per square inch	0.578
Inches of water	Pounds per square foot	5.2
Inches of mercury	Inches of water	13.6
Inches of mercury	Feet of water	1.1333
Inches of mercury	Feet of water	0.4914
Ounces per square inch	Pounds per square inch	0.127
Ounces per square inch	Inches of mercury	1.733
Pounds per square inch	Inches of water	27.72
Pounds per square inch	Feet of water	2.310
Pounds per square inch	Inches of mercury	2.04
Pounds per square inch	Atmospheres	0.0681
Feet of water	Pounds per square inch	0.434
Feet of water	Pounds per square foot	62.5
Feet of water	Inches of mercury	0.8824
Atmospheres	Pounds per square inch	14.696
Atmospheres	Inches of mercury	29.92
Atmospheres	Feet of water	34
Long tons	Pounds	2240
Short tons	Pounds	2000
Short tons	Long tons	0.89285

D-1 *Continued.*

Metric Symbols

Quantity	Unit	Symbol
Length	Millimetre	mm
	Centimetre	cm
	Metre	m
	Kilometre	km
Area	Square millimetre	mm^2
	Square centimetre	cm^2
	Square decimetre	dm^2
	Square metre	m^2
	Square kilometre	km^2
Volume	Cubic centimetre	cm^3
	Cubic decimetre	dm^3
	Cubic metre	m^3
Mass	Milligram	mg
	Gram	g
	Kilogram	kg
	Tonne	t
Temperature	Degree Celsius	°C
	Kelvin	K
Time	Second	s
Plane angle	Radius	rad
Force	Newton	N

D-2 *Metric symbols.*

Quantity	Unit	Symbol
Energy, work, quantity of heat	Joule	J
	Kilojoule	kJ
	Megajoule	MJ
Power, heat flow rate	Watt	W
	Kilowatt	kW
Pressure	Pascal	Pa
	Kilopascal	kPa
	Megapascal	MPa
Velocity, speed	Metre per second	m/s
	Kilometre per hour	km/h
Revolutional frequency	Revolution per minute	r/min

D-2 *Continued.*

Decimal Equivalents of Fractions

Inches	Decimals of an inch	Inches	Decimals of an inch
1/64	0.0156	11/64	0.1718
1/32	0.0312	3/16	0.1875
3/64	0.0468	13/64	0.2031
1/16	0.0625	7/32	0.2187
5/64	0.0781	15/64	0.2343
3/32	0.0937	1/4	0.2500
7/64	0.1093	17/64	0.2656
1/8	0.1250	9/32	0.2812
9/64	0.1406	19/64	0.2968
5/32	0.1562	5/16	0.3125

D-3 *Decimal equivalents of fractions.*

Inches Converted to Decimals of Feet

Inches	*Decimal of a foot*	*Inches*	*Decimal of a foot*
⅛	0.01042	1⅝	0.13542
¼	0.02083	1¾	0.14583
⅜	0.03125	1⅞	0.15625
½	0.04167	2	0.16666
⅝	0.05208	2⅛	0.17708
¾	0.06250	2¼	0.18750
⅞	0.07291	2⅜	0.19792
1	0.08333	2½	0.20833
1⅛	0.09375	2⅝	0.21875
1¼	0.10417	2¾	0.22917
1⅜	0.11458	2⅞	0.23959
1½	0.12500	3	0.25000

NOTE: To change inches to decimals of a foot, divide by 12. To change decimals of a foot to inches, multiply by 12.

D-4 *Inches converted to decimals of feet.*

Decimal Equivalents of Fractions of an Inch

Inches	Decimal of an inch	Inches	Decimal of an inch
1/64	0.015625	11/64	0.171875
1/32	0.03125	3/16	0.1875
3/64	0.046875	13/64	0.203125
1/16	0.0625	7/32	0.21875
5/64	0.078125	15/64	0.234375
3/32	0.09375	1/4	0.25
7/64	0.109375	17/64	0.265625
1/8	0.125	9/32	0.28125
9/64	0.140625	19/64	0.296875
5/32	0.15625	5/16	0.3125

NOTE: To find the decimal equivalent of a fraction, divide the numerator by the denominator.

D-5 *Decimal equivalents of fractions of an inch.*

Board Lumber Measure

Nominal size	Actual size	Board feet per linear foot	Linear feet per 1000 board feet
1 × 2	¾ × 1½	⅙ (0.167)	6000
1 × 3	¾ × 2½	¼ (0.250)	4000
1 × 4	¾ × 3½	⅓ (0.333)	3000
1 × 6	¾ × 5½	½ (0.500)	2000
1 × 8	¾ × 7¼	⅔ (0.666)	1500
1 × 10	¾ × 9¼	⅚ (0.833)	1200
1 × 12	¾ × 11¼	1 (1.0)	1000

D-6 *Board lumber conversions.*

Dimensional Lumber Board Measure

Nominal size	Actual size	Board feet per linear foot	Linear feet per 1000 board feet
2 × 2	1½ × 1½	⅓ (0.333)	3000
2 × 3	1½ × 2½	½ (0.500)	2000
2 × 4	1½ × 3½	⅔ (0.666)	1500
2 × 6	1½ × 5½	1 (1.0)	1000
2 × 8	1½ × 7¼	1⅓ (1.333)	750
2 × 10	1½ × 9¼	1⅔ (1.666)	600
2 × 12	1½ × 11¼	2 (2.0)	500

D-7 *Board measures.*

Approximate Weights of Building Materials

Material	Lbs./sq. ft.
Roof with wood or asphalt shingles	10
Roof with ³⁄₁₆ slate	15
Roof with tar and gravel	15
Concrete wall—8"	100
Concrete wall—10"	125
Concrete wall—12"	150
Concrete block wall—8"	55
Brick wall—4"	35
Brick wall—8"	75
Exterior wood frame wall (4" studs)	10
Interior partitions (per sq. ft. of floor area)	20

D-8 *Weights of building materials.*

Residential Live Loads

Area/activity	Live load, psf
First floor	40
Second floor and habitable attics	30
Balconies, fire escapes, and stairs	100
Garages	50

D-9 *Residential live loads.*

Design Loads

Usage	Live load (lbs./sq. ft.)
Bedrooms	30
Other rooms (residential)	40
Ceiling joists (no attic use)	5
Ceiling joists (light storage)	20
Ceiling joists (attic rooms)	30
Retail stores	75–100
Warehouses	125–250
School classrooms	40
Offices	80
Libraries	
Reading rooms	60
Book stacks	150
Auditoriums, gyms	100
Theater stage	150
Most corridors, lobbies, stairs, exits, fire escapes, etc. in public buildings	100

D-10 *Design loads.*

Screw Lengths and Available Gauge Numbers

Length	Gauge numbers	Length	Gauge numbers
¼"	0 to 3	1¾"	8 to 20
⅜"	2 to 7	2"	8 to 20
½"	2 to 8	2¼"	9 to 20
⅝"	3 to 10	2½"	12 to 20
¾"	4 to 11	2¾"	14 to 20
⅞"	6 to 12	3"	16 to 20
1"	6 to 14	3½"	18 to 20
1¼"	7 to 16	4"	18 to 20
1½"	6 to 18		

D-11 *Screw lengths.*

Nail Sizes and Number Per Pound

Penny size "d"	Length	Approximate number per pound, Common	Approximate number per pound, Box	Approximate number per pound, Finish
2	1"	875	1000	1300
3	1¼"	575	650	850
4	1½"	315	450	600
5	1¾"	265	400	500
6	2"	190	225	300
7	2¼"	160		
8	2½"	105	140	200
9	2¾"	90		
10	3"	70	90	120
12	3¼"	60	85	110
16	3½"	50	70	90
20	4"	30	50	60
30	4½"	25		
40	5"	20		
50	5½"	15		
60	6"	10		

NOTE: Aluminum and c.c. nails are slightly smaller than other nails of the same penny size.

D-12 *Nail sizes.*

Converting Inches to Decimals of a Foot

Inches	Decimals of a foot	Inches	Decimals of a foot
1"	0.083	7"	0.583
2"	0.167	8"	0.667
3"	0.250	9"	0.750
4"	0.333	10"	0.833
5"	0.417	11"	0.917
6"	0.500	12"	1.0

D-13 *Conversion for inches to decimals of a foot.*

Decimals to Millimeters

Decimal equivalent	Millimeters	Decimal equivalent	Millimeters
0.0625	1.59	0.5625	14.29
0.1250	3.18	0.6250	15.87
0.1875	4.76	0.6875	17.46
0.2500	6.35	0.7500	19.05
0.3125	7.94	0.8125	20.64
0.3750	9.52	0.8750	22.22
0.4375	11.11	0.9375	23.81
0.5000	12.70	1.000	25.40

D-14 *Decimals to millimeters.*

Conversion Table

0.001 in.	0.025 mm	1 mi.^{2}	2.590 km^2
1 in.	25.400 mm	1 in.^{3}	16.387 cm^3
1 ft.	30.48 cm	1 ft.^{3}	0.0283 m^3
1 ft.	0.3048 m	1 yd.^{3}	0.7647 m^3
1 yd.	0.9144 m	1 U.S. oz.	29.57 ml
1 mi.	1.609 km	1 U.S. pint	0.4732 l
1 in.^{2}	6.4516 cm^2	1 U.S. gal.	3.785 l
1 ft.^{2}	0.0929 m^2	1 oz	28.35 g
1 yd.^{2}	0.8361 m^2	1 lb.	0.4536 kg
1 acre	0.4047 ha		

D-15 *Conversion table.*

Measurement Conversions

Imperial to Metric

Length	1 inch	25.4 mm
	1 foot	0.3048 m
	1 yard	0.9144 m
	1 mile	1.609 km
Mass	1 pound	0.454 kg
	1 U.S. short ton	0.9072 tonne
Area	1 ft^2	0.092 m^2
	1 yd^2	0.836 m^2
	1 acre	0.404 hectare (ha)
Capacity	1 ft^3	0.028 m^3
Or	1 yd^3	0.764 m^3
Volume	1 liquid quart	0.946 litre (l)
	1 gallon	3.785 litre (l)
Heat	1 Btu	1055 joule (J)
	1 Btu/hr	0.293 watt (W)

D-16 *Measurement conversions.*

Inches to Millimetres

Inches	Millimetres	Inches	Millimetres
1	25.4	11	279.4
2	50.8	12	304.8
3	76.2	13	330.2
4	101.6	14	355.6
5	127.0	15	381.0
6	152.4	16	406.4
7	177.8	17	431.8
8	203.2	18	457.2
9	228.6	19	482.6
10	254.0	20	508.0

D-17 *Converting inches to millimeters.*

Fractions to Decimals

Fractions	Decimal equivalent	Fractions	Decimal equivalent
$\frac{1}{16}$	0.0625	$\frac{9}{16}$	0.5625
$\frac{1}{8}$	0.1250	$\frac{5}{8}$	0.6250
$\frac{3}{16}$	0.1875	$\frac{11}{16}$	0.6875
$\frac{1}{4}$	0.2500	$\frac{3}{4}$	0.7500
$\frac{5}{16}$	0.3125	$\frac{13}{16}$	0.8125
$\frac{3}{8}$	0.3750	$\frac{7}{8}$	0.8750
$\frac{7}{16}$	0.4375	$\frac{15}{16}$	0.9375
$\frac{1}{2}$	0.5000	1	1.000

D-18 *Converting fractions to decimals.*

Square Inches to Approximate Square Centimeters

Square inches	Square centimeters	Square inches	Square centimeters
1	6.5	8	52.0
2	13.0	9	58.5
3	19.5	10	65.0
4	26.0	25	162.5
5	32.5	50	325.0
6	39.0	100	650.0
7	45.5		

D-19A *Converting square inches to square centimeters.*

Square Feet to Approximate Square Meters

Square feet	Square meters	Square feet	Square meters
1	0.925	8	0.7400
2	0.1850	9	0.8325
3	0.2775	10	0.9250
4	0.3700	25	2.315
5	0.4650	50	4.65
6	0.5550	100	9.25
7	0.6475		

D-19B *Converting square feet to square meters.*

Measurement Conversion Factors

	To	Multiply by
Inches	Feet	0.0833
Inches	Millimeters	25.4
Feet	Inches	12
Feet	Yards	0.3333
Yards	Feet	3
Square inches	Square feet	0.00694
Square feet	Square inches	144
Square feet	Square yards	0.11111
Square yards	Square feet	9
Cubic inches	Cubic feet	0.00058
Cubic feet	Cubic inches	1728
Cubic feet	Cubic yards	0.03703
Gallons	Cubic inches	231
Gallons	Cubic feet	0.1337
Gallons	Pounds of water	8.33
Pounds of water	Gallons	0.12004
Ounces	Pounds	0.0625
Pounds	Ounces	16
Inches of water	Pounds per square inch	0.0361
Inches of water	Inches of mercury	0.0735
Inches of water	Ounces per square inch	0.578
Inches of water	Pounds per square foot	5.2

D-20 *Helpful conversion factors.*

	To	Multiply by
Inches of mercury	Inches of water	13.6
Inches of mercury	Feet of water	1.1333
Inches of mercury	Pounds per square inch	0.4914
Ounces per square inch	Inches of mercury	0.127
Ounces per square inch	Inches of water	1.733
Pounds per square inch	Inches of water	27.72
Pounds per square inch	Feet of water	2.310
Pounds per square inch	Inches of mercury	2.04
Pounds per square inch	Atmospheres	0.0681
Feet of water	Pounds per square inch	0.434
Feet of water	Pounds per square foot	62.5
Feet of water	Inches of mercury	0.8824
Atmospheres	Pounds per square inch	14.696
Atmospheres	Inches of mercury	29.92
Atmospheres	Feet of water	34
Long tons	Pounds	2240
Short tons	Pounds	2000
Short tons	Long tons	0.89295

D-20 *Continued.*

Decimal Equivalents of Fractions

Fraction	Decimal	Fraction	Decimal
1/64	0.015625	13/64	0.203125
1/32	0.03125	7/32	0.21875
3/64	0.046875	15/64	0.234375
1/20	0.05	1/4	0.25
1/16	0.0625	17/64	0.265625
1/13	0.0769	9/32	0.28125
5/64	0.078125	19/64	0.296875
1/12	0.0833	5/16	0.3125
1/11	0.0909	21/64	0.328125
3/32	0.09375	1/3	0.333
1/10	0.10	11/32	0.34375
7/64	0.109375	23/64	0.359375
1/9	0.111	3/8	0.375
1/8	0.125	25/64	0.390625
9/64	0.140625	13/32	0.40625
1/7	0.1429	27/64	0.421875
5/32	0.15625	7/16	0.4375
1/6	0.1667	29/64	0.453125
11/64	0.171875	15/32	0.46875
3/16	0.1875	31/64	0.484375
1/5	0.2	1/2	0.5

D-21 *Decimal equivalents of fractions.*

Fraction	Decimal	Fraction	Decimal
$^{33}\!/_{64}$	0.515625	$^{5}\!/_{8}$	0.625
$^{17}\!/_{32}$	0.53125	$^{41}\!/_{64}$	0.640625
$^{35}\!/_{64}$	0.546875	$^{21}\!/_{32}$	0.65625
$^{9}\!/_{16}$	0.5625	$^{43}\!/_{64}$	0.671875
$^{37}\!/_{64}$	0.578125	$^{11}\!/_{16}$	0.6875
$^{19}\!/_{32}$	0.59375	$^{45}\!/_{64}$	0.703125
$^{39}\!/_{64}$	0.609375		

D-21 *Continued.*

Circumference of Circle

Diameter (inches)	Circumference	Diameter (inches)	Circumference
⅛	0.3927	3¾	11.78
¼	0.7854	4	12.56
⅜	1.178	4½	14.13
½	1.570	5	15.70
⅝	1.963	5½	17.27
¾	2.356	6	18.84
⅞	2.748	6½	20.42
1	3.141	7	21.99
1⅛	3.534	7½	23.56
1¼	3.927	8	25.13
1⅜	4.319	8½	26.70
1½	4.712	9	28.27
1⅝	5.105	9½	29.84
1¾	5.497	10	31.41
1⅞	5.890	10½	32.98
2	6.283	11	34.55
2¼	7.068	11½	36.12
2½	7.854	12	37.69
2¾	8.639	12½	39.27
3	9.424	13	40.84
3¼	10.21	13½	42.41
3½	10.99	14	43.98

D-22 *Circumference of a circle.*

Diameter (inches)	Circumference	Diameter (inches)	Circumference
14½	45.55	24	75.39
15	47.12	24½	76.96
15½	48.69	25	78.54
16	50.26	26	81.68
16½	51.83	27	84.82
17	53.40	28	87.96
17½	54.97	29	91.10
18	56.54	30	94.24
18½	58.11	31	97.38
19	59.69	32	100.5
19½	61.26	33	103.6
20	62.83	34	106.8
20½	64.40	35	109.9
21	65.97	36	113.0
21½	67.54	37	116.2
22	69.11	38	119.3
22½	70.68	39	122.5
23	72.25	40	125.6
23½	73.82		

D-22 *Continued.*

Surface Measure

144 sq. in.	1 sq. ft.	160 sq. rd.	1 acre
9 sq. ft.	1 sq. yd.	640 acres	1 sq. mile
30½ sq. yd.	1 sq. rd.	43,560 sq. ft.	1 acre

D-23 *Surface measure.*

Area of Circle

Diameter	Area	Diameter	Area
⅛	0.0123	3¾	11.044
¼	0.0491	4	12.566
⅜	0.1104	4½	15.904
½	0.1963	5	19.635
⅝	0.3068	5½	23.758
¾	0.4418	6	28.274
⅞	0.6013	6½	33.183
1	0.7854	7	38.484
1⅛	0.9940	7½	44.178
1¼	1.227	8	50.265
1⅜	1.484	8½	56.745
1½	1.767	9	63.617
1⅝	2.073	9½	70.882
1¾	2.405	10	78.54
1⅞	2.761	10½	86.59
2	3.141	11	95.03
2¼	3.976	11½	103.86
2½	4.908	12	113.09
2¾	5.939	12½	122.71
3	7.068	13	132.73
3¼	8.295	13½	143.13
3½	9.621	14	153.93

D-24 *Area of a circle.*

Diameter	Area	Diameter	Area
14½	165.13	24	452.39
15	176.71	24½	471.43
15½	188.69	25	490.87
16	201.06	26	530.93
16½	213.82	27	572.55
17	226.98	28	615.75
17½	240.52	29	660.52
18	254.46	30	706.86
18½	268.80	31	754.76
19	283.52	32	804.24
19½	298.6	33	855.30
20	314.16	34	907.92
20½	330.06	35	962.11
21	346.36	36	1017.8
21½	363.05	37	1075.2
22	380.13	38	1134.1
22½	397.60	39	1194.5
23	415.47	40	1256.6
23½	433.73		

D-24 *Continued.*

Conversion Factors in Converting from Customary (U.S.) Units to Metric Units

To find	Multiply	By
Microns	Mils	25.4
Centimeters	Inches	2.54
Meters	Feet	0.3048
Meters	Yards	0.19144
Kilometers	Miles	1.609344
Grams	Ounces	28.349523
Kilograms	Pounds	0.4539237
Liters	Gallons (U.S.)	3.7854118
Liters	Gallons (imperial)	4.546090
Milliliters (cc)	Fluid ounces	29.573530
Milliliters (cc)	Cubic inches	16.387064
Square centimeters	Square inches	6.4516
Square meters	Square feet	0.09290304
Square meters	Square yards	0.83612736
Cubic meters	Cubic feet	2.8316847×10^{-2}
Cubic meters	Cubic yards	0.76455486
Joules	BTU	1054.3504
Joules	Foot-pounds	1.35582
Kilowatts	BTU per minute	0.01757251
Kilowatts	Foot-pounds per minute	2.2597×10^{-5}
Kilowatts	Horsepower	0.7457
Radians	Degrees	0.017453293
Watts	BTU per minute	17.5725

D-25 *Converting customary units to metric units.*

Inch and Metric Scales

Scales used for detail drawings		
Inch scale		*Metric scale*
1"	is full size	1:1
3"	is closest to	1:5
1½"	is closest to	1:10*
¾"	is used for	1:10*
½"	is closest to	1:20
Scales used for building plans		
Inch scale		*Metric scale*
¼"	is closest to	1:50
⅛"	is closest to	1:100
Scale used for site plans		
Inch scale		*Metric scale*
⅟₁₆"	is closest to	1:200

*The 1:10 is used for both ¾" and the 1½" scales.

D-26 *Inch and metric scales.*

Cubic Measure

1728 cu. in.	1 cu. ft.
27 cu. in.	1 cu. yd.
128 cu. ft.	1 cord

D-27 *Cubic measures.*

Metric-Customary Equivalents

1 meter	39.3 inches 3.28083 feet 1.0936 yards
1 centimeter	0.3937 inch
1 millimeter	0.03937 inch, or nearly ⅕₅ inch
1 kilometer	0.62137 mile
1 foot	0.3048 meter
1 inch	2.54 centimeters 25.40 millimeters
Measures of surface	
1 square meter	10.764 square feet 1.196 square yards
1 square centimeter	0.155 square inch
1 square millimeter	0.00155 square inch
1 square yard	0.836 square meter
1 square foot	0.0929 square meter
1 square inch	6.452 square centimeter 645.2 square millimeter
Measures of volume and capacity	
1 cubic meter	35.314 cubic feet 1.308 cubic yards 264.2 U.S. gallons (231 cubic inches)
1 cubic decimeter	61.0230 cubic inches 0.0353 cubic feet
1 cubic centimeter	0.061 cubic inch
1 liter	1 cubic decimeter 61.0230 cubic inches

D-28 *Measurement conversions.*

	0.0353 cubic foot 1.0567 quarts (U.S.) 0.2642 gallon (U.S.) 2.2020 lb. of water at 62°F
1 cubic yard	0.7645 cubic meter
1 cubic foot	0.02832 cubic meter 28.317 cubic decimeters 28.317 liters
1 cubic inch	16.383 cubic centimeters
1 gallon (British)	4.543 liters
1 gallon (U.S.)	3.785 liters
Measures of weight	
1 gram	15.432 grains
1 kilogram	2.2046 pounds
1 metric ton	0.9842 ton or 2240 pounds 19.68 cwts. 2204.6 pounds
1 grain	0.0648 gram
1 ounce avoirdupois	28.35 grams
1 pound	0.4536 kilograms
1 ton or 2240 lb.	1.1016 metric tons 1016 kilograms

D-28 *Continued.*

Formulas
Circle
Circumference = diameter × 3.1416
Circumference = radius × 6.2832
Diameter = radius × 2
Diameter = square root of; (area ÷ 0.7854)
Diameter = square root of area × 1.1283
Diameter = circumference × 0.31831
Radius = diameter ÷ 2
Radius = circumference × 0.15915
Radius = square root of area × 0.56419
Area = diameter × diameter × 0.7854
Area = half of the circumference × half of the diameter
Area = square of the circumference × 0.0796
Arc length = degrees × radius × 0.01745
Degrees of arc = length ÷ (radius × 0.01745)
Radius of arc = length ÷ (degrees × 0.01745)
Side of equal square = diameter × 0.8862
Side of inscribed square = diameter × 0.7071
Area of sector = area of circle × degrees of arc ÷ 360
Cone
Area of surface = one half of circumference of base × slant height + area of base.
Volume = diameter × diameter × 0.7854 × one-third of the altitude.

D-29 *Formula functions.*

Cube
Volume = width × height × length
Cylinder
Area of surface = diameter × 3.1416 × length + area of the two bases
Area of base = diameter × diameter × 0.7854
Area of base = volume ÷ length
Length = volume ÷ area of base
Volume = length × area of base
Capacity in gallons = volume in inches ÷ 231
Capacity of gallons = diameter × diameter × length × 0.0034
Capacity in gallons = volume in feet × 7.48
Ellipse
Area = short diameter × long diameter × 0.7854
Hexagon
Area = width of side × 2.598 × width of side
Parallelogram
Area = base × distance between the two parallel sides
Pyramid
Area = ½ perimeter of base × slant height + area of base
Volume = area of base × ⅓ of the altitude
Rectangle
Area = length × width
Rectangular prism
Volume = width × height × length

D-29 *Continued.*

Sphere
Area of surface = diameter × diameter × 3.1416
Side of inscribed cube = radius × 1.547
Volume = diameter × diameter × diameter × 0.5236
Square
Area = length × width
Triangle
Area = one-half of height times base
Trapezoid
Area = one-half of the sum of the parallel sides × the height

D-29 *Continued.*

Weights & Measures

Linear measure

12 inches = 1 foot

3 feet = 1 yard

5½ yards = 1 rod

320 rods = 1 mile

1 mile = 1760 yards

1 mile = 5280 feet

Square measure

144 sq. inches = 1 sq. foot

9 sq. feet = 1 sq. yard

1 sq. yard = 1296 sq. inches

4840 sq. yards = 1 acre

640 acres = 1 sq. mile

Cubic measure

1728 cubic inches = 1 cubic foot

27 cubic feet = 1 cubic yard

Avoirdupois weight

16 ounces = 1 pound

100 pounds = 1 hundredweight

20 hundredweight = 1 ton

1 ton = 2000 pounds

1 long ton = 2240 pounds

D-30 *Weights and measures.*

Liquid measure
4 gills = 1 pint
2 pints = 1 quart
4 quarts = 1 gallon
31½ gallons = 1 barrel
1 gallon = 231 cubic inches
7.48 gallons = 1 cubic foot
1 gallon water = 8.33 pounds
1 gallon gasoline = 5.84 pounds

D-30 *Continued.*

Weights of Building Materials

Framing and Floor

Component	Material	Load, psf
Framing (16" oc)	2 × 4 and 2 × 6	2
	2 × 8 and 2 × 10	3
Floor-ceiling	Softwood, per inch	3
	Hardwood, per inch	4
	Plywood, per inch	3
	Concrete, per inch	12
	Stone, per inch	13
	Carpet	0.5
	Drywall, per inch	5

D-31 *Weights of various building materials.*

Estimating Cubic Yards of Concrete for Slabs, Walks and Drives

Slab thickness Inches	Slab area Square feet				
	10	50	100	300	500
2	0.1	0.3	0.6	1.9	3.1
3	0.1	0.5	0.9	2.8	4.7
4	0.1	0.6	1.2	3.7	6.2
5	0.2	0.7	1.5	4.7	7.2
6	0.2	0.9	1.9	5.6	9.3

D-32 *Estimating concrete needs.*

Grades for Traffic Surface

Surface	Minimum	Maximum
Driveways in the north	1%	10%
Driveways in the south	1%	15%
Walks	1%	4%
Ramps		15%
Wheelchair ramps		8%
Patios	1%	2%

D-33 *Recommended elevation grades.*

Wheelchair Ramps

Maximum slope	1 in 12
Minimum clear width	3'0"
Minimum curb height	2"
Railing	2'8"
Maximum length	30'0"
Minimum width of passage	2'8"
Approximate length of chair	3'8"
Seat height	17" to 18"
Maximum comfortable reach	5'4"
Eye level	3'9" to 4'3"

D-34 *Suggestions for wheelchair ramps.*

- *Polyurethane:*
  - ~Expensive
  - ~Resists water
  - ~Durable
  - ~Scratches are difficult to hide
- *Varnishes:*
  - ~Less expensive than polyurethane
  - ~Less durable than polyurethane
  - ~Resists water
  - ~Scratches are difficult to hide
- *Penetrating sealers:*
  - ~Provide a low-gloss sheen
  - ~Durable
  - ~Scratches touch up easily

D-35 *Qualities of various wood finishes.*

Reconstituted Wood
Panels with Typical Uses

Particleboard	Wood particles and resin. a. Industrial grade—Cabinets and counter tops under plastic laminates. b. Underlayment—Installed over subfloor under tile or carpet.
Wafer board	Wood wafers and resin. Inexpensive sheathing, craft projects, etc.
Oriented Strand Board (OSB)	Thin wood strands oriented at right angles with phenolic resin. Same uses as above.
Hardboard	Wood fiber mat compressed into stiff, hard sheets. a. Service—Light weight—Cabinet backs, etc. b. Standard—Stronger with better finish quality. c. Tempered—Stiffer and harder for exterior use.
Fiberboard (Grayboard)	Molded wood fibers—Underlayment, sound deadening panels.
Composite plywood	A core of particleboard with face and back veneers glued directly to it.

D-36 *Typical uses of wood panels.*

Types of Plywood with Typical Uses

Softwood veneer	Cross laminated plies or veneers— Sheathing, general construction and industrial use, etc.
Hardwood veneer	Cross laminated plies with hardwood face and back veneer— Furniture and cabinet work, etc.
Lumbercore plywood	Two face veneers and 2 crossband plies with an inner core of lumber strips—Desk and table tops, etc.
Medium-density overlay (MDO)	Exterior plywood with resin and fiber veneer—Signs, soffits, etc.
High-density overlay (HDO)	Tougher than MDO—Concrete forms, workbench tops, etc.
Plywood siding	T-111 and other textures used as one step sheathing and siding where codes allow.

D-37 *Typical uses of plywood.*

Potential Life Spans for Gutters

Material	Expected life span	Material	Expected life span
Aluminum	15 to 20 years	Copper	50 years
Vinyl	Indefinite	Wood	10 to 15 years
Steel	Less than 10 years		

All estimated life spans depend on installation procedure, maintenance, and climatic conditions.

D-38 *Potential life spans of gutters.*

Price Ranges for Gutters

Material	Price range	Material	Price range
Aluminum	Moderate	Copper	Very expensive
Vinyl	Expensive	Wood	Moderate to expensive
Steel	Inexpensive		

All estimated life spans depend on installation procedure, maintenance, and climatic conditions.

D-39 *Price ranges of gutters.*

E

Zone regulations

States in Zone One

Washington	Iowa
Oregon	Nebraska
California	Kansas
Nevada	Utah
Idaho	Arizona
Montana	Colorado
Wyoming	New Mexico
North Dakota	Indiana
South Dakota	Parts of Texas
Minnesota	

E-1 *List of states normally governed by the plumbing code in zone one tables.*

Zone One's Fixture-Unit Requirements on Trap Sizes

1¼" trap	One fixture-unit
1½" trap	Three fixture-units
2" trap	Four fixture-units
3" trap	Six fixture-units
4" trap	Eight fixture-units

E-2 *Zone one fixture-unit requirements on trap sizes.*

Trap-to-Vent Distances in Zone One

Grade on drain pipe	Size of trap arm	Maximum distance between trap and vent
¼"	1¼"	2'6"
¼"	1½"	3'6"
¼"	2"	5'
¼"	3"	6'
¼"	4" and larger	10'

E-3 *Zone one trap-to-vent distances.*

Recommended Trap Sizes for Zone One

Type of fixture	Trap size
Bathtub	1½"
Shower	2"
Residential toilet	Integral
Lavatory	1¼"
Bidet	1½"
Laundry tub	1½"
Washing-machine standpipe	2"
Floor drain	2"
Kitchen sink	1½"
Dishwasher	1½"
Drinking fountain	1¼"
Public toilet	Integral

E-4 *Zone one recommended trap sizes.*

Approved Materials for Storm-Water Drainage in Zone One

Materials approved for use inside buildings, above ground	
Galvanized materials	Cast-iron materials
Wrought-iron materials	ABS materials*
Brass materials	PVC materials*
Copper materials	Lead materials

*Note—ABS and PVC may not be used in buildings that have more than three floors above grade.

E-5 *Zone one approved materials for interior, above-grade storm-water drainage.*

Approved Materials for Storm-Water Drainage in Zone One

Materials approved for use inside buildings, below ground	
Service-weight cast-iron materials	PVC materials
DWV copper materials	Extra-strength vitrified-clay materials
ABS materials	

E-6 *Zone one approved materials for interior, below-grade storm-water drainage.*

Approved Materials for Storm-Water Drainage in Zone One

Materials approved for use on the exterior of buildings
Sheet metal with a minimum gauge of 26

E-7 *Zone one approved materials for exterior storm-water drainage.*

Materials Approved for Underground Vents in Zone One

Cast-iron materials	PVC materials*	Brass materials
ABS materials*	Copper materials	Lead materials

*Note—these materials may not be used with buildings having more than three floors above grade.

E-8 *Zone one approved underground vent materials.*

Materials Approved for Above-Ground Vents in Zone One

Cast-iron materials	Copper materials	Lead materials
ABS materials*	Galvanized materials	Brass Materials
PVC materials*		

*Note—these materials may not be used with buildings having more than three floors above grade.

E-9 *Zone one approved above-ground vent materials.*

Zone One's Minimum Drainage-Pipe Pitch

Pipes under 4" in diameter	¼" to the foot
Pipes 4" or larger in diameter	⅛" to the foot

E-10 *Minimum pipe pitch in zone one.*

Vertical Pipe-Support Intervals in Zone One

Type of drainage pipe	Maximum distance of supports
Lead pipe	4'
Cast iron	At each story
Galvanized	At least every other story
Copper	At each story*
PVC	Not mentioned
ABS	Not mentioned

*Note—support intervals may not exceed 10 feet.
Note—all stacks must be supported at their bases.

E-11 *Zone one vertical pipe supports.*

Horizontal Pipe-Support Intervals in Zone One

Type of drainage pipe	Maximum distance of supports
ABS	4'
Cast iron	At each pipe joint*
Galvanized (1" and larger)	12'
Galvanized (¾" and smaller)	10'
PVC	4'
Copper (2" and larger)	10'
Copper (1½" and smaller)	6'

*Note—Cast-iron pipe must be supported at each joint, but supports may not be more than ten feet apart.

E-12 *Zone one horizontal pipe supports.*

Support Intervals for
Supporting Water Pipe in Zone One

Type of pipe	Vertical support interval	Horizontal support interval
Threaded pipe (¾" and smaller)	Every other story	10'
Threaded pipe (1" and larger)	Every other story	12'
Copper tube (1½" and smaller)	Every story, not to exceed 10'	6'
Copper tube (2" and larger)	Every story, not to exceed 10'	10'
Plastic pipe	Not mentioned	4'

E-13 *Zone one support intervals for water pipes.*

Vertical Pipe-Support Intervals in Zone One

Type of vent pipe	Maximum distance of supports
Lead pipe	4'
Cast iron	At each story
Galvanized	At least every other story
Copper	At each story*
PVC	Not mentioned
ABS	Not mentioned

*Note—support intervals may not exceed 10 feet.
Note—all stacks must be supported at their bases.

E-14 *Zone one vertical pipe supports.*

Horizontal Pipe-Support Intervals in Zone One

Type of vent pipe	Maximum distance of supports
ABS	4'
Cast iron	At each pipe joint*
Galvanized	12'
Copper (1½" and smaller)	6'
PVC	4'
Copper (2" and larger)	10'

*Note—Cast-iron pipe must be supported at each joint, but supports may not be more than 10 feet apart.

E-15 *Zone one horizontal pipe supports.*

Fittings Approved for Vertical to Horizontal Changes in Zone One

Forty-five-degree branches
Sixty-degree branches and offsets, if they are installed in a true vertical position

E-16 *Fittings allowed for vertical to horizontal changes in direction in zone one.*

Fittings Approved for Horizontal Changes in Zone One

Forty-five-degree wye
Combination wye and eighth-bend
Note—other fittings with similar sweeps may also be approved.

E-17 *Fittings approved for horizontal changes in direction in zone one.*

Fittings Approved for Horizontal to Vertical Changes in Zone One

Forty-five-degree wye
Sixty-degree wye
Combination wye and eighth-bend
Sanitary tee
Sanitary tapped-tee branches
Note—cross fittings, like double sanitary tees, cannot be used when they are of a short-sweep pattern. However, double sanitary tees can be used if the barrel of the tee is at least two pipe-sizes larger than the largest inlet.

E-18 *Fittings approved for horizontal to vertical changes in direction in zone one.*

States in Zone Two

Alabama	Mississippi	Parts of Maryland
Arkansas	Georgia	Parts of Delaware
Louisiana	Florida	Parts Of Oklahoma
Tennessee	South Carolina	Parts of West Virginia
North Carolina	Parts of Texas	

E-19 *List of states normally governed by the plumbing code in zone two tables.*

Zone Two's Minimum Drainage-Pipe Pitch

Pipes under 3" in diameter	¼" to the foot
Pipes 3" or larger in diameter	⅛" to the foot

E-20 *Minimum pipe pitch in zone two.*

Zone Two's Fixture-Unit Requirements on Trap Sizes

1¼" trap	One fixture-unit
1½" trap	Two fixture-units
2" trap	Three fixture-units
3" trap	Five fixture-units
4" trap	Six fixture-units

E-21 *Fixture-unit requirements on trap sizes in zone two.*

Recommended Trap Sizes for Zone Two

Type of fixture	Trap size
Bathtub	1½"
Shower	2"
Residential toilet	Integral
Lavatory	1¼"
Bidet	1½"
Laundry tub	1½"
Washing-machine standpipe	2"
Floor drain	2"
Kitchen sink	1½"
Dishwasher	1½"
Drinking fountain	1"
Public toilet	Integral

E-22 *Recommended trap sizes in zone two.*

Trap-to-Vent Distances in Zone Two

Grade on drain pipe	Fixture's drain size	Trap size	Maximum distance between trap and vent
¼"	1¼"	1¼"	3' 6"
¼"	1½"	1¼"	5'
¼"	1½"	1½"	5'
¼"	2"	1½"	8'
¼"	2"	2"	6'
⅛"	3"	3"	10'
⅛"	4"	4"	12'

E-23 *Trap-to-vent distances in zone two.*

Vertical Pipe-Support Intervals in Zone Two

Type of drainage pipe	Maximum distance of supports
Lead pipe	4'
Cast iron	At each story*
Galvanized	At each story**
Copper (1¼" and smaller)	4'
Copper (1½" and larger)	At each story
PVC (1½" and smaller)	4'
PVC (2" and larger)	At each story
ABS (1½" and smaller)	4'
ABS (2" and larger)	At each story

*Note—support intervals may not exceed 15 feet.

**Note—support intervals may not exceed 30 feet.

Note—all stacks must be supported at their bases.

E-24 *Vertical pipe support requirements in zone two.*

Horizontal Pipe-Support Intervals in Zone Two

Type of drainage pipe	Maximum distance of supports
ABS	4'
Cast iron	At each pipe joint
Galvanized (1" and larger)	12'
PVC	4'
Copper (2" and larger)	10'
Copper (1½" and smaller)	6'

E-25 *Horizontal pipe support requirements in zone two.*

Support Intervals for
Supporting Water Pipe in Zone Two

Type of pipe	Vertical support interval	Horizontal support interval
Threaded pipe	30'	12'
Copper tube (1¼" and smaller)	4'	6'
Copper tube (1½")	Every story	6'
Copper tube (larger than 1½")	Every story	10'
Plastic pipe (2" and larger)	Every story	4'
Plastic pipe (1½" and smaller)	4'	4'

E-26 *Support intervals for water pipe in zone two.*

Vertical Pipe-Support Intervals in Zone Two

Type of vent pipe	Maximum distance of supports
Lead pipe	4'
Cast iron	At each story*
Galvanized	At each story**
Copper (1¼")	4'
Copper (1½" and larger)	At each story
PVC (1½" and smaller)	4'
PVC (2" and larger)	At each story
ABS (1½" and smaller)	4'
ABS (2" and larger)	At each story

*Note—support intervals may not exceed 15 feet.
**Note—support intervals may not exceed 30 feet.
Note—all stacks must be supported at their bases.

E-27 *Vertical pipe support intervals in zone two.*

Horizontal Pipe-Support Intervals in Zone Two

Type of vent pipe	Maximum distance of supports
ABS	4'
Cast iron	At each pipe joint
Galvanized	12'
PVC	4'
Copper (2" and larger)	10'
Copper (1½" and smaller)	6'

E-28 *Horizontal pipe support intervals in zone two.*

Materials Approved for
Above-Ground Vents in Zone Two

Cast-iron materials	Lead materials
ABS materials	Aluminum materials
PVC materials	Borosilicate-glass materials
Copper materials	Brass materials
Galvanized materials	

E-29 *Materials for above-ground vents approved in zone two.*

Example of Horizontal-Branch
Sizing Table in Zone Two

Pipe size	Maximum number of fixture units on a horizontal branch
1¼"	1
1½"	3
2"	6
3"	20*
4"	160
6"	620

*Note—no more than two toilets may be connected to a single 3" horizontal branch. Any branch connecting with a toilet must have a minimum diameter of 3 inches.

Note—table does not represent branches of the building drain, and other restrictions apply under battery-venting conditions.

E-30 *Sizing table for horizontal drain branches in zone two.*

Stack-Sizing Tall Stacks in Zone Two
(Stacks with more than three branch intervals)

Pipe size	Fixture-unit discharge on stack from a branch	Total fixture-units allowed on stack
1½"	2	8
2"	6	24
3"	16*	60*
4"	90	500

*Note—no more than two toilets may be placed on a 3" branch, and no more than six toilets may be connected to a 3" stack.

E-31 *Sizing table for drainage stacks in zone two.*

Stack-Sizing Table for Zone Two

Pipe size	Fixture-unit discharge on stack from a branch	Total fixture-units allowed on stack
1½"	3	4
2"	6	10
3"	20*	30*
4"	160	240

*Note—no more than two toilets may be placed on a 3" branch, and no more than six toilets may be connected to a 3" stack.

E-32 *Sizing table for drainage stacks in zone two.*

Materials Approved for Underground Vents in Zone Two

Cast-iron materials	Copper materials
ABS materials	Aluminum materials
PVC materials	Borosilicate-glass materials

E-33 *Materials approved for underground vents in zone two.*

Table for Sizing a Vent Stack for Wet-Venting in Zone Two

Wet-vented fixtures	Vent-stack size requirements
1–2 bathtubs or showers	2"
3–5 bathtubs or showers	2½"
6–9 bathtubs or showers	3"
10–16 bathtubs or showers	4"

E-34 *Sizing table for wet vents in zone two.*

Table for Sizing a Wet Stack-Vent in Zone Two

Pipe size of stack	Fixture-unit load on stack	Maximum length of stack
2"	4	30
3"	24	50
4"	50	100
6"	100	300

E-35 *Sizing table for wet stack-vents in zone two.*

Stack-Venting without
Individual Vents in Zone Two

Fixtures allowed to be stack-vented without individual vents*

Water closets

Basins

Bathtubs

Showers

Kitchen sinks, with or without dishwasher and garbage disposal

*Note—restrictions apply to this type of installation.

E-36 *Fixtures that don't require individual vents in zone two.*

Approved Materials for
Storm-Water Drainage in Zone Two

Materials approved above-ground use	
Galvanized materials	ABS materials
Black-steel materials	PVC materials
Brass materials	Aluminum materials
DWV copper materials or thicker types of copper	Lead materials
Cast-iron materials	

E-37 *Materials approved for above-ground storm-water drainage in zone two.*

Approved Materials for
Storm-Water Drainage in Zone Two

Materials approved for underground use	
Cast-iron materials	Copper materials*
Coated aluminum materials	Concrete materials*
ABS materials*	Asbestos-cement materials*
PVC materials*	Vitrified-clay materials*
Note—these materials may be allowed for use, subject to local code authorities.	

E-38 *Materials approved for underground storm-water drainage in zone two.*

Approved Materials for
Storm-Water Drainage in Zone Two

Materials approved for building storm sewers	
Cast-iron materials	Vitrified-clay materials
Aluminum materials*	Concrete materials
ABS materials	Asbestos-cement materials
PVC materials	
Note—buried aluminum must be coated.	

E-39 *Materials approved for building storm sewers.*

States in Zone Three

Virginia	New York	New Jersey
Kentucky	Connecticut	Parts of Delaware
Missouri	Massachusetts	Parts of West Virginia
Illinois	Vermont	Parts of Maine
Michigan	New Hampshire	Parts of Maryland
Ohio	Rhode Island	Parts of Oklahoma
Pennsylvania		

E-40 *List of states normally governed by the plumbing code in zone three tables.*

Trap-to-Vent Distances in Zone Three

Grade on drain pipe	Fixture's drain size	Trap size	Maximum distance between trap and vent
¼"	1¼"	1¼"	3' 6"
¼"	1½"	1¼"	5'
¼"	1½"	1½"	5'
¼"	2"	1½"	8'
¼"	2"	2"	6'
⅛"	3"	3"	10'
⅛"	4"	4"	12'

E-41 *Trap-to-vent distances in zone three.*

Recommended Trap Sizes for Zone Three

Type of fixture	Trap size
Bathtub	1½"
Shower	2"
Residential toilet	Integral
Lavatory	1¼"
Bidet	1¼"
Laundry tub	1½"
Washing-machine standpipe	2"
Floor drain	2"
Kitchen sink	1½"
Dishwasher	1½"
Drinking fountain	1¼"
Public toilet	Integral
Urinal	2"

E-42 _Recommended trap sizes in zone three._

Zone Three's Fixture-Unit Requirements on Trap Sizes

1¼" trap	One fixture-unit
1½" trap	Two fixture-units
2" trap	Three fixture-units
3" trap	Five fixture-units
4" trap	Six fixture-units

E-43 _Fixture-unit requirements on trap sizes in zone three._

Horizontal Pipe-Support Intervals in Zone Three

Type of vent pipe	Maximum distance of supports
PB pipe	32"
Lead pipe	Continuous
Cast iron	5' or at each joint
Galvanized	12'
Copper tube (1¼")	6'
Copper tube (1½" & larger)	10'
ABS	4'
PVC	4'
Brass	10'
Aluminum	10'

Vertical Pipe-Support Intervals in Zone Three

Type of vent pipe	Maximum distance of supports
Lead pipe	4'
Cast iron	15'
Galvanized	15'
Copper tubing	10'
ABS	4'
PVC	4'
Brass	10'
PB pipe	4'
Aluminum	15'

E-44 *Horizontal and vertical pipe support intervals in zone three.*

Vertical Pipe-Support Intervals in Zone Three

Type of vent pipe	Maximum distance of supports
Lead pipe	4'
Cast iron	15'
Galvanized	15'
Copper tubing	10'
ABS	4'
PVC	4'
Brass	10'
Aluminum	15'

E-45 *Vertical pipe support intervals in zone three.*

Horizontal Pipe-Support Intervals in Zone Three

Type of vent pipe	Maximum distance of supports
Lead pipe	Continuous
Cast iron	5'
Galvanized	12'
Copper tube (1¼")	6'
Copper tube (1½" & larger)	10'
ABS	4'
PVC	4'
Brass	10'
Aluminum	10'

E-46 *Horizontal pipe support intervals in zone three.*

Stack-Sizing Tall Stacks in Zone Three (Stacks with more than three branch intervals)

Pipe size	Fixture-unit discharge on stack from a branch	Total fixture-units allowed on stack
1½"	2	8
2"	6	24
3"	20*	72*
4"	90	500

*Note—no more than two toilets may be placed on a 3" branch, and no more than six toilets may be connected to a 3" stack.

E-47 *Table for stack sizing tall stacks in zone three.*

Stack-Sizing Table for Zone Three

Pipe size	Fixture-unit discharge on stack from a branch	Total fixture-units allowed on stack
1½"	2	4
2"	6	10
3"	20*	48*
4"	90	240

*Note—no more than two toilets may be placed on a 3" branch, and no more than six toilets may be connected to a 3" stack.

E-48 *Table for stack sizing in zone three.*

Materials Approved for
Underground Vents in Zone Three

Cast-iron materials	PVC materials
ABS materials	Copper materials

E-49 *Approved underground vent materials in zone three.*

Materials Approved for
Above-Ground Vents in Zone Three

Cast-iron materials	Copper materials	Aluminum materials
ABS materials	Galvanized materials	Brass materials
PVC materials	Lead materials	

E-50 *Approved above-ground vent materials in zone three.*

Vent Sizing Table for Zone Three
(For use with individual, branch, and circuit vents for horizontal drain pipes)

Drain pipe size	Drain pipe grade per foot	Vent pipe size	Maximum developed length of vent pipe
1½"	¼"	1¼"	Unlimited
1½"	¼"	1½"	Unlimited
2"	¼"	1¼"	290'
2"	¼"	1½"	Unlimited
3"	¼"	1½"	97'
3"	¼"	2"	420'
3"	¼"	3"	Unlimited
4"	¼"	2"	98'
4"	¼"	3"	Unlimited
4"	¼"	4"	Unlimited

E-51 *Vent sizing table in zone three.*

Vent Sizing Table for Zone Three
(For use with vent-stacks and stack-vents)

Drain pipe size	Fixture-unit Load on drain pipe	Vent pipe size	Maximum developed length of vent pipe
1½"	8	1¼"	50'
1½"	8	1½"	150'
1½"	10	1¼"	30'
1½"	10	1½"	100'
2"	12	1½"	75'
2"	12	2"	200'
2"	20	1½"	50'
2"	20	2"	150'
3"	10	1½"	42'
3"	10	2"	150'
3"	10	3"	1,040'
3"	21	1½"	32'
3"	21	2"	110'
3"	21	3"	810'
3"	102	1½"	25'
3"	102	2"	86'
3"	102	3"	620'
4"	43	2"	35'
4"	43	3"	250'
4"	43	4"	980'
4"	540	2"	21'
4"	540	3"	150'
4"	540	4"	580'

E-52 *Vent sizing table in zone three.*

Building-Drain Sizing Table for Zone Three

Pipe size	Pipe grade to the foot	Maximum number of fixture-units
2"	¼"	21
3"	¼"	42*
4"	¼"	216

*Note—no more than two toilets may be installed on a 3" building drain.

E-53 *Sizing table for building drains in zone three.*

Fixture-Unit Ratings in Zone Three

Bathtub	2	Kitchen sink	2
Shower	2	Dishwasher	2
Residential toilet	4	Clothes washer	3
Lavatory	1	Laundry tub	2

E-54 *Fixture-unit ratings in zone three.*

Zone Three's Minimum Drainage-Pipe Pitch

Pipes under 3" in diameter	¼" to the foot
Pipes 3" to 6" in diameter	⅛" to the foot
Pipes 8" or larger in diameter	¹⁄₁₆" to the foot

E-55 *Minimum pipe pitch in zone three.*

Index

Illustration page numbers are in **boldface**.

About the author

R. Dodge Woodson has nearly 20 years' experience as a homebuilder, contractor, master plumber, and real estate broker. He is also the author of many books, including *Home Plumbing Illustrated, Roofing Contractor: Start and Run a Money-Making Business, Troubleshooting & Repairing Heat Pumps,* and *The Master Plumber's Licensing Exam Guide,* among others.